Partition and Making Modern South Asia

Refugees,phenomens reflection

Partition and Making Modern South Asia

Refugees, Phenomens Reflections

Brig. S. D. Lal (Retd.)

Gaurav Book Centre Pvt Ltd

Delhi

Publisher
GAURAV BOOK CENTRE PVT LTD
4832/24,Prahlad Lane,S-207 Ansari
Road, Daryaganj, Delhi-110002
Ph.: 43570976, 23278261
Email: gauravbookcentre@gmail.com

Edition: 2015

ISBN: 978-93-83316-18-2

Laser Typesetting
JEE-VEE Graphics, Delhi

Price: 1195/-

Printed
Vikas Computers, Delhi

Preface

Along with the desire for independence, tensions between Hindus and Muslims had also been developing over the years. The Muslims had always been a minority within the subcontinent, and the prospect of an exclusively Hindu government made them wary of independence; they were as inclined to mistrust Hindu rule as they were to resist the foreign Raj, although Gandhi called for unity between the two groups in an astonishing display of leadership. The British, extremely weakened by the Second World War, promised that they would leave and participated in the formation of an interim government. The British Indian territories gained independence in 1947, after being partitioned into the Union of India and Dominion of Pakistan.

However another reason for this arrangement was to avoid the appearance that Pakistan was seceding from a sovereign India. Therefore Pakistan celebrates Independence Day on 14 August, while India celebrates it on 15 August. Another reason for Pakistan celebrating independence on 14 August is the adoption of new standard time in Pakistan after partition.

Modern Bangladesh emerged as an independent nation in 1971 after achieving independence from Pakistan in the Bangladesh Liberation War. The country constitutes with the major portion of the ancient and historic region of Bengal in the eastern part of the Indian subcontinent, wherecivilization dates back over four millennia, to the Copper Age. The history of the region is closely intertwined with the history of Bengal and the history of India.

It is further hoped that the book will prove to be of immense value to teachers, students and researchers.

—*Editor*

Contents

1

History of South Asia

In South Asia — which includes the land that makes up the modern-day nations of India, Pakistan, Bangladesh, Bhutan, Nepal, and Sri Lanka — colourful distinctions are apparent and even celebrated. When India crashed into Asia 50 million years ago, the collision created the Himalayan Mountains and made India a subcontinent. Under the layers of diversity lies a solid core of South Asian tradition. Traditions have endured for over 5,000 years — from the earliest known Indian civilization to the present day.

The Indus Valley civilization dates back to about 3000 B.C.E. The archaeological evidence from this period provides exemplary evidence that many aspects of South Asian culture have endured through changing times. Remnants of ancient bathhouses and sophisticated sanitation systems point to the long history of South Asian culture — admiration of purity and cleanliness, and abhorrence of all things polluted. Ancient statues representing the god Shiva are proof that the religious traditions of today's South Asia, too, have been around for millennia.

THE SOUL OF SOUTH ASIA

To understand the history and cultures of ancient South Asia, it is essential to consider the development of Hinduism and Buddhism. These two religions encompassed far more than spirituality. They became the lifeblood of the people and the backbone of social, political, and economic structures. These religions pervaded all aspects of life and shaped the evolution of the region. Some have called Hinduism the "soul of India." One of the most powerful and influential developments of ancient Hinduism was the institution of the caste system. The caste system became deeply incorporated into Hindu tradition and created an enduring framework of ascribed social status.

Buddhism emerged as a rejection of the injustices created by caste system sanctioned by Hinduism. It was a response to discontentment and a search for new answers to the mysterious and complex questions that define human experience.

Organized power structures arose from the conflict and confusion that followed the growth of new religions and the challenging of social structures. These power structures led to the formation of state systems and even triggered the development of vast empires. Few regions in the world have histories as ancient and diverse as South Asia's. And few people realize that South Asia's roots can be traced to the beginnings of human civilization. Marked by integration, intellectualism, and spirituality, South Asia's ancient history begs to be explored.

INDEPENDENCE AND PARTITION (1947-PRESENT)

Along with the desire for independence, tensions between Hindus and Muslims had also been developing over the years. The Muslims had always been a minority within the subcontinent, and the prospect of an exclusively Hindu government made them wary of independence; they were as inclined to mistrust Hindu rule as they were to resist the foreign Raj, although Gandhi called for unity between the two groups in an astonishing display of leadership.

The British, extremely weakened by the Second World War, promised that they would leave and participated in the formation of an interim government. The British Indian territories gained independence in 1947, after being partitioned into the Union of India and Dominion of Pakistan. Following the controversial division of pre-partition Punjab and Bengal, rioting broke out between Sikhs, Hindus and Muslims in these provinces and spread to several other parts of India, leaving some 500,000 dead. Also, this period saw one of the largest mass migrations ever recorded in modern history, with a total of 12 million Hindus, Sikhs and Muslims moving between the newly created nations of India and Pakistan (which gained independence on 15 and 14 August 1947 respectively). In 1971, Bangladesh, formerly East Pakistan and East Bengal, seceded from Pakistan.

HISTORY OF PAKISTAN

The history of Pakistan encompasses the history of the region constituting modern Pakistan. Prior to independence in 1947, the land that is now Pakistan was a part of India and ruled in different periods by local kings and numerous imperial powers. The ancient history of the region comprising present-day Pakistan also includes some of the oldest empires of Indian Subcontinent and some of its major civilizations. By the 18th century the land was incorporated into British India. Pakistan's political history began with the birth of the All India Muslim League in 1906 to protect "Muslim interests, amid neglect and under-representation" and to oppose Congress and growing Indian nationalism in return the British Raj would decide to grant local self-rule. On 29 December 1930, philosopher Sir Muhammad Iqbal called for an autonomous new state in "northwestern India for Indian Muslims". The League rose to popularity in the late 1930s. Muhammad Ali Jinnah espoused the *Two Nation Theory* and led the League to adopt the *Lahore Resolution* of 1940, demanding the formation of independent states in the East and the West of British India. Eventually, a successful movement led by Jinnah resulted in the partition of India and independence from Britain, on 14 August 1947.

On 12 March 1949, the second constituent assembly of Pakistan passed the Objectives Resolution which was proposed by the first Prime Minister Liaquat Ali Khan, proclaimed that the future constitution of Pakistan would not be modelled entirely on a European pattern, but on the ideology and democratic faith of Islam. The legislative elections in 1954 saw the Awami League coming to power and its leader Huseyn Suhrawardy becoming country's first Bengali Prime minister. Promulgation of Constitution in 1956 lead to Pakistan declaring itself Islamic republic (official name) with the adoption of parliamentary democratic system of government. The constitution transformed the Governor-General of Pakistan into President of Pakistan (ashead of state). Subsequently, Iskander Mirza became the first president as well as first Bengali in 1956, but the democratic system was stalled after President Mirza imposed the military coup d'état and appointed Ayub Khan as an enforcer of martial law. Two weeks later, President Mirza was ousted by Ayub Khan; his presidency saw an era of internal instability and a second war with India in 1965. Economic grievances and political disenfranchisement in East Pakistanled to violent political tensions and armed repression, escalating into guerrilla war followed by the third war with India. Pakistan's defeat in the war ultimately led to the secession of East Pakistan and the birth of Bangladesh.

Democracy again returned which was resumed from 1972 to 1977 under leftist PPP led by Zulfikar Ali Bhutto, until he was vanquished by General Zia-ul-Haq, who became the country's third military president. Pakistan's banished-secular policies were replaced by the new Islamic Shariah legal code, which increased religious influences on the civil service and the military. With the death of President Zia-ul-Haq in 1988, the new general elections announced the victory of PPP led by Benazir Bhutto who was elevated as the country's first female Prime Minister of Pakistan. Over the next decade, she alternated power with conservative Pakistan Muslim League-N (PML(N)) led by Nawaz Sharif, as the country's political and economic situation becoming worsen. Military tensions in the Kargil conflict with India were followed by a 1999 coup d'état in which General Pervez Musharraf assumed executive powers.

Self-appointing himself as President after the resignation of President Rafiq Tarar, Musharraf held nation-wide general elections in 2002 to transfer the executive powers to newly elected Prime Minister Zafarullah Khan Jamali, who was succeeded in the 2004 by Shaukat Aziz. During the election campaign in 2007 following the parliament completing its term on 15 November 2007, Benazir Bhutto was assassinated which resulted in a series of important political developments when left-wing alliance led by PPP. The historic general elections held in 2013 marked the return of PML(N) coming to national prominence with Prime Minister Nawaz Sharif assuming the leadership of the country for the third time in the history.

HISTORY OF BANGLADESH

Modern Bangladesh emerged as an independent nation in 1971 after achieving independence from Pakistan in the Bangladesh Liberation War. The country constitutes with the major portion of the ancient and historic region of Bengal in the eastern part of the Indian subcontinent, where civilization dates back over four millennia, to the Copper Age. The history of the region is closely intertwined with the history of Bengal and the history of India.

The area's early history featured a succession of Indian empires, internal squabbling, and a tussle between Hinduism and Buddhism for dominance. Islam made its appearance during the 8th century when Sufi missionaries arrived. Later, Muslim rulers reinforced the process of conversion by building mosques, madrassas and Sufi Khanqah.

The borders of modern Bangladesh were established with the partition of Bengal and India in August 1947, when the region became East Pakistan as a part of the newly formed State of Pakistan following the Radcliffe Line. However, it was separated from West Pakistan by 1,600 km (994 mi) of Indian territory. Due to political exclusion, ethnic and linguistic discrimination, as well as economic neglect by the politically dominant westerin-wing, popular agitation and civil disobedience led to the war of independence in 1971. After independence, the new state endured famine, natural disasters and widespread poverty, as well as political turmoil and military coups. The restoration of democracy in 1991 has been followed by relative calm and economic progress.

Movement for Self Rule and Establishment of Pakistan

As the independence movement throughout British-controlled India began in the late 19th century gained momentum during the 20th century, Bengali politicians played an active role in Mohandas Gandhi's Congress Party and Mohammad Ali Jinnah's Muslim League, exposing the opposing forces of ethnic and religious nationalism. By exploiting the latter, the British probably intended to distract the independence movement, for example by partitioning Bengal in 1905 along religious lines. Partition of Bengal (1905) divided Bengal Presidency into an overwhelmingly Hindu west (including present-day Bihar and Odisha) and a predominantly Muslim east (including Assam). Dhaka was made the capital of the new province of Eastern Bengal and Assam. But the split only lasted for seven years.

Creation of Pakistan

The All-India Muslim League was founded on 30 December 1906, in the aftermath of partition of Bengal, on the sidelines of the annual All India Muhammadan Educational Conference in Shahbagh, Dhaka. At first the Muslim League sought only to ensure minority Muslim rights in the future nation of independent India. However, in 1940 the Muslim League passed the Lahore Resolution which envisaged one or more Muslim majority states in South Asia. The resolution unambiguously rejected the concept of a United India because of increasing inter-religious violence The resolution was moved in the general session by *Sher-e-Bangla* A. K. Fazlul Huq, the then Chief Minister of Bengal, and was adopted on 23 March 1940. Non-negotiable was the inclusion of the Muslim parts of Punjab and Bengal in these proposed states. The stakes grew as a new Viceroy Lord Mountbatten of Burma was appointed expressly for the purpose of effecting a graceful British exit. Sectarian violence in Noakhali and Calcutta sparked a surge in support for the Muslim League, which won the majority seats in Bengal legislature in the 1946 election. This surge of support also emerged as a reaction against the British decision to reverse the 1905 Partition of Bengal, which the League regarded as a betrayal of the Bengali Muslims. At the last moment Huseyn Shaheed Suhrawardy and Sarat Chandra Bose came up with the idea of an independent and unified Bengal state, which was endorsed by Jinnah. This idea was vetoed by the Indian National Congress.

British India was partitioned and the independent states of India and Pakistan were created in 1947; the region of Bengal was divided along religious lines. The predominantly Muslim eastern half of Bengal became the East Bengal (later renamed East Pakistan) state of Pakistan and the predominantly Hindu western part became the Indian state of West Bengal. Most of the Sylhet District of Assam also joined East Pakistan following a referendum .

Pakistan's history from 1947 to 1971 was marked by political instability and economic difficulties. In 1956 a constitution was at last adopted, making the country an "Islamic republic within the Commonwealth". The nascent democratic institutions foundered in the face of military intervention in 1958, and the government imposed martial law between 1958 and 1962, and again between 1969 and 1971.

Almost from the advent of independent Pakistan in 1947, frictions developed between East and West Pakistan, which were separated by more than 1,000 miles of Indian territory. East Pakistanis felt exploited by the West Pakistan-dominated central government. Linguistic, cultural, and ethnic differences also contributed to the estrangement of East from West Pakistan.

The Bengali Language Movement

The Bengali Language Movement, also known as the Language Movement *Bhasha Andolon,* was a political effort in Bangladesh (then known as East Pakistan), advocating the recognition of the Bengali language as an official language of Pakistan. Such recognition would allow Bengali to be used in government affairs. Movement was led by Mufti Nadimul Quamar Ahmed. When the state of Pakistan was formed in 1947, its two regions, East Pakistan (also called East Bengal) and West Pakistan, were split along cultural, geographical, and linguistic lines. In 1948, the Government of Pakistan ordained Urdu as the sole national language, sparking extensive protests among the Bengali-speaking majority of East Pakistan. Facing rising sectarian tensions and mass discontent with the new law, the government outlawed public meetings and rallies. The students of the University of Dhaka and other political activists defied the law and organised a protest on 21 February 1952. The movement reached its climax when police killed student demonstrators on that day. The deaths provoked widespread civil unrest led by the Awami Muslim League, later renamed the Awami League. After years of conflict, the central government relented and granted official status to the Bengali language in 1956. On 17 November 1999, UNESCO declared 21 February International Mother Language Day for the whole world to celebrate, in tribute to the Language Movement and the ethno-linguistic rights of people around the world.

Republic of Bangladesh

Constitution

After Bangladesh achieved recognition from major countries, Sheikh Mujibur Rahman briefly assumed the provisional presidency. He charged the provisional parliament to write a new constitution. The constitution proclaims Bangladesh as a secular democratic republic, declares the fundamental rights and freedoms of Bangladeshi citizens, spells out the fundamental principles of state policy, and establishes the structure and functions of the executive, legislative and judicial branches of the republic. Passed by the Constituent Assembly of Bangladesh on November 4, 1972, it came into effect from December 16, 1972, on the first anniversary of Bangladesh's victory over Pakistan in the Liberation War. The constitution proclaims nationalism, democracy, socialism and secularity as the national ideals of the Bangladeshi republic. When adopted in 1972, it was one of the most liberal constitutions of the time.

Sheikh Mujib Administration (1971–1975)

Sheikh Mujibur Rahman came to office with immense personal popularity but had difficulty transforming this popular support into the political strength needed to function as head of government. The new constitution, which came into force on 16 December 1972, created a strong executive prime minister, a largely ceremonial presidency, an independent judiciary, and a unicameral legislature on a modified Westminster model. The 1972 constitution adopted as state policy the Awami League's (AL) four basic principles of nationalism, secularism, socialism, and democracy. The first parliamentary elections held under the 1972 constitution were in 7 March 1973, with the Awami League winning a massive majority. No other political party in Bangladesh's early years was able to duplicate or challenge the League's broad-based appeal, membership, or organizational strength. Relying heavily on experienced civil servants and members of the Awami League, the new Bangladesh government focused on relief, rehabilitation, and reconstruction of the economy and society. Economic conditions remained precarious, however. In December 1974, Mujib decided that continuing economic deterioration and mounting civil disorder required strong measures. After proclaiming a state of emergency, Mujib used his parliamentary majority to win a constitutional amendment limiting the powers of the legislative and judicial branches, establishing an executive presidency, and instituting a one-party system, the Bangladesh Krishak Sramik Awami League (BAKSAL), which all members of Parliament (and senior civil and military officials) were obliged to join.

Despite some improvement in the economic situation during the first half of 1975, implementation of promised political reforms was slow, and criticism of government policies became increasingly centered on Mujib. In 15 August 1975, Mujib, and most of his family, were assassinated by mid-level army officers. His daughters, Sheikh Hasina and Sheikh Rehana, were out of the country. A new government, headed by former Mujib associate Khondaker Mostaq Ahmad, was formed.

Democratic era (1991–present)

A constitutional referendum was held in Bangladesh on 15 September 1991. Voters were asked "Should or not the President assent to the Constitution (Twelfth Amendment) Bill, 1991 of the People's Republic of Bangladesh?" The amendments would lead to the reintroduction of parliamentary government, with the President becoming the constitutional head of state, but the Prime Minister the executive head. It also abolished the position of Vice-President and would see the President elected by Parliament. Since then, Bangladesh has reverted to a parliamentary democracy. Zia's widow, Khaleda Zia, led the Bangladesh Nationalist Party to parliamentary victory at the general election in 1991 and became the first female Prime Minister in Bangladeshi history. However, the Awami League, headed by Sheikh Hasina, one of Mujib's surviving daughters, won the next election in 1996. The Awami

League lost again to the Bangladesh Nationalist Party in 2001. Widespread political unrest followed the resignation of the BNP in late October 2006, but the caretaker government worked to bring the parties to election within the required ninety days. At the last minute in early January, the Awami League withdrew from the election scheduled for later that month. On 11 January 2007, the military intervened to support both a state of emergency and a continuing but neutral caretaker government under a newly appointed Chief Advisor, who was not a politician. The country had suffered for decades from extensive corruption, disorder, and political violence. The caretaker government worked to root out corruption from all levels of government. It arrested on corruption charges more than 160 people, including politicians, civil servants, and businessmen, among whom were both major party leaders, some of their senior staff, and two sons of Khaleda Zia.

After working to clean up the system, the caretaker government held what was described by observers as a largely free and fair election on 29 December 2008. The Awami League's Sheikh Hasina won with a two-thirds landslide in the elections; she took the oath of Prime Minister on 6 January 2009.

HISTORY OF BHUTAN

Bhutan's early history is steeped in mythology and remains obscure. It may have been inhabited as early as 2000 BC and there is a legend that it was ruled or controlled by a Cooch-Behar king, Sangaldip, around the 7th century B.C., but not much was known until the introduction of Tibetan Buddhism in the 9th century, when turmoil in Tibet forced manymonks to flee to Bhutan. In the 12th century, the Drukpa Kagyupa school was established and remains the dominant form of Buddhism in Bhutan today. The country's political history is intimately tied to its religious history and the relations among the various monastic schools and monasteries.

Bhutan are the only countries which have been independent throughout their history, never conquered, occupied, or governed by an outside power (notwithstanding occasional [nominal] tributary status). Although there has been speculation that it was under the Kamarupa Kingdom or the Tibetan Empire in the 7th to 9th centuries, firm evidence is lacking. From the time historical records are clear, Bhutan has continuously and successfully defended its sovereignty.

The consolidation of Bhutan occurred in 1616 when Ngawanag Namgyal, a lama from western Tibet known as the Zhabdrung Rinpoche, defeated three Tibetan invasions, subjugated rival religious schools, codified the Tsa Yig, an intricate and comprehensive system of law, and established himself as ruler over a system of ecclesiastical and civil administrators. After his death, infighting and civil war eroded the power of the Zhabdrung for the next 200 years when in 1885, Ugyen Wangchuck was able to consolidate power and cultivated closer ties with the British in India.

In 1907, Ugyen Wangchuck was elected as the hereditary ruler of Bhutan, crowned on December 17, 1907, and installed as the head of state Druk Gyalpo (Dragon King). In 1910, King Ugyen and the British signed the Treaty of Punakha which provided that British Indiawould not interfere in the internal affairs of Bhutan if the country accepted external advice in its external relations. When Ugyen Wangchuck died in 1926, his son Jigme Wangchuck became the next ruler, and when India gained independence in 1947, the new Indian Government recognized Bhutan as an independent country. In 1949, India and Bhutan signed the Treaty of Peace and Friendship, which provided that India would not interfere in Bhutan's internal affairs but would be guided by India in its foreign policy. Succeeded in 1952 by his son Jigme Dorji Wangchuck, Bhutan began to slowly emerge from its isolation and began a program of planned development. Bhutan became a member of the United Nations in 1971, and the National Assembly was established and a new code of law, as well as the Royal Bhutanese Army and the High Court.

In 1972, Jigme Singye Wangchuck ascended the throne at age 20. He emphasized moderneducation, decentralization of governance, the development of hydroelectricity and tourism and improvements in rural developments. He was perhaps best known internationally for his overarching development philosophy of "gross national happiness." It recognizes that there are many dimensions to development and that economic goals alone are not sufficient. Satisfied with Bhutan's transitioning democratization process, he abdicated in December 2006 rather than wait until the promulgation of the new constitution in 2008. His son, Jigme Khesar Namgyel Wangchuck, became King upon his abdication.

HISTORY OF AFGHANISTAN

The written history of Afghanistan , can be traced back to around 500 BCE when the area was under the Achaemenid Empire, although evidence indicates that an advanced degree of urbanized culture has existed in the land since between 3000 and 2000 BCE. Alexander the Great and his Macedonian army arrived to what is now Afghanistan in 330 BCE after conquering Persia during the Battle of Gaugamela. Since then, many empires have established capitals inside Afghanistan, including the Greco-Bactrians, Mauryas, Kushans, Kabul Shahi, Saffarids, Samanids, Ghaznavids, Ghurids, Timurids, Mughals, Hotakis and Durranis.

Afghanistan (meaning "land of the Afghans") has been a strategically important location throughout history. The land served as "a gateway to India, impinging on the ancient Silk Road, which carried trade from the Mediterranean to China". Sitting on many trade and migration routes, Afghanistan may be called the 'Central Asian roundabout' since routes converge from the Middle East, from the Indus Valley through the passes over the Hindu Kush, from the Far East via the Tarim Basin, and from the adjacent Eurasian Steppe.

The Aryans arrived to Afghanistan from the north after the 20th century BCE, who left their languages that survived in the form of Pashto and Dari. The Arab invasions influenced theculture of Afghanistan, as its Zoroastrian, Macedonian and Buddhist past had long vanished, or had just started to decline, as it went with Buddhism. Turkic empire-builders such as the Ghaznavids, Ghurids and Timurids made the region now called Afghanistan of major importance.

Mirwais Hotak followed by Ahmad Shah Durrani unified Afghan tribes and founded the last Afghan Empire in the early

18th century CE. Afghanistan's sovereignty has been held during the Anglo-Afghan Wars, the 1980s Soviet war, and the 2001-present war by the country's many and diverse people: the Pashtuns, Tajiks, Hazaras, Uzbeks, Turkmen, Aimak, Baloch and others. The Pashtuns form the largest group, claiming to be descendants of ancient Israelites or Qais Abdur Rashid but scholars believe that they are a confederation of various peoples from the past who united under Pashtunwali.

Contemporary era (1973–present)

Republic of Afghanistan and the end of monarchy

Amid charges of corruption and malfeasance against the royal family and poor economic conditions created by the severe 1971–72 drought, former Prime Minister Mohammad Sardar Daoud Khanseized power in a non-violent coup on July 17, 1973, while Zahir Shah was receiving treatment for eye problems and therapy for lumbago in Italy. Daoud abolished the monarchy, abrogated the 1964 constitution, and declared Afghanistan a republic with himself as its first President and Prime Minister. His attempts to carry out badly needed economic and social reforms met with little success, and the new constitution promulgated in February 1977 failed to quell chronic political instability.

As disillusionment set in, in 1978 a prominent member of the People's Democratic Party of Afghanistan (PDPA), Mir Akbar Khyber (or "Kaibar"), was killed by the government. The leaders of PDPA apparently feared that Daoud was planning to exterminate them all, especially since most of them were arrested by the government shortly after. Nonetheless, Hafizullah Amin and a number of military wing officers of the PDPA's Khalq faction managed to remain at large and organize a military coup.

Democratic Republic and Soviet war

On 27 April 1978, the PDPA, led by Nur Mohammad Taraki, Babrak Karmal and Amin Taha overthrew the government of Mohammad Daoud, who was assassinated along with all his family members in a bloody military coup. The coup became known as the Saur Revolution. On 1 May, Taraki became President, Prime

Minister and General Secretary of the PDPA. The country was then renamed the Democratic Republic of Afghanistan (DRA), and the PDPA regime lasted, in some form or another, until April 1992.

In March 1979, Hafizullah Amin took over as prime minister, retaining the position of field marshaland becoming vice-president of the Supreme Defence Council. Taraki remained President and in control of the Army. On 14 September, Amin overthrew Taraki, who was killed. Amin stated that "the Afghans recognize only crude force." Afghanistan expert Amin Saikal writes: "As his powers grew, so apparently did his craving for personal dictatorship ... and his vision of the revolutionary process based on terror."

Once in power, the PDPA implemented a liberal and Marxist-Leninist agenda. It moved to replace religious and traditional laws with secular and Marxist-Leninist ones. Men were obliged to cut their beards, women could not wear a chador, and mosques were placed off limits. The PDPA made a number of reforms on women's rights, banning forced marriages, giving state recognition of women's right to vote, and introducing women to political life. A prominent example was Anahita Ratebzad, who was a major Marxist leader and a member of the Revolutionary Council. Ratebzad wrote the famous *New Kabul Times* editorial (May 28, 1978) which declared: "Privileges which women, by right, must have are equal education, job security, health services, and free time to rear a healthy generation for building the future of the country ... Educating and enlightening women is now the subject of close government attention." The PDPA also carried out socialist land reforms and moved to promote state atheism. They also prohibited usury and took a number of measures in favor of women's rights, by declaring equality of the sexes and introducing women to political life. The PDPA invited the Soviet Union to assist in modernizing its economic infrastructure (predominantly its exploration and mining of rare minerals and natural gas). The USSR also sent contractors to build roads, hospitals and schools and to drill water wells; they also trained and equipped the Afghan army. Upon the PDPA's ascension to power, and the establishment of the DRA, the Soviet Union promised monetary aid amounting to at least $1.262 billion.

At the same time, the PDPA imprisoned, tortured or murdered thousands of members of the traditional elite, the religious establishment, and the intelligentsia. The government launched a campaign of violent repression, killing some 10,000 to 27,000 people and imprisoning 14,000 to 20,000 more, mostly at Pul-e-Charkhi prison. In December 1978 the PDPA leadership signed an agreement with the Soviet Union which would allow military support for the PDPA in Afghanistan if needed. The majority of people in the cities including Kabul either welcomed or were ambivalent to these policies. However, the Marxist-Leninist and secular nature of the government as well as its heavy dependence on the Soviet Union made it unpopular with a majority of the Afghan population. Repressions plunged large parts of the country, especially the rural areas, into open revolt against the new Marxist-Leninist government. By spring 1979 unrests had reached 24 out of 28 Afghan provinces including major urban areas. Over half of the Afghan army would either desert or join the insurrection. Most of the government's new policies clashed directly with the traditional Afghan understanding of Islam, making religion one of the only forces capable of unifying the tribally and ethnically divided population against the unpopular new government, and ushering in the advent oflslamist participation in Afghan politics.

In the wake of the Iranian Revolution, the US sought rapprochement with the Afghan government—a prospect that the USSR found unacceptable due to weakening Soviet leverage over the regime. In February 1979, U.S. Ambassador Adolph "Spike" Dubs was murdered in Kabul after Afghan security forces burst in on his kidnappers. The U.S. then reduced bilateral assistance and terminated a small military training program.

HISTORY OF THE MALDIVES

The Maldives is a nation consisting of 26 natural atolls, comprising 1192 islands.

Historical setting

Since very ancient times, the Maldives were ruled by kings (Radun) and occasionally queens (Ranin). Historically Maldives has had a strategic importance because of its location on the major marine routes of the Indian Ocean. Maldives' nearest neighbors are Sri Lankaand India, both of which have had cultural and economic ties with Maldives for centuries. The Maldives provided the main source of cowrie shells, then used as a currency throughout Asia and parts of the East African coast.

After the 16th century, when European colonial powers took over much of the trade in the Indian Ocean, first the Portuguese, and then the Dutch, and the French occasionally meddled with local politics. However, these interferences ended when the Maldive became a British Protectorate in the 19th century and the Maldivian monarchs were granted a good measure of self-governance.

Maldives gained total independence from the British in 1965. However, they continued to maintain an air base on the island of Gan in the southernmost atoll until 1976. The British departure in 1976 at the height of the Cold War almost immediately triggered foreign speculation about the future of the air base. Apparently the Soviet Union made a move to request the use of the base, but the Maldives refused.

The greatest challenge facing the republic in the early 1990s was the need for rapid economic development and modernization, given the country's limited resource base in fishing, agriculture and tourism. Concern was also evident over a projected long-term rise in sea level, which would prove disastrous to the low-lying coral islands.

HISTORY OF NEPAL

The history of Nepal has been influenced by its position in the Himalayas and its two neighbors, India and China.

Due to the arrival of disparate settler groups from outside through the ages, it is now a multiethnic, multicultural, multi religious, and multilingual country. Central Nepal was split in three kingdoms from the 15th century until the 18th century, when it was unified under the Shah monarchy. The national language of Nepal is Nepali, which is also the most spoken language of Nepal.

Nepal experienced a struggle for democracy in the 20th century. During the 1990s and until 2008, the country was in civil strife. A peace treaty was signed in 2008 and elections were held in the same year.In a historical vote for the election of the constituent assembly, Nepal voted to oust the monarchy in June 2008. Nepal was formally renamed the Federal Democratic Republic of Nepal when it became a federal republic.

HISTORY OF SRI LANKA

The history of Sri Lanka begins around 30,000 years ago when the island was first inhabited. Chronicles, including the Mahawansa, the Dipavamsa, the Culavamsa and the Rajaveliya, record events from the beginnings of the Sinhalese monarchy in the 6th century BC; through the arrival of European Colonialists in the 16th century; and to the disestablishment of the monarchy in 1815. Some mentions of the country are found in the Ramayana, the Mahabharata and the Lankavatara Sutra Mahayana Buddhism texts of Gautama Buddha's teachings. Buddhism was introduced in the 3rd century BC by Arhath Mahinda (son of the Indian emperor Ashoka the Great).

From the 16th century, some coastal areas of the country were ruled by the Portuguese, Dutchand British. Sri Lanka was ruled by 181 Kings and Queens from the Anuradhapura to Kandy periods. After 1815 the entire nation was under British colonial rule and armed uprisings against the British took place in the 1818 Uva Rebellion and the 1848 Matale Rebellion. Independence was finally granted in 1948 but the country remained a Dominion of the British Empire.

In 1972 Sri Lánka assumed the status of a Republic. A constitution was introduced in 1978 which made the Executive President the head of state. The Sri Lankan Civil War began in 1983, including an armed youth uprising in 1987–1989, with the 25 year-long civil war ending in 2009.

2

The Fading Memory of South Asia's Partition

This week, Indians and Pakistanis have been showering the night sky with fireworks, singing patriotic songs, and memorializing national heroes in observation of their respective independence days (Pakistan's was Thursday, India's Friday).

But the 67th birthday of the antagonistic South Asian neighbors is also the grim anniversary of their divorce in the partition of 1947, when the British hastily and arbitrarily divided up the landmass formerly known as India along religious lines while leaving behind their former colony. The new borders created roughly 14 million refugees as Muslims in India and Hindus in Pakistan found themselves on the wrong side of the line, in what some historians have called thelargest mass migration in human history. Estimates vary, but hundreds of thousands of civilians died in the process.

The legacy of tension has persisted for nearly seven decades, but one thing people on both sides of the India-Pakistan border have shared is the memory of partition's trauma. Now, though, people who were children in 1947 are in their seventies and eighties, meaning that these common memories are fading.

Guneeta Singh Bhalla hopes to preserve them. Born in India, Bhalla grew up hearing her grandmother recount fleeing Pakistan at independence. When Bhalla moved to the U.S. in middle school, she wondered why what her grandmother had called "an apocalypse" wasn't covered in history classes alongside other important world events. On a trip to Hiroshima in college, Bhalla saw a memorial to the victims of the atomic bomb, with a collection of writings and videos from survivors. "That's when it hit home," Bhalla told me in an interview. "Watching these survivors talk about how their lives had completely turned upside down just for being at the wrong place at the wrong time made it real." She wanted to make partition real and understandable in the same way.

Thus was born the 1947 Partition Archive, a library of videos and audio clips capturing the memories of migrants who crossed the subcontinent's new borders during partition. Sukhmander Singh, who was in second grade at the time, recounts memories of "fear... apprehension, not knowing what was going to happen," and visiting empty houses where Muslims had lived in his village, which ended up on the Indian side of the border. "One Muslim boy was my friend.... We were together in the same class, you know? And he never showed up, but where did he go? We don't know."

Shane Ali recounts learning to forgive after watching a man shoot his mother and brother. "I forgive... the evil people who killed my family," he says. "My own thinking is, just love everyone, hate no one."

The subcontinent's demographics are making these kinds of stories increasingly rare. The populations of both India and Pakistan are among the youngest in the world: 29.9 percent of Indians and 33.8 percent of Pakistanis are under the age of 14.

This does not mean suspicion has faded on the subcontinent, however; 80 percent of Indians still view Pakistan as a very serious threat. For their part, only 13 percent of Pakistanis hold a favorable view of India.

But Bhalla, who is in her mid-30s, notes the enduring lesson of partition for people who never experienced it firsthand. "We are pretty lucky to be living in a time and a place where it's not so fragile that you have to up and leave your house and everything behind because of total chaos that is beyond our control."

TRANSFER OF POPULATIONS SURROUNDING THE PARTITION OF INDIA

The transfer of populations surrounding the Partition of India on August 14-15, 1947 created at least ten million refugees, and resulted in at least one million deaths. This is, perhaps, as much as we can quantify the tragedy. The bounds of the property loss, even if they were known, could not compass the devastation. The number of persons beaten, maimed, tortured, raped, abducted, exposed to disease and exhaustion, and otherwise physically brutalized remains measureless. The emotional pain of severance from home, family and friendships is by its nature unmeasurable. Fifty years have passed and the Partition remains unrequited in the historical experience of the subcontinent.

This is, in one sense, as it should be, for the truth remains that the Partition unleashed barbarism so cruel, indeed so thorough in its cruelty, and complementary acts of compassion so magnificent—in short a complex of impulses so pernicious, so heroic, so visceral, so human—that they cannot easily be assimilated into normal life. Neither can they be forgotten.

And so, ingloriously, the experience of the Partition has been perhaps most clearly assimilated in the perpetuation of communal hostility within both India and Pakistan, for which it serves as the defining moment. The hope for a different assimilation has motivated the recent spate of publications on the literature of the Partition—three major anthologies in the past two years, with others promised for the upcoming anniversary year. These collections attest not only to the resurgence of literary interest in the Partition, and the emergence of Partition writings as a genre in modern South Asian literature in translation, but of a different approach to the event itself: an unbridled reclamation, a direct gaze at ugliness and survival. The hope is that a just remembrance mandates a better future.

The historical benefits of these publications are not for Indians and Pakistanis alone. In wider perspective, the Partition stands as the archetype of what I would call nationalist fratricide, the conflict between people of a common cultural heritage—usually also the common subjects of foriegn domination—in competition as "nations" for political control of land and government. (The other principal type of ethnic conflict, nationalist genocide, is characterized by state-sponsored persecution or slaughter of cultural or religious minorities—epitomized by the destruction of the European Jews).

Those looking for historical lessons and for the depths of the human impact of current conflicts in the former Yugoslavia, in Chechnya, in Armenia and Azerbaijan, in Kurdistan, in Rwanda and Burundi, in the Sudan and in Israel, have much to gain in a close study of the Partition. A decent number, perhaps even a growing number of Pakistani and Indian historians will take exception to my characterization of the Partition as a case of fratricide. In their view, Pakistanis and Indians were not and are not one people, but two—different in their ways of life, in their religious ideals and in their historical destiny—whose separation at the end of colonial rule was right, if regrettable in its execution. If one idea emerges from the body of Partition writings taken as a whole, it is this: such a view is historically disingenuous, politically opportunistic, apologetic for crimminal behavior committed in the name of "destiny," compatible with resignation in the face of preventable suffering, and a mockery of religious values. Not that the anthologized literature is outwardly polemic—most of it is not—but the majority of it is necessarily politicized. And this is good: the Partition was an event so great in its human consequences that its literature rightly forces us to reckon sides and to choose. It is, after all, the literature's job to raise the event psychologically and emotionally, to tie us into its complex of choices and pain. So knotted we may learn to discriminate the day when (God willing) fratricide no longer appears a reasonable approach to the fact, indeed the joy of cultural difference.

However unified the literature itself, though, important and even fractious differences remain between the editorial viewpoints of these anthologies. Because these differences are critical in determining the climate of the literature's reception, it is worthwhile to examine them in some detail before turning to evocation and discussion of the texts themselves.

Cowasjee and Duggal's fine collection of stories from Urdu, Hindi and Panjabi emerges as the least editorially wieghted of the three. The collection as a whole offers what the stories individually offer: the psychologies of characters in the midst of the events, the drama and pathos of their human impact, trauma in various hues. It offers, plainly, the plainspoken truths of the Partition experience, namely that it was a maze of brutality, loss, jealousy, cupidity, cunning, death by butchery, by rape, by deracination.

Cowasjee and Duggal's Introduction is not particularly analytical philosophically or politically. If anything the collection rides editorially on the disgust, disillusionment and horror that were central concerns of the Progressive Writers movement, the dominant literary school in South Asian literature from the twenties through the forties, and the single greatest literary origin of Partition writing.

Both Cowasjee and Duggal were well known Progressive writers—Duggal's work in particular achieving critical acclaim—and it comes as no surprise that their collection should stand as a clear statement of the Progressive perspective on the Partition. In general the collection presents Progressive writing at its best, avoiding the sometimes melodramatic excesses of Progressive sentiment, offering a selection of stories that is nuanced, rich, difficult.

Bhalla has compiled an ambitious anthology, successfully hunting down works from every major and some minor Indian languages, presenting the perspective of Muslim, Hindu and Sikh writers. The anthology is not comprehensive, but does succeed in representating diverse points of view, bringing together some of the best authors and the best stories.

Bhalla wants more than this achievement, however. He intends his collection to stand as a categorical indictment of communal hatred, as well as a vindication of his own Gandhian views, and of Gandhi himself. Thus Bhalla offers himself in his Introduction as a committed partisan of the one-people perspective: that Hindus, Muslims and Sikhs, Pakistanis, Indians and Bangladeshis, are culturally a single people with different languages, religions and customs. The evidence of this single peoplehood is, in Bhalla's eyes, overwhelming: evident in the deep intermingling of lives, of cultural expression, of ethos in everday life, in literature, music, architecture, commerce. The violence of the Partition occurred because a single people was torn into separate nations in a spasm of religious hysteria, self-interest, panic, bloodlust, greed.

Bhalla's own focus on the phenomenology of the Partition places him squarely within the Progressive tradition. But where the Progressives simply offer shock and outrage at the failure of civilized behavior, and leave the Partition as an unrequited event, Bhalla offers along with his quotient of shock and outrage a philosophy to redeem both the past and the future. He observes, trenchantly, that cultural chauvanism arises when inclusion and exclusion become the mediating criteria according to which a culture is defined: "[e]ntrapped by the logic of exlusive nationalism, [migrants] learn[ed] too late that neither the community of religion nor the shared idioms of language can offer a secure guarantee of a just society and so become the basis of a firm identity.

Religious and linguistic definitions...succeed only in establishing shifting grounds for the inclusion of some and making all others expendable...[t]hese definitions...can be manipulated for the purposes of political power by the unscrupulous". Bhalla's true concern thus is articulating the rudiments of a just society. Bhalla does not get very far in such an articulation, but indicates that achieving a just society demands, at the least, exploding myths of cultural purity, and denuding any self-enchantment that "sublime feelings about our particular faiths alone [could] lead us to social justice".

Stated positively, social justice proceeds from admitting the selfish error of construing another community as essentially other, from admitting our essential connectedness to one another, and from correct remembrance of our mistakes. Making human connectedness and self-critical memory central to the building of a just society, we fence ourselves off from any suspicion that another community is less worthy of justice, which is to say less holy, than our own. First and foremost, with regard to the Partition, Bhalla implores us to accept "the absurdity of constructing fundamental entities called the Muslims or the Hindus who could easily be separated into nation states", and that the Partition forced members of both communities "to leave behind a human world...in return [for] an empty allegory of a religious community".

Approaching the Partition as a task of defining social justice is doubtless right, and Bhalla deserves commendation. Bhalla begins to stray, however, with the suggestion that religious faith, cultural pride, the essential connectedness of Muslim, Hindu and Sikh life in the subcontinent, the incomprehensibility of the notion that there was always hatred between the communities in everyday life, should together have been enough to prevent the degeneration into violence during the Partition. "Why did we not, as a people, resist?" Bhalla asks incredulously.

The stories themselves and a basic knowledge of history suggest a number of answers for the violence and the lack of resistance that are perfectly compatible with the one-people approach. First, the political climate of the freedom struggle was violent to begin with. The British government met the Indian nationalist movement with violent repression consistently throughout the freedom struggle, from the Khilafat/Noncooperation activism of 1918-22, through the Noncooperation movement of 1930-34, and the widespread revolts following the arrests of Gandhi, Nehru, Azad and other leaders at the start of the Quit India movement in 1942. In addition there were continuous, if rogue acts of revolutionary terrorism, as well as trade union militancy, communist agitation, and regular outbreaks of communal rioting. The militant voices of Muslim separatism became exceedingly important, as we know, after the 1940 Lahore Resolution, in addition to the voices of Hindu chauvanism in the Hindu Mahasabha and the RSS, whose message dovetailed with the more moderate voices of the Hindu religious revival that began in the nineteenth century. Add to the political turbulence the economic suffering the country experienced under the British regime, the most obvious consequence of which was a series of devastating famines causing an estimated thirty million deaths between 1857 and 1947, with three million in 1943 alone—and the result is a condition of extraordinary explosiveness.

It is quite possible that no force in the world could have prevented the ignition of such a concentration of social and political discontents. Second, the exchange of populations during the Partition introduced a social vacuum uniquely habitable to thugs and goons.

If the aggressions of an organized few are usually enough to frighten the unorganized many in times of stability, they are enough to terrorize in times of social upheaval. Thus, self-protection alone must account for a great deal of the nonresistance. Such self-protection, while perhaps not noble, is also not a vice. Third, there was legitimate confusion over the future of the country given the erratic policy of the British government and the brinksmanship between the League and the Congress.

Likewise there was legitimate confusion over cultural identity, particularly given that tensions by 1947 had risen to a point where extreme views had managed to win the tacit if not explicit support of moderates. Confusion is eminently permissive of ethical failure. Fourth, the incendiary quality of media coverage only hastened the collapse of good judgment. Finally, distinctions must be made between the overt perpetration of violence and the willing allowance of violence, and also between first and retaliatory acts of violence. The original perpetration of violence is unquestionably to be condemned. But the allowance of violence and retaliatory violence are not necessarily indicative of pure ethical rot: they may just as well proceed from the gross error in judgment of people acting in anger who did in fact know better. While such errors are not justified, they are perhaps more easily understood as products of war.

All five violence-begetting elements—the ambient political and social violence, the terror of an organized few and the self-protective reaction of the many, political and cultural confusion, inflammatory media reportage, the natural retaliatory impulse in the face of violence—do not in any way contradict the thesis of shared history and essential amity between groups. But Bhalla fails to consider these or other sources of violence when he asks, "why did we not, as a people, resist?" Rather he asks the question as if the only answer were either that the violence remains essentially inexplicable, or that the Partition shows human nature itself intrinsically weak and depraved. For Bhalla there is apparently no explanation for the violence, short of a nihilistic conclusion about human nature, which Bhalla is loathe to make. Indeed it seems that Bhalla considers himself noble for not making such a conclusion, which the horror of the events would warrant.

In fact Bhalla's question is rhetorical, and he offers only naive answers because the question is a sieve into his own agenda: rehabilitating Gandhi as an ethical model and a martyr to hatred. Directly following his query about the failure of resistance, Bhalla asks, "Why did we not follow Gandhi, as we had done often before, on his pilgrimmage to Noakhali and gather around him at Srirrampur to pledge to uphold the peace?". The only way Bhalla can ask this question seriously is if Gandhi has himself become a mythical figure of universal unification. The "we" of Bhalla's question cries for definition: not only did Gandhi not enjoy the uncritical support of the Congress leadership, much of which rejected his Luddite economics and his political strategy (not to mention his personal idiosyncracies), but his detractors included B.R. Ambedkar, who criticized him for his support of the varna system and gender inequalities, and mainstream Muslims who were justifiably suspicious of his trading on Hindu symbolism to rally political support.

To make Gandhi into a model universalist is to take him entirely on his own terms, which is a sport for the gullible. I do not think, however, that Bhalla is merely a dupe of Gandhian myth. Rather I believe that he himself, while asserting that secularism is the only acceptable political solution to the challenge of multi-culturalism, is sympathetic with Gandhi's personal religious orthodoxy, and with a Hindu religiosity modeled on it. Bhalla says, in effect, that Gandhi represents the pinnacle of Hindu ethical consciousness, which is a pure achievement beyond its political manifestation, and so deserves to be embraced by members of all faiths as a solution compatible with secularism to the problem of communal hatred.

Because I respect that Bhalla offers his opinions sincerely, I hesitate to call them arrogant. But the question remains open whether Gandhi's legacy can be laundered so that Gandhi emerges as a prophet of social inclusiveness acceptable to secularists and to non-Hindus. Trying to make Gandhian Hinduism the true path of ethical universalism, and the natural handmaiden of political secularism is a dicey proposition, if only in the effort to be true to the historical record, as Bhalla insists we must be. Whatever Gandhi's personal religious feelings, his politics were not evident to all parties as the politics of universal love.

And even his personal ethics are not universally lovable, at least as Gandhi presents them in his Autobiography, where he frequently appears egocentric, rigid, unforgiving and exceedingly authoritarian. That aside, Bhalla's efforts are certainly questionable in the current political climate, in which there is no more guarantee than there was fifty years ago that Gandhi will not be revered narrowly as a Hindu hero rather than as a Hindu universalist. Bhalla risks playing into the hands of those fundamentalists he opposes.

The least that Bhalla owes his readers in the way of Gandhi therapy is a thorough criticism of Bhalla's own Hindu community both during and after the Partition. Bhalla's analysis of Hindu fundamentalist history is curiously abrupt, and off the mark. First, the problem is not that Hindu fundamentalist historians falsely construct entities called Hindus and Muslims, as Bhalla claims, but that they distort differences that do exist for the sake of creating enmity. Second, Bhalla fails to consider that not only was Muslim resistance to the Hinduized politics of the Indian National Congress not a betrayal of India, as the Hindu historians claim, but it was a legitimate forum of resistance.

That is, if Gandhi's Hindu religiosity formed a legitimate, indeed desirable basis of resistance, then some form of Muslim-centered consciousness must also be admitted. Third, and perhaps most seriously, Bhalla has the temerity to attack current Pakistani historians who justify the violence of the Partition in defense of Pakistan as an historical destiny, without decrying the ways that hindutva history is currently used to justify the persecution of the Muslim minority in India—indeed without mentioning the appalling levels of communal violence in the 1990s that such history has abetted. We are left to wonder whether it is merely accidental that Bhalla's Gandhian humanism seems remarkably like Indian nationalism, more concerned with discrediting Pakistani ideology than setting its own house right.

Where Bhalla positions himself as a lone ethical hero trapped in a universe of parochial fiends, and then fails to live up to the self-critical standards he expects of others, Mushirul Hasan emerges as a sober critic who clearly understands the gravity of the ethical failure the Partition played out—without self-righteousness.

The clear editorial strength of Hasan's new volumes is his willingness to peer critically into the political tectonics of the Partition from the Muslim perspective, with a courage that delineates precisely who won and who lost with the partition of the country.

Hasan has collected two thoughtful, compelling volumes of literary and documentary material from Urdu, Hindi, Panjabi and English, that enable a deep consideration of the social configuration of the Partition, largely but not exclusively from the Muslim perspective. Together with the collection of academic papers he edited in 1993, India's Partition: Process, Strategy and Mobilization (New Delhi: Oxford), the new volumes will remain a landmark in Partition studies for some time to come.

Hasan's scholarship into the politics that won Pakistan hovers in the background of his project in these volumes, and provides a light on events that the stories themselves generally do not shine, namely the politics of the Muslim League's success, and the political brinksmanship of Muhammad Ali Jinnah, the Congress leadership, Lord Mountbatten and the British government.

Neither Hasan nor his collegues question that the status of the Muslim minority raised a nearly intractable dilemma in the context of rising Indian nationalist consciousness: such consciousness grew, on the one hand, as against the colonial regime, but on the other along the contours of internal cultural differences.

Where the colonial status quo involved reducing all groups to minority parties, encouraging them to make their separate peaces with the British regime—gaining privelege, protection, or being ignored—Indian nationalists divided between builders of an integrated, pan-Indian coalition, and builders of a mass majority with pronounced minority exclusion. Hasan describes the Muslim League's three-pronged response, which succeeded in mobilizing the Muslim middle and working classes, and polarizing the overall political climate after the Lahore Resolution.

First, the League galvanized the fears of the Urdu-speaking muhajir bourgeoisie that they were in direct competition with and mortally outnumbered by a tightly knit, conspiratorial Hindu bania.

Second, it swayed self-seeking local lanndlords and political henchmen, particularly in the Panjab, by capitalizing on the electoral miscalculations of its opponents (the Congress, the Panjabi Unionist Party), and by secretly promising not to enact land reforms in Muslim controlled areas.

Third, it sent pirs together with Aligarh students to canvass the countryside. The pirs, whom the League paid tens of thousands of rupees, convinced large numbers of people that dedication to the Muslim League was a religious duty.

The students transformed the League's popular appeal into an anti-Hindu hysteria, drumming up a paranoia that could only be solved by Muslim secession from the rest of India and the creation of a fundamentalist theocracy to save the "endagered" Muslim people.

What Hasan and others call into question is how much Jinnah actually wanted partition. They suggest that Jinnah after 1937 was hemmed in from two sides: by provincial Muslim bosses, particularly in the Panjab, and by the provincial Congress ministries, which sought on the strength of the Congress' showing in the 1937 elections to marginalize Jinnah and the League.

The secular, liberal Jinnah, according to the new thinking, was imperfectly committed, even perhaps uncommitted—but in any case far less committed than the Muslim religious right—to the two nation theory of essential cultural and political differences between Hindus and Muslims, and the picture of Islam in danger—of, that is, Muslims as hapless victims of communal riots perpetrated by a hostile Hindu majority, of the Muslim salariat in a losing battle with the dominant caste Hindu salariat, and of

Urdu under seige. (Incidentally, he was also far less committed than the Hindu religious right, which viciously attacked not only Muslims but secularists also).

In the revisionist perspective, Jinnah did not embrace religious mobilization and the demand for partition because he was wedded to a sovereign Muslim religious homeland, but because he needed to win support for the League in Muslim dominated areas, and to break the Congress' grip on the post-independence central government. In short, Jinnah made a bargaining chip of the spectre of partition in his effort to make a place for himself and the League in a united, free India. Jinnah's India would have been characterized by provincial autonomy, benefitting the League in the Muslim dominated provinces, accompanied by parity between the League and the Congress at a weak center. Additionally, separate Muslim provinces within a united India would facilitate the League's other principal charge, the protection of Indian Muslims where they were in the minority.

For the Congress, the reverse would be true: a partition of the country would certify its control over a strong central governement. Such control, Hasan and his corps argue, ultimately proved more important to the Congress than Indian unity.

The genius of the Congress strategy was to force Jinnah to wear the black mark of division, putting up a facade of unity while deliberately pushing Jinnah toward his Pakistan. Thus both Nehru's and Gandhi's reactions to the Lahore Resolution were from the beginning calculating. Shortly after the passage of the Resolution, Gandhi, realizing that partition promised fratricide, effectively equated his nonviolence with nonprotection of the innocent, and with a willingness to accept blood as the price of the Congress' leadership:

"Unless the rest of India wishes to engage in internal fratricide, the others will have to submit to the Muslim dictation, if the Muslims will resort to it...The Muslims must have the same right to self-determination that the rest of India has. We are at present a joint family. Any member may claim a division... As a man of non-violence, I cannot forcibly resist the proposed partition if the Muslims of India really [insist] upon it [sic]... My whole soul rebels against the idea that Hinduism and Islam

represent two antagonistic cultures and doctrines... But that is my belief. I cannot thrust it down the throats of the Muslims who think that they are a different nation."

Likewise, on April 15, 1940, Nehru was reported to be

"pleased, not because he liked [the Lahore Resolution]—on the contrary he considered it to be the most insane suggestion—but because it very much simplified the problem. They were now able to get rid of the demands about proportionate representation in legislatures, services, cabinets, etc... [He] asserted that if people wanted such things as suggested by the Muslim League at Lahore...they and people like him[self]...could not live together in India."

So too, Maulana Abul Kalam Azad, in the thirty pages of his 1957 memoir, India Wins Freedom, disclosed in 1988, points his finger at Nehru's responsibility, and gives the lie to the myth of "the Congress for Unity, the League for Partition:"

I warned Jawaharlal [in 1946] that...if we agreed to Partition...[t]he verdict would be that India was not divided by the Muslim League but by the Congress.

Finally, in 1960, Nehru himself made the opprobrious confession: "The truth is that...the plan for partition offered a way out and we took it."

Jinnah, along with the Congress leadership, accepted the Cabinet Mission Plan in June, 1946, which did not call for partition. The Congress then destroyed the option by refusing to accede to parity with the League in the interim government, or to a compulsory grouping of the six Muslim provinces. In 1947, Jinnah was willing to accept a united India with a "dominion" of the six provinces. So it was that Jinnah remained obstinate in public and considerably more pliable behind the scenes. The final outcome of negotiations, mandating the dual transfer of power to a bifurcated Pakistan and an Indian state, followed from Congress policy and the British government's acquiescence to it.

Whether the League, the Congress or the British were the most culpable in the high level brinksmanship, the new scholarship makes clear the extradordinary recklessness of the demand for partition, fuelling as it did social engines of hatred beyond anyone's control, soliciting communal hatred as the best outlet for the social tensions of the period. The scholarship suggests the following answer to the question of whether Pakistan was an historical destiny: bloodshed was the destiny of the politics of arrogance and deceit. And so like Bhalla, Hasan believes that Hindus and Muslims in the subcontinent formed a single people, sharing a culture in which linguistic, regional and fraternal bonds crossing religious communities were socially foundational, and indeed, in which folk religious worship was frequently a fusion of Hindu and Muslim practice.

Who were the losers in the Partition? Without question it was the great majority of common people who had lived side by side for generations, and had cultivated deep attachments to land, language, friendship and a shared cultural heritage. Hasan writes: "It is undeniable that most people, Hindus and Muslims alike, were largely unconcerned with or indifferent to the newly created geographical entities.

Most were caught up in the cross fire of religious hate. Most were driven out of their homes and drifted from one place to another out of fear, panic and a sense of hopelessness. They were indeed hapless victims of a triangular game plan, worked out by the British, the Congress and the League without care or consideration for huge number [sic] of people who had no commitment to a Hindu homeland or fascination for an imaginary dar al-Islam. They had no destination to reach, no mirage to follow". It is only natural that Hasan like Bhalla should strive with his collection to fathom "the immediate and the long term impact of Partition on the silent majority, uprooted from home and field and driven by sheer fear of death to seek safety across a line they had neither drawn nor desired".

"Somewhere the wave of the slow night will melt the shore and somewhere the boat of the heart's grief will anchor..." —Faiz Ahmad Faiz

It is well that the high politics of the Partition hang in the background of the majority of the stories themselves, which dwell in the affective experience of the events and their consequences for ordinary people. It is, after all, in drawing forth the ways the

Partition felt, beyond debate about what caused it and what it caused, that it reaches a universal accessibility, and gets lodged in a broad section of humanity's historical memory.

Across the anthologized material, three central thematic areas emerge: rupture, protest and repair. Though none of the anthologies is thematically arranged, these three motifs taken in a progression form a natural response to the Partition, a continuum from pain to healing. Stories of rupture involve a basic confusion, a groping for sense and sanity amid personal, social and sometimes existential loss. Stories of protest grow fundamentally from anger, and decry human savagery, the vitiation of values, the betrayal of social contract. Stories of repair, finally, remind us of the sparks of ethical conscience that dwell in the human soul, even in the most degraded of times, and of the healing power of positive memory. Of course, many stories include more than one of these themes.

The three anthologies do differ slightly in their thematic emphases. Cowasjee and Duggal include mainly stories of rupture and protest. Bhalla includes stories of all three types, with perhaps a larger quotient of stories of repair. Hasan's volumes are weighted in favor of stories of protest. It should be said to the credit of all the editors and translators that their selections are, in general, literarily sophisticated as English works. Indeed, in the 136 stories the three anthologies together offer, only one seems to treat the Partition entirely superficially, at the level of its crimes and atrocities, even exploiting them for literary shock value, proffering the easy answer of indignation in the face of the Partition's complexities. This is Krishan Chander's "The Peshawar Express," in which a personified train narrates a putrid journey of murder and woe from Peshawar to Bombay. The story is simplistic and specular in a literal sense: it describes events as a mute passerby might see them. By literarily sophisticated I mean not that the other stories are all successful, but that they are dramatically, emotionally, psychologically or philosophically skilled. Within such skill is a range of success. Many plot-driven works read well, perhaps because they are relatively easy to translate. Of the emotionally driven works, those focussing on anger tend to be more successful than those based in melancholy, which easily beçomes facile sentimentality. Alok Bhalla's and Vishwmitter Adil's translation of Ismat Chugtai's "Roots," for example, seems concertedly on the saccharine side. The same can be said for their translation of Gurmukh Singh Musafir's "The Abandoned Child," for Mihir Bhattacharya's translation of "The White Horse," and Bhisham Shahni's own translation of his "Pali." Likewise Faruq Hassan's translation of Qudrat Ullah Shahan's "Ya Khuda," which contains moments of extraordinary pathos, is uneven and at times cloying in its portrayal of its protagonist's wizened numbness. Luckily, nearly all the stories that work primarily as psychological and philosophical studies are decently translated, particularly those of Intizar Husain. The notable exception is Kamleshwar's "How Many Pakistans?"—which despite being included in all three collections—is in none of them quite able to marry the protagonist's directionlessness in the last scene with his knowing tenderness in first.

Hasan's collection raises special concerns because it, unlike the others, treats fictional and nonfictional writing, combining stories, exerpts from long fiction, poems, oral histories, interviews and memoir material. Hasan's editorial choice to include both types of writing brings us face to face with an essential problem of writing the Partition as the human experience it was, namely that the overwhelming majority of its events went unrecorded, unverbalized.

The writer of historical fiction strives to make particular events resound with the vast catalogue of silent events, to make the writing conjure what can never be fully spoken, and historical fiction thereby validates historical truth precisely in its power to represent. Documentary writing, on the other hand, remains closely attached to particular persons, particular contexts, and achieves a sense of representation only when the person relating the events is especially insightful. When the two genres are combined, what might seem like poetic license in the fiction—for example, in descriptions of violence and crimminality—reads true to the personal experiences of the nonfiction.

At the same time, the nonfiction, when informed by the fiction, seems to describe not just the particular experience of an individual, but also commonplace experience. As tempting as it might be to privilege fictional investigation for its aesthetic and philosophic richness, Hasan's volumes abundantly bear out that the fiction's power is, if anything, increased when offered together with nonfictional accounts. This is particularly true in the case of oral history, interview and other testimonial texts, which are experiential and nonanalytical, and so are strikingly close in their feeling to much of the short fiction. The juxtaposition draws attention to the different truths different sorts of writing tell—and is one of Hasan's collection's principal achievements.

For those with limited time to study the anthologized material, the following are, I think, the finest pieces.5 It is, naturally, impossible here to relate the works in their fullness, or to do justice to the many extraordinary characters and scenes the stories impart.

Abbas' "Revenge" is the terse tale of Hari Das, a prominent Panjabi lawyer who has lost his entire family in the massacres: his wife drowned herself, and a bloodthirsty crowd raped and murdered his daughter. Consumed with the desire for revenge, Hari Das becomes fixed on the notion of stabbing a Muslim girl in her naked breasts. Living as a refugee in Delhi, it happens that he receives a sum money from a rehabilitation fund. He decides to spend it in lavish fulfillment of his violent fantasy. He goes to a brothel and sets his sight on an extraordinarily beautiful Muslim prostitute.

He enters into a seductive drama with her, gracing her dance with note after note, until, at the end of the evening, he accompanies her to her bedroom. With his knife in his pocket, and a manic gloss in his eyes, he bolts the door and orders her to undress, piece by piece, under the electric light. When only her brassiere remains, the girl covers her face with her hands and begins to sob. Hari Das raises the knife above her, and grabs at her hands to see the look of terror on her face as he kills her. The girl shrieks. Hari Das intuitively recognizes more than terror in her look—but also fear, hate, a plea for mercy, hopelessness—a look her face had borne before, and the very look he had seen on his own daughter's face. When he snatches away her brassiere, his dagger still poised above her, he can only avert his eyes: "beneath the brassiere where he was going to stab her, there were no breasts...there was nothing—nothing but two horrible round scars." We imagine that Hari Das realizes that revenge only contributes an economy of mutilation, but Abbas leaves open whether such a realization can match the force of tears and shame. Revenge, Abbas suggests, may be a poor response to the pain, but poor because there is no reclaiming such pain. We see that the urge for revenge veils the pain. Abbas in his story lifts the veil, but gives no direction for living with the pain more directly felt.

Perhaps the finest writer of pithy, biting stories, Saadat Hasan Manto, receives considerable attention in these collections. Manto's achievement—and the reason for treating him foremost as writer of rupture—is to place his readers in the heat of depraved, senseless and twisted universes from which he offers—in what is perhaps his own vengeance— no clear escape. We are left only with speed and violence coursing in the blood of his characters, spun off without soothing messages or disclaimers. "Cold Meat" brilliantly traces the thin line between sexual urge and bloodlust, as a jealous woman murders her usually virile lover, who has become impotent after abducting a woman, killing her family and raping her with such lust he fails to notice she too is dead.

"Open It" tells the dark story of a refugee who hires a group of self-appointed social workers to find his missing daughter. The men locate her, feed her and—her father discovers in the end—brutally rape her. "Toba Tek Singh" relates with acid humor the story of a lunatic (perhaps any of us who tries to rationalize the Partition, Manto suggests), who in the exchange of asylum inmates between the two countries, answers the official queries of which country he belongs to with repeated nonsensical sputter, only to be left lying in a no man's land between barbed wire fences. In "Black Margins," Manto strings together a series of gritty vignettes, sometimes fragments of vignettes, of Partition evils. The piece is perhaps not as refined as his other work—which may account for why Hasan includes only twentytwo of the original thirty-two pieces, and why Bhalla includes only two6—but reveals the character of the moral hell Manto sees in the Partition. The following segment of the story, titled "Reformed," recounts a pitiless mob interrogation, in this case by Hindus, of a captive:

"Who are you?"

"But who are you?"

"Har Har Mahadev! Har Har Mahadev!"

"Har Har Mahadev!"

"What's the proof?"

"Proof? My name is Dharamchand."

"But this is no proof."

"I'm well versed in the four Vedas. Ask me about them."

"We don't know about the Vedas. We demand proof."

"What?"

"Loosen your pyjamas."

A cry went up when the pyjama was lowered. "Kill him! Kill him!"

"Wait, wait I am one of you. I swear I am one of you."

"Then what's all this?"

"The locality I live in is full of enemies. So I was forced to do it—to save my life. This is my only mistake. For the rest I'm just fine."

"Chop off his mistake!"

The mistake was chopped off. So was Dharamchand.

Where the stories of Manto, as well as Samaresh Basu, Krishna Sobti, Mumtaz Mufti, M.A. Sarna and others offer profound confusion in the form of unrequited violence or madness, Intizar Husain, Umm-e-Ummara, Qudrat Ullah Shahaz and others offer it as philosophic and existential crisis, or as boundless meditation on sorrow. Intizar Husain's "The City of Sorrow" is a disembodied, Beckett-like story of violence sustained and suspended in a memory that not only fails to forgive, but fails even in its fixation to numb. Husain's brilliant "An Unwritten Epic" begins as the epic novel of a hero murdered internally by the contradictions of the Partition, and then literally murdered—when the work is truncated and continued as the author's diary entries telling of his difficulties and finally his decision to abandon writing, in what he considers the inhumanity of life in Pakistan. The story leaves us in realm in which all efforts to recuperate the tragedy of the Partition through writing have failed: the effort to write the character of a hero capable of transcending the pain, a man who could "fight the wind with a lamp;" the effort to write supposedly only for oneself, diaristically; finally the effort even to write inability. Abandoning writing, the author claims he has "come to his senses." Husain's particular genius in this and many of his pieces is to mum and straightjacket us, and at the same time engender a strange feeling of release and completion in perpetual unfulfillment. In this way Husain, in stringing us in confusion along to infinity, perfectly complements Manto's punching us in the stomach with it.

The high minded Rafiquddin is motivated not just by friendship, but by the dictates of universal justice: "We will not let you go," he insists, "...[i]t is the duty of the majority to protect the minority...If we can't protect our neighbors, how can we possibly protect our country? I am sure that the Hindus in Panjab, where they are in the majority, must be thinking and acting in the same way." Devenderlal accepts his friends reassurances, only to see his own house soon looted.

As the atmosphere in the city becomes increasingly vicious, a band comes and threatens Rafiquddin for hiding Devenderlal. Rafiquddin has no choice but to move Devenderlal to a small room in the compound of a friend who works as a police clerk. Devenderlal finds himself imprisoned indefinitely in solitary confinement—in the newly "free" Pakistan—his only companion a cat. Time goes by. One day he finds a cryptic note in his food, which turns out to be an act of mercy. He feeds the cat, and the cat dies. Devenderlal gathers his things and jumps over the compound wall into an unknown future, his friendship having been overpowered by the enmity of strangers, and the generosity of other strangers liable at any time to poison him.

Bhisham Sahni's "The Train Has Reached Amritsar" masterfully describes the breakdown of civil amity in a confined public space. Riding in a train through western Panjab east to Amritsar, three jovial Pathans poke fun at a mirthless Hindu. From the train window, passengers see the smoke of burning villages, and panic on the platforms of rural stations. At one stop, a Hindu family fleeing a mob attempts to board the compartment. One of the Pathans approaches the family, swearing and claiming the compartment is full, then gratuituously kicks the woman of the family in the stomach, sending her screaming to the floor in pain, and begins throwing the family's baggage out of the train. The family tries to recover its baggage, but fails.

As the train begins to pull away from the station, the family frantically disembarks, crippled and terrified. The Hindu seethes with anger, abuses the Pathans verbally, and resolves to take revenge. The compartment becomes grim and silent. When the train reaches Amritsar, both the Hindu and the Pathans leave the compartment.

The Hindu returns with a metal rod to find that his adversaries have relocated. He roundly abuses the other passengers on the train for letting them "escape." The train leaves the station and soon most of the passengers are sleeping, except the Hindu, who is restless. In the middle of the night, as the train is moving slowly through the countryside with its lights out, there is a banging on the door, and the plead of a refugee who has caught the door handle, his wife running beside the train, "In the name of Allah, open the door! Open the door!... There is a woman with me. She'll be left behind..." The Hindu opens the door. Suddently his rod flashes and comes down hard on the man's head. The man grimaces in terror at his anonymous assailant, and falls from the footboard in a heap. The babu surveys the compartment, and then flings the rod into the night.

Yaspal's "A Holy War" is likewise a microcosmic study of hatred, this time in a dense, integrated lane in Lahore in 1947. Communal terror has driven all the Muslims from their locale, with the exception of the dyer, Fazzay, who has lived in the lane for forty years, and his son, Nasru. The humble, peaceful Fazzay stays in the confidence that the tumoil is only temporary. Nasru, however, years to do what other Muslims of the city are doing: to burn, loot and kill in the "holy war" for the creation of Pakistan. Fazzay scolds him intensely: "Shut up. You stupid son of a pig!...don't talk nonsense... This shop was set up by your father.

You were born in this room. It's the women of this lane who...looked after your mother. She...died in this very room. It is this Gali which has given us shelter and helped us earn our bread. Wait patiently, things will settle down." When Hindus begin to flee the city, Fazzay becomes despondent, while Nasru becomes elated, and gleefully joins in the looting.

Troops occupy the city, curfew is imposed, and Fazzay becomes sick with worry. When Nasru returns, the two are confined with one another in their small shop. They fan each other, and quarrel. After a sleepless night, Nasru opens the door for air, and sees a well known, old Hindu widow of the lane stealing away, wrapped in a bedsheet, carrying her money in a bundle. "Let her go, why should you care?"

Fazzay asks. "May Allah protect her."...When Fazzay, staggering on his old legs, finally reaches the bazaar, Nasru has not only caught up with the old woman, but stabbed her and taken her bundle. Trembling with rage, Fazzay drags his son back to their room. Nasru is overjoyed with himself: "Bitch...the kafir was running away with the stone idol of her God," he laughs derisively. Fazzay is alternately exhausted and burning with rage. "May a pig—your mother," he curses. "May you burn in Hell... The kafir was running away with the stone idol of her God. She should have smashed your head with her stone idol..." The story powerfully telegraphs the pain of the Partition, conveying the impairment of judgment in communal disintigration so rapid it dissolves not only tightly woven communities, but even single families.

Ganda Singh's "Diary of Partition Days," a nonfictional narrative, documents the grim toll of the religious hate rhetoric in Panjab from April, 1947 through January, 1948. From personal observations, newpaper accounts and astute political intuition, Singh pieces together the month to month political developments with details of the mounting campaign of death, showing how the forces of destruction proceeded with their own momentum, aided by the rancor of political contention. In March, 1947 we see the first Muslim armed offenses in Panjab; in April and May, riots in Amritsar, and then in Lahore, with stabbings of 200 and more at a time. By October the violence has reached epidemic proportions, including, for example, the massacre of 2000 Hindus and Sikhs in a special envoy train by a Muslim mob. By January mobs of greater than 25,000 are roaming Karachi, looting and massacring, with the police standing by the wayside, taking their share. The narrative clearly shows that after April, 1947, if the brutal communal violence in Bihar, Calcutta and Noakhali in 1946 were not enough, no one could mistake the upshot of a religious partition of the country.

Unlike most of the other texts in these collections, "Diary of Partition Days" does leave the impression that one group, in this case the Muslims, was more culpable than other groups in the violence. Other texts with discernable communal allegiances include Shorish Kashmiri's "Humiliated and Harassed They Left" (H2), Ishtiaq Husain Qureshi's "Hindu-Muslim Social Relations 1935-47" (H2), both pro-Muslim in their orientation, as well as the collection of League propaganda poems, "It's Voting Day: Let's March... Mukhiaji" (Urdu propaganda poems, H1). Hasan's decision to include these texts, particularly the poems, is justified because they provide important documentary material—even their bias proves informative.

Whether inclusion of such texts would be justified were they fictional remains an open question. Bhalla strongly disapproves of including communally charged stories, believing that they perpetuate "codes of fraud" by insufficiently describing the communally shared and reciprocal nature of the Partition's crimes. To prove his point he attacks certain stories in his own volumes, for example Krishna Sobti's "Where is my Mother?", the story of a Pathan murderer's acts of mercy toward an innocent Hindu child who refuses to trust him.

Also he makes a point of stating his exclusion of other stories he deems communal, claiming they are poor literature. While he is right to condemn such stories, it is not clear that they should be excluded: as Hasan demonstrates, when properly contextualized they may aid the discriminating reader. Bhalla's criteria for judging a story communal also demands refinement. First, it is not clear that the literary value of so-called communal stories would improve with demonstrations the author's knowledge of history. For example Sobti's story, in what I would consider a plain and reasonable reading, gains its effectiveness precisely because it is terse. Second, many stories are told largely from the point of view of a single community, and this in itself cannot be considered a communal liability.

Attia Hosain's "After the Storm" is an exquisitly told vignette of the first meetings between a resettled housewife (or so it seems—the narrator's gender is not given) and a child servant who lost her family during the riots. Winsomely and innocently the girl cannot help but seed new life—despite the brutality she has witnessed—bringing flowers and garlands, mixing her responses to questions about the violence she has seen with talk of sweets and bangles. The story avoids sentimentality superbly. We truly feel that we are being led by the child into liminal realms of the human spirit so pure that they survive unspeakable trauma and educate us in the release of our bigotry and grief.

Lalithambika Antharjanam's "A Leaf in the Storm" is likewise a sensitive and powerfully told story of survival. Jyoti arrives pregnant and despondent in a refugee camp, having been betrayed, abducted and raped in her transport across the border. The life inside her, "conceived in...inhuman rape and ignorance," tortures her as she watches births and deaths in the camp and grows increasingly bitter at the corruption that put and keeps her there. She is likewise tortured by her own idealism, her ardent, long-cultivated desire for "freedom from slavery for her community, indeed for the whole human race," which has been rudely dashed and has been reticulated back into her very body as the physical pain of her pregnancy. When the child is born she herself is thrust into a profound and spontaneous confrontation with the value of life. Miraculously, almost despite herself, she chooses life, taking the child in her arms, letting her life-blood flow "like fresh milk."

The interviews in Hasan's second volume with Partition survivors, as well as fictional pieces such as Mohan Rakesh's "The Owner of Rubble" and Ismat Chughtai's "Roots," reveal the healing power of memory—which is separate from the justice-producing power of memory. In these texts, memories of a shared communal life, of friendhips, of a civilization based on mutuality becomes not just salve for wounds, but life forces in themselves. Such memory-driven passion emerges in complex ways from "We are Still Theirs," an interview with Amrik Singh originally of Doberan Village near Rawalpindi, which was seriously affected by riots in March, 1947. In long, digressive and somehow still pointed passages, Singh recounts the past and also his conviction, born from his travels through Pakistan in the 1970s and 1980s, that great affection still remains at the popular level between citizens of the two countries:

"That shop where we were sitting at that time—this is of 1976 that I am speaking—I said to them, now you must be happy. They said, 'What do you mean?' I said, 'Earlier the angrez were rulers, now you have your own rulers. Bhutto Saheb is Prime Minister.' He said, 'So what? After all, what was there earlier, the same thing.' So I asked him what he wanted. He said, "We want many things, but we won't get them. What we want is to become what we once were, to be together again. But that will not happen...these are battles to win power, these people want their kursis here, your people want their kursis there, and we're just caught in between. We really feel that it was best as it was before. If we can become like that again, we'll really be happy, we'll celebrate.' They told us, he went on, that our lane was still empty. The village is full of people, but we have not let that lane be settled. You people are still there...and we keep hoping that one day you will come. We will help you with your work... There was so much love in their hearts for us..."

If the upshot of the renascent interest in the literature of the Partition is reclamation of the single peoplehood of the subcontinent, in its shared culture as well as shared violence, then the reclamation proves both a liberation—of the everyday life not imprinted either Hindu or Muslim—and a yoke—the recoupling of the grand narrative of the freedom struggle with the complexities that made freedom an experience of slaughter and inhumanity for many. Of course political debate will continue to penetrate the contributions of the various players—the British government's longstanding policy of sewing political divisiveness and haste in leaving India; the fanaticism of Muslim Leaguers and Hindu fascists who with gross lack of political sagacity ignored the evidence that partition would result in massive death and destruction precisely because of the density of the bicultural fabric; Hindu communalists disguising themselves as Congressmen and preventing the national movement from becoming truly inclusive; moderate muhajirs and landlords who allowed themselves to be polarized by extremist propaganda; Gandhi's and Jinnah's inabilities to guide the movements they initiated away from the forces of reactionary communalism; the newly formed Indian and Pakistani governments' failure to guarantee the security of their citizens, including government officials who profited personally from the unrest; all the individuals who killed, raped and looted, whether out of ideological conviction, personal greed, the idiotic aping of others, or retaliation as if for interpolative balance. Such debate will likewise go some distance in sussing out the psychology of the upheaval—what happened in thousands of villages and towns when thugs and extremists entered the question of the common man and woman, "to go or not to go?", and forced a decision that ensured counter violence on the other side of the border, a vicious cycle of fear and terror.

What political debate will never fully do—and the reason we so badly need the literature— is defeat the urge to lay blame, which keeps animosity alive. Only the literature truly evokes the suffering of the innocent, whose pain is more universal and ultimately a vehicle of more honest reconciliation than political discourse. The literary work on the Partition affirms that the subject of the Partition was first the human being—not the Hindu human being, or the Muslim, or the Sikh. In the world of the stories, the experiences of each community distinctly mirror one another, indeed reach out and clutch at one another. No crime, no despair, no grief at exile belongs uniquely to anyone. On the one hand, then, the stories seem to suggest that secularism puts a fence around the sanctity of life often more effectively than religious devotion—when, that is, secular thinking destroys religious myths of destiny and privilege that justify violence. At the same time they remind us that secular nationalism is not without its own mythology, including justification of foundational violence and violence deemed necessary for national sustenance. Perhaps we emerge from the literature with a mefiance toward group solidarity of an oppositional bent. If so we must emerge at the same time, paradoxically, with a conviction to oppose such mefiance with trust in the goodness of the human life-urge wherever we find it. Indeed, we emerge from the literature as searchers for such trust. If we find it in the solitary dissidence of even a single person—we feel obliged to offer him or her our compionship. And if we find it stitched into whole communities—we come away not necessarily more pious, but inspired. The literature as a whole seeds pathos for the suffering and inhumanity of the Partition, and related instances of cultural chauvanism, but not merely so. It also sprouts a countervailing protest, a voice of justice that must be the surging of our humanity itself—something greater than our beastiality—within us. In this sense the literature does what religious leaders in each community failed to do: to make communities forces for the affirmation of humanity broadly, and to forge nations- -if nations are the destinies of cherished traditions—dedicated to human improvement, dedicated precisely to virtuous conduct with those of different faith. If religious politics worked nefariously in favor of partition, it was because an ecumenical religious politics never developed. We are in a different position than the men and women of August, 1947. Our choices are not limited to exile, death or resignation. If the literature of the Partition can teach that committed people of different faiths serve God far more effectively when they face one another in prayer than when they face their respective temples, we can learn to exercise such a choice.

3

Partition and Making of India and Pakistan

PAKISTAN AND INDIA

Two self governing countries legally came into existence at the stroke of midnight on 15 August 1947.

The ceremonies for the transfer of power were held a day earlier in Karachi, at the time the capital of the new state of Pakistan, so that the last British Viceroy, Lord Mountbatten of Burma, could attend both the ceremony in Karachi and the ceremony in Delhi.

However another reason for this arrangement was to avoid the appearance that Pakistan was seceding from a sovereign India. Therefore Pakistan celebrates Independence Day on 14 August, while India celebrates it on 15 August.

Another reason for Pakistan celebrating independence on 14 August is the adoption of new standard time in Pakistan after partition.

The new standard time of West Pakistan (modern 'Pakistan') was behind Indian standard time by 30 minutes and the new standard time of East Pakistan (modern 'Bangladesh') was ahead of Indian standard time by 30 minutes, so technically on the stroke of midnight falling between 14 August and 15, when India became independent, it was still 11:30 p.m. on 14 August in West Pakistan.

BACKGROUND

Late 19th and early 20th century

The All India Muslim League (AIML) was formed in Dhaka in 1906 by Muslims who were suspicious of the Hindu-majority Indian National Congress. They complained that Muslim members did not have the same rights as Hindu members. A number of different scenarios were proposed at various times.

Among the first to make the demand for a separate state was the writer/philosopher Allama Iqbal, who, in his presidential address to the 1930 convention of the Muslim League said that a separate nation for Muslims was essential in an otherwise Hindu-dominated subcontinent.

The Sindh Assembly passed a resolution making it a demand in 1935. Iqbal, Jouhar and others then worked hard to draft Mohammad Ali Jinnah, who had till then worked for Hindu-Muslim unity, to lead the movement for this new nation. By 1930, Jinnah had begun to despair of the fate of minority communities in a united India and had begun to argue that mainstream parties such as the Congress, of which he was once a member, were insensitive to Muslim interests.

The 1932 communal award which seemed to threaten the position of Muslims in Hindu-majority provinces catalysed the resurgence of the Muslim League, with Jinnah as its leader. However, the League did not do well in the 1937 provincial elections, demonstrating the hold of the conservative and local forces at the time.

1932–1942

In 1940, Jinnah made a statement at the Lahore conference that seemed to call for a separate Muslim 'nation'. However, the document was ambiguous and opaque, and did not evoke a Muslim nation in a territorial sense. This idea, though, was taken up by Muslims and particularly Hindus in the next seven years, and given a more territorial element. All Muslim political parties including the Khaksar Tehrik of Allama Mashriqi opposed the partition of India Mashriqi was arrested on 19 March 1940.

Hindu organisations such as the Hindu Mahasabha, though against the division of the country, were also insisting on the same chasm between Hindus and Muslims. In 1937 at the 19th session of the Hindu Mahasabha held at Ahmedabad, Veer Savarkar in his presidential address asserted: "India cannot be assumed today to be Unitarian and homogeneous nation, but on the contrary there are two nations in the main – the Hindus and the Muslims."

Most of the Congress leaders were secularists and resolutely opposed the division of India on the lines of religion. Mohandas Gandhi and Allama Mashriqi believed that Hindus and Muslims could and should live in amity. Gandhi opposed the partition, saying, "My whole soul rebels against the idea that Hinduism and Islam represent two antagonistic cultures and doctrines. To assent to such a doctrine is for me a denial of God." For years, Gandhi and his adherents struggled to keep Muslims in the Congress Party (a major exit of many Muslim activists began in the 1930s), in the process enraging both Hindu Nationalists and Indian Muslim nationalists. (Gandhi was assassinated soon after Partition by Hindu nationalist Nathuram Godse, who believed that Gandhi was appeasing Muslims at the cost of Hindus.)

Politicians and community leaders on both sides whipped up mutual suspicion and fear, culminating in dreadful events such as the riots during the Muslim League's *Direct Action Day* of August 1946 in Calcutta, in which more than 5,000 people were killed and many more injured. As public order broke down all across northern India and Bengal, the pressure increased to seek a political partition of territories as a way to avoid a full-scale civil war.

1942–1946

Until 1946, the definition of Pakistan as demanded by the League was so flexible that it could have been interpreted as a sovereign nation Pakistan, or as a member of a confederated India.

Some historians believe Jinnah intended to use the threat of partition as a bargaining chip in order to gain more independence for the Muslim dominated provinces in the west from the Hindu dominated centre.

Other historians claim that Jinnah's real vision was for a Pakistan that extended into Hindu-majority areas of India, by demanding the inclusion of the East of Punjab and West of Bengal, including Assam, a Hindu-majority country. Jinnah also fought hard for the annexation of Kashmir, a Muslim majority state with Hindu ruler; and the accession of Hyderabad and Junagadh, Hindu-majority states with Muslim rulers.

The British colonial administration did not directly rule all of "India". There were several different political arrangements in existence: Provinces were ruled directly and the Princely States with varying legal arrangements, like paramountcy.

The British Colonial Administration consisted of Secretary of State for India, the India Office, the Governor-General of India, and the Indian Civil Service. The British were in favour of keeping the area united. The 1946 Cabinet Mission was sent to try and reach a compromise between Congress and the Muslim League. A compromise proposing a decentralized state with much power given to local governments won initial acceptance, but Nehru was unwilling to accept such a decentralized state and Jinnah soon returned to demanding an independent Pakistan.

The Indian political parties were:

- All India Muslim League,
- Communist Party of India,
- Hindu Mahasabha,
- Indian National Congress,
- Khaksar Tehrik, and
- Unionist Muslim League (mainly in the Punjab).

LAHORE: A SKETCH

The legendary origin of Lahore is traced to *Lav* or *Loh* a son of Rama, the king of Ayodhya and the hero of *Ramayana,* the second major Hindu epic from the pre-historical period. At the time of the first Ghaznivid invasion in the beginning of the 11th century a fortified city existed in the same place where the old walled city is located today. From that time onwards, Lahore remained under Muslim rule and a Muslim majority was always to be found in it. Until the British takeover in mid 18th century, Lahore was ravaged and razed time and again by Turks, Afghans, Persians and Sikhs.

A Hindu, and later Sikh, presence can also be traced in it throughout the post-Ghaznivid period. Real glory as a great city was attained by Lahore under Akbar (d. 1605) and thereafter it remained a prominent provincial capital of the Mughal Empire. It seems that notwithstanding periodic anarchy and disorder which followed when central authority weakened and petty warlords and chiefs fought each other for control over taxes and other dues, things returned to normality and communal concord was restored. The interplay between various sufi, sadhu and sant movements of those times created a scope for peaceful coexistence and a fair degree of interaction between the various religious communities, especially during festivals and holy occasions. The famous gay love affair between the sufi-poet, Lal Hussain, and the Hindu Brahmin boy, Madho, during the 16 century is some indication of the pluralistic environment of that time.

To this day an annual festival is held to commemorate their union. Both are buried in the same tomb and thousands of people flock to it. This is not to deny that dogmatic rules and regulations were also observed at all levels of society, especially by the clerics and upper strata of each community and communal boundaries were marked clearly through manifest rites, rituals and practices. In 1799 the Sikh leader Ranjit Singh defeated the Muslim garrison at Lahore and made it the capital of his kingdom.

After his death in 1839, a battle of succession began among the various claimants to the throne. Some Sikh chieftains began to extort heavy taxes and other dues from parts of the walled city in which they maintained their military presence. Chaos and disorder prevailed. The British were waiting in the wings to march on to Lahore. On 29 March 1849 a treaty was signed between Maharaja Dalip Singh and the British whereby the kingdom passed into the possession of the English East India Company. At that time, Lahore was in a state of chronic dilapidation, economic misery and overall decay. The buildings, streets, sewerage system and other facilities were in complete disrepair.

Under British patronage Lahore again prospered and became the most important city of northwestern India. The *Gazetteer of Lahore District 1883-4* gives the total population of Lahore town as 149,369. The communal composition of the three major groups was as follows: 86,413 Muslims, 53,641 Hindus, and 4,627 Sikhs. At the beginning of the 20th century many modern government offices, public and private banks, insurance companies, warehouses and educational institutions were built in Lahore.

People from other parts of Punjab and beyond were drawn towards it. The emerging new middle class and retired government preferred to settle in it. Punjab University, the engineering, medical and general colleges and a number of public and charitable hospitals and libraries rendered it a city of progressive art, culture and learning.

In that rapid economic transformation the Hindus and Sikhs enjoyed a head-start over Muslims. They had taken to modern education much earlier and were culturally better placed to function within a capitalist economy.

As Lahore expanded beyond the confines of the walled city and new localities sprang up it was the upwardly mobile Hindu and Sikh groups which settled them. The nationalist currents and communal revivals apace all over India invariably headed towards Lahore, where followers could be found from amongst its variegated citisenry comprising different religions, castes, communities and sects.

Following the massacre at Jalianwala Bagh in Amritsar in 1919 there was a flurry of political activity in Lahore, which brought all the communities together. Hindu, Muslim and Sikh speakers addressed agitated crowds from the pulpit of the Badshahi Mosque. The famous December 1929 Lahore session of the Congress in which the demand for the freedom of India was first formally made drew large inter-communal crowds.

The 1920s and 1930s was also a period of intensification of communal and religious revivals that had begun even earlier. The Arya Samaj, Hindu Mahasabha, the RSS and many other Hindu organisations were active in Lahore. Among Muslims the Ahrar,

Khaksar and various other Islamist movements had emerged. The Muslim League was also present but until the mid-1930s its support was confined to a few intellectuals and elite politicians. The Singh Sabha and the Akali Dal echoed Sikh communal aspirations.

Culture and society in Lahore from the 1920s and until 1947: written accounts and interviews

Agha Ashraf's autobiography, *Aik Dil Hazaar Dastan* (One Heart and a Thousand Stories) begins with a detailed description of his childhood in the 1920s, spent within the walled city. Children of all communities studied together in the local schools. He describes some of his Hindu and Sikh teachers at the Dayal Singh School in saintly terms.

He played truant along with his Hindu, Muslim and Sikh class-fellows. They went around, among other things, visiting Hindu temples all over Lahore on such occasions. Drinking, opium eating, gambling and other such deviations were widespread in the inner city. Ashraf himself indulged in drinking bouts along with his friends.

In another major autobiography, *Mera Shehr Lahore* (My City of Lahore), Yunas Adeeb covers mostly the period from the late 1930s onwards. As a young lad, he could casually enter orthodox Brahmin homes and go to the temple with the older, unmarried sister of his neighbour Pandit Bhagat Ram. He notes that the people had evolved their own peculiar ways and means of circumventing the strictures of orthodox Hinduism, Islam and Sikhism and as a result a composite, heterodox way of life had emerged in the process.

In the local mohallas help and sympathy to the poor and distressed was given without reference to the various prejudices, although communal pride could sometimes prevent members of one group from taking help from the other community. Commenting upon the multiculturalism of Lahore, he recalls that Hindus would shower flowers on the Muharram procession while Muslims flocked to the great Ram Leela festival held in the Minto Park behind the Badshahi Mosque, and many took part in the Diwali and Dusera celebrations.

He personifies traditional multiculturalism in the following inimitable words:

- I remember in particular Lala Gunpat Rai because of his typical Hindu dress and appearance. He wore narrow pajama-type trousers, a kurta (long shirt), a waist-coat, and a black pointed cap on his head. Looking at his face one new that he was extremely cordial and friendly. It was his routine that when he passed the mosque in Kucha Darzian (locality of the tailors) he would stop, bend down to touch the steps of the mosque with his hands, and then with both hands pressed together pay his respect.

For those seeking exit from the conventions of regular society the various sufi shrines and abodes (called takkias), Hindu and Sikh non-conformist groups, training centres of wrestlers (called akharas), the quarters of the courtesans and prostitutes and various hideouts of opiumeaters and users of other intoxicants, offered a range of outlets. Among these marginal enclaves orthodox beliefs and practices were ignored.

Interviews

The veteran song-writer and music-director of the Bombay film industry Prem Dhawan told the present author that as a young man he came in contact with revolutionaries in the Lahore jail where his father was the superintendent. By the time he graduated from the Forman Christian College in 1942, he had been converted to Marxism.

About Lahore of the 1930s and early 40s he remarked:

- The atmosphere in F. C. College was cosmopolitan. The students came from all the communities. Most of us got along very well. Things were the same in most other parts of Lahore. It was indeed a city of tolerance and light. I left for Bombay in 1943. That four years later Hindus and Sikhs would have to leave Lahore forever never occurred to me. It could never have occurred, could it?

The world-famous sculptor, artist and poet Amar Nath Sehgal, with many internationally acclaimed works devoted to peace and solidarity to his credit remembered Lahore in very fond terms:

- I am originally from Campbellpur. In 1939 I arrived in Lahore to study at the Government College and graduated from there in 1941. Lahore was a paragon of brotherhood. Hindus, Muslims, Sikhs and others lived in peace and harmony. Things began to change by 1944 when the first slogans about Pakistan where chanted in Lahore. By 1946 things had changed fundamentally. Simply a suspicion that you doubted the feasibility of Pakistan could mean that some diehard Muslim Leaguer would get at your throat. In May 1947 I left Lahore because stabbing, looting and burning had become a daily routine. It was a shattering exit from a place I had learnt to love dearly. However, when I arrived in eastern Punjab things were no better. In the Kangra-Kulu Valley a wholesale slaughter of the Muslim minority took place between August and September. Out of 35,000 only 9000 managed to escape alive to Pakistan. The Beas was littered with dead bodies and a foul odour was in the air for weeks after the massacres.

Communal conflicts before the Partition riots

Occasionally communal riots did take place in Lahore. At such times interaction between Muslims and non-Muslims became tense and volatile. One such occasion was the publication of the book *Rangeela Rasul (The Merry Messenger of God).* Its Hindu publisher Raj Pal was sentenced on 18 January 1927 to eighteen months imprisonment and a fine of Rs 1000 for provoking enmity between Hindus and Muslims. The book was found to be a scurrilous satire on the founder of the Muslim religion.

On 6 April 1929 a Muslim youth Ilam Din stabbed him to death with a knife. The Lahore High Court found him guilty and sentenced him to death on 17 July 1929, and on 31 October the same year he was hanged in the Mianwali jail and buried there. Only persistent processions and demonstrations, on the one hand, and assurances by the notables of the Muslim community, on the other, that peace and order will not be disturbed if his body were returned to his family and buried in Lahore convinced the British authorities to comply with that demand. Ilam Din received a hero's burial and was given the honorific title of Ghazi Ilam Din Shaheed by the Muslims.

During those two years Hindu and Muslim relations were very hostile. A few years later, in 1935, the Masjid Shaheed Ganj dispute between Sikh and Muslim zealots turned into a bloody conflict. It has its origins in conflicting claims to a place claimed as sacred by both. Many people were killed and a veritable threat to law and order existed for some days.

High ethical standards of elite politics

Notwithstanding occasional outbursts of communal friction and confrontation, the Punjab in general and Lahore in particular maintained peace and normality until the riots of 1947. The credit for such a state of affairs went largely to the consociational model of power sharing which the Punjab Unionist Party had established in the province since, its foundation in 1923. It was the leading pro-British inter-communal party representing the powerful rural elite of Punjab. Tahir Lahori notes that whether Hindu, Muslim or Sikh, the politicians of the 1930s observed high standards of honesty.

He remarks:

- The finance minister was Sir Monohar Lal. His only son was an employee in a bank, but he did not hold any high position. If the finance minister had wanted he could have found him any high position. Sir Choutu Ram owned some agricultural land before he became a minister. When he left that job he still had the same piece of land. All leaders were of strong character. Muslim leaders were also of firm and exemplary patriotic character. Sir Sikandar Hayat's son was a major in the army.

Lahori records that after March 1940, when the Muslim League passed the Lahore Resolution demanding the creation of a Muslim state, the parting of ways between Hindus and Muslims began. The former reacted with great alarm to the idea of a separate Muslim state. On the other hand the Muslim League became very popular among the Muslims of Lahore. Seven years later, the idea of Pakistan had become a fact.

The time to leave

Pran Nevile, who in his Lahore

A Sentimental Journey reminisces the city of his birth and youth in the best of spirits - lavishly praising its joyous and boisterous citisenry and telling many a tale of fun and scandal involving Hindus, Muslims and Sikhs alike—expressed the pathos and trauma of Hindus and Sikhs who left Lahore in 1947 in the following words:

- It was for us a heart-rending experience to leave our beloved Lahore for good and seek refuge across the border which was created to divide the subcontinent. In the city which had been the home of our near and dear ones for centuries, there was no one left now to look back to. Suddenly, Lahore had become a foreign land.

Som Anand also expresses the profound sense of loss which Hindus and Sikhs felt when they were forced to flee Lahore:

- Communal riots became more intense after March '47 and it seemed that the Muslim leadership was out to clear the city of its non-Muslim inhabitants. That is not to say that every Muslim in Lahore liked what was happening. There were some who dreaded the prospect of the Hindus and Sikhs leaving the city for good. But such people could not speak of their feelings.

He pays tributes especially to the editor of the Urdu literary magazine, *Adabi Dunya,* Maulana Salahuddin Ahmed and the popular Punjabi poet Ustad Daman both of whom were deeply saddened when the non-Muslims left Lahore. He observes that although Hindus and Sikhs had begun to realise that Lahore may remain in Pakistan, it did not mean that they were willing to accept such a fate easily. Many of their leaders continued to believe that they will get Lahore on the basis of their overwhelming economic claims on that city.

Others, including his father argued that come what may, non-Muslims could continue to live on in Pakistan. The communal violence however made that choice virtually impossible. He admits that Hindus and Sikhs also carried out terrorism against Muslims. An attack on the Muslims of Rajgarh, a suburb of Lahore, made the situation explosive. The RSS and other militant Hindu and organisations were behind such activities.

The cultural basis of communal violence

Thus far, we have been examining accounts, which suggest a robust composite, multicultural environment prevalent in Lahore, which at times was put to the test by communal clashes. For understanding, why collective insanity imploded in Lahore during 1947 and enveloped its variegated citisenry into a horrendous bloodbath, we need to bring into the picture other aspects of the situation.

In this regard, we need to examine the extent to which Lahore constituted a plural society, that is, one marked by cleavages and tension, which Leo Kuper theorises can suddenly rip apart under strain. Som Anand provides some clues in this regard. He remarks that the Hindu and Muslim communities, 'lived like two streams, flowing side by side but never meeting at any point'.

He dilates further:

- To keep themselves away from the Muslims' "polluting touch", the Hindus had set-up many barriers in their daily life. My mother, for example, would never allow any Muslim to enter her kitchen. No cooked food was accepted from them. I remember how, if any of our Muslim neighbours even sent any special dish for my father, it never went beyond the dining table, a place where she did not take her own food. While eating she would never allow any of her Muslim friends or neighbours to touch her. During my childhood such inhibitions were generally not observed by male members of educated Hindu families. (Women have always been more conservative in these matters.) Some decades earlier these rules formed a strict code of conduct for all, no matter how educated or enlightened a person might be....
- The absurdities of such Hindu restrictions notwithstanding, the Muslims had come to accept them as a law of nature.

Their older generation knew the limits of a relationship with the Hindus and considered it improper even to offer them drinking water from their utensils.... The Hindus have always complained of Muslim fanaticism but they have never understood that the walls they raised around themselves could have not resulted in any other attitude....

- It took many centuries for the Hindus of Punjab to realise how absurd and harmful their anti-Muslim prejudices were. In this respect the first current of change was felt during the Khilafat movement in the early twenties. Though the spirit of Hindu-Muslim amity received many reverses in later years, at the social level the urban elite had changed its code of conduct for the better. This was due, in part, [to] Western education. What this change meant was evident in my father's attitude. When he was young, my mother used to recall, he would come back to change his clothes if a Muslim had touched him while walking in the bazaar; but during my childhood in Model Town, father had several Muslim friends and he considered my mother's inhibitions a sign of backwardness.

The economic basis of communal violence

The economic structure in Lahore surely compounded the social cleavages. Yunas Adeeb writes, ' The Hindus dominated money lending, import and export of cloth, the business in gold and silver and in food-grain.... The Muslims worked outside Lahore city in the fields. They cultivated vegetables and wheat, and most were craftsmen and artisans'.

Pran Nevile makes similar comments on the socio-economic structure:

- While the majority of the city population were Muslims, very few of them were engaged in business, civil services and the professions. It was only after the Government's job reservation policy came into force that the number of Muslims in the services increased. The Muslims constituted the majority of workers and artisan, being either employed in craft industries or in factories owned by Hindus. However, they controlled the fruit and vegetable markets, milk supply, furniture shops, tent manufacture and the tailoring business. There was also a sizeable Muslim landed aristocracy which owed its wealth and status to the British government.

The economic contradictions between Hindu-Sikh and Muslim groups had led the Communist Party of India to adopt a resolution declaring the movement for Pakistan as 'progressive'. Many prominent Muslim members of the Congress and Communist parties had subsequently joined the Muslim League.

This was particularly noticeable in Lahore where many of them were based. They started appearing in public meetings of the Muslim League, preaching from its platform the emancipation of the oppressed Muslim masses. According to their analysis, the movement for Pakistan represented the national aspirations of the Muslim people to self-determination.

The attitude of the Muslims of Lahore to the expulsion of Hindus and Sikhs

In Pakistan, official ideology based on the Two-Nation Theory looks upon Partition as necessary and inevitable: Hindus and Muslims were two separate nations and hence, entitled to separate states. This conviction has been imbibed through the education system in the later generations of Pakistani Muslims. Further, they have been indoctrinated to believe that the Hindus and Sikhs were the culprits and Muslims the victims of the Partition massacres.

Undoubtedly the perceptions of the younger people in Lahore to those times are imbued with the crass propaganda disseminated through textbooks.

As regards those who were in their late teens or more when rioting took place in Lahore, the perceptions are more varied. I have been discussing over the years with a cross-section of the people of Lahore on this theme. The dominant perception of the Muslims is that had the Hindus and Sikhs stayed behind they would have hindered and obstructed the progress and economic advancement of the Muslims.

A section of Muslims was attracted to the idea of Pakistan because it was going to be an Islamic state, a utopian polity where only piety and Islamic justice were to prevail. Some veteran

Communist-turned-Muslim Leaguers persist with their 'class analysis': the oppressed Muslim community overthrew the Hindu and Sikh bourgeoisie: simple and neat. The older Muslim nationalism school, with its most sophisticated exponents among the senior politicians and civil servants, emphasises the irreconcilability of the Hindu and Islamic worldviews. Among them a regret for the sufferings of people on all sides in 1947 is present, but the Congress and Hindus are held responsible for the failure of a power-sharing arrangement within a united India or a peaceful division and separation as two states.

The less-often heard critical voices in Lahore dissent from the nationalist version. Some of them bluntly state that the attacks on Hindus and Sikhs were motivated primarily by the desire to loot and plunder and that it was the criminal element, the depressed sections of society and Muslim League activists and partisan state functionaries who, in various combinations, conducted the raids.

It is interesting to note that the apologists of the attacks on Hindus and Sikhs justify the extensive use of petrol to lit fires as the 'poor man's weapon' against the better armed Hindus and Sikhs. It is pointed out that large-scale employment of arson became the chief weapon against Hindus and Sikhs only after the RSS had carried out several bomb blasts during May-June in the inner city.

On the more social and less politically theorised level, I have often heard the complaint that devout caste-conscious Hindus routinely humiliated the Muslims through their neurotic concerns for pollution by the latter. Even trivial matters such as drinking of water had to be done separately. Once in a while, however, the elderly generation does recall its Hindu and Sikh contemporaries with a tinge of nostalgia and sadness.

It is not entirely uncommon that some of those non-Muslims continue to be mentioned as models of gentleness and kindness. Among them Hindu and Sikh teachers, doctors, dispensers and philanthropists figure prominently. On the whole, the upward economic mobility achieved by large numbers of Muslims in Lahore with the departure of the non-Muslims seems to be the strongest argument for believing in Partition as necessary and inevitable.

INDIAN NATIONAL CONGRESS AND PARTITION OF INDIA

Inconsistent Opinions of Congressmen

When Moti Lal Nehru's daughter wished to marry Syed Hussain, the editor of a newspaper Independent, Moti Lal Nehru threatened that he would commit suicide. Gandhiji later persuaded Syed Hussain to forget about his marriage and to leave the country. Similarly when Gandhiji's son embraced Islam Gandhiji ostracized him and was reconciled to him only when he was brought back to the Hindu fold under Birla's influence. There was a tendency in Congress circles to overlook the communal character of Muslim leaders. Especially an attempt was made to portray Syed Ahmed Khan and Muhammad Iqbal as nationalists, who later became communalists due to the influence of Britishers, that too Beck, the principal of Aligarh college. But both these persons were too strong willed to play in the hands of any Britisher. As early as in 1867 Syed Ahmed Khan had said that he was convinced that these communities (Hindus and Muslims) cannot cooperate in any work. Iqbal, in an interview given to Bombay Chronicle in September 1931 said "In my college days I was a zealous nationalist, which I am not now.

The change is due to mature thinking." Jawaharlal Nehru in one of his letters to Padmaja in 1929 said-" I have never met Iqbal. He was always been one of the many problems I could not solve. How can a real poet be so extraordinary communal and narrow minded and earthly? And yet he happens to be both. Though Gandhiji had said in Harijan (January 6th, 1940) that it was Hindu's cowardice that had made the Musalman a 'bully' leading to Hindu Muslim riots, yet his advise to girls menaced with rape in the Punjab (after Partition) was to bite their tongue and hold their breath until they died. Even with regards to partition, while Gandhiji said that it could happen only over his dead body, at the same time he backed Rajaji's formula which agreed for a separate state for Muslims after a plebescite. As early as in April 1942 the Congress working committee had declared that even though it was wedded to Indian unity and regarded any division of India as injurious to all concerned, it could not "think in terms of compelling the people in any territorial unit to remain in an Indian union against their declared and established will" In July 1945, Nehru made his stand explicit in the context of Pakistan: "If those areas which have predominant Muslim majorities are utterly bent on separation no power on earth can stop them" and even more explicitly in August 1945: "If the Muslims insist on it (Pakistan) they will have it". It was these types of inconsistent view and conflicting opinions which caught the masses unaware and ill prepared when partition actually took place, resulting in the genocide of the century.

Was Partition Unavoidable?

Partition could have been avoided, provided, the men in the Congress, some, of great intellectual stature had tried to analyze the rapid growth of Islam in the subcontinent and adopt remedial measure to counter it. As the Census Report revealed, unabated conversion during British regime proved beyond doubt that Islam was bound to grow in Bengal whether the backing of political power was available of not. (Ram Gopal, Indian Muslims. A Political History (1858-1947), Asia Publishing House, 1964. p. People dissatisfied with the rigours of a caste-ridden society and a religion based on vulgar ritualism turned to the new faith which promised common brotherhood, liberation from the offensive yoke of the Brahman priests and some material incentives such as easy appointments to government jobs.

The process of conversion was facilitated by the practices of Hindu society, such as the one that closed the doors of the society to anyone who had been forcibly fed beef or who had taken food or water from the hands of a Muslim, or any woman who had been abducted by force and wished to return to her home and faith but was denied that right. Islam also offered young widows, the prospect of a normal and honoured life which, the Hindu society had denied and imposed upon them a life of privation and indignity. Early Smriti writers had stated that if a woman was criminally assaulted, she was not to be socially ostracized and readmitted into the family and society after some penance and purification. This procedure was followed in the beginning in the case of women forcibly converted and violated. The Devala Smriti went to the extent of declaring that women of this unfortunate category should be readmitted to the fold of Hinduism even if their violation was followed by pregnancy. This liberal viewpoint was however given up by 1000 A.D. From that time onwards, Hindu women once carried away by force into the fold of Islam had no hope of return to the religion of their birth. They had to reconcile themselves with their captors and live a miserable life, not much different from a concubine. In Kashmir also the majority of the people were forced to give up the religion of their forefathers in the 17th and 18th century under the rule of fanatic Mughal emperor Aurangzeb.

In the later part of the 19th century, a delegation of Kashmiri Muslims went to Varanasi, to get the approval of Brahmins there to return to Hindu fold, but the priests declined their request. Even today most common family name in Kashmir is Butt, a distortion of Bhatt, a Hindu surname common amongst the Brahmins in India. The converts in Bengal remained as ignorant of Islam as of Hinduism. "Some of them" says the Imperial Gazetteer of India Vol I (1885) "have never heard of Mohammed; some regard him as a person corresponding in their system of religion to Rama or Lakshman of the Hindus. The Koran is hardly read even in Bengali and in the original Arabic not at all. Many of those who have heard of it cannot tell who wrote it. Yet any Muslim peasant is able to repeat a few scraps of prayer in Arabic. This prayer gave him a sense of religion and he considered himself as a member of a socio cum religious system, which he did not have it when he was, a Hindu. In fact the Jamait ul ulema was opposed to Pakistan, as it would affect its propagation of Islam. Maulana Madani delivering a speech on 19th September 1945 in Delhi on the occasion of the formation of the Azad Muslim Parliamentary Board to fight the last constitutional battle against the demand of Pakistan said that at the termination of the Muslim rule, there were about 25 million Muslims in India. Within a period of less than a century their number increased up to 100 millions.

The missionary work of the Jamait has a great share in this increase. The great object of an overall spread of Islam in the whole of India cannot be realized by appealing to passion of hatred and antagonism. It is the non-Muslims who are the field of action for the tabligh (spread of Islam) and form the raw material for this splendid activity. The above factors definitely reveal that lack of social cohesion had weakened the Hindu society and evangelists of various faiths had reaped its advantage. The Arya Samaj was the first organization to recognize the need of Shuddhi, to bring back into the Hindu fold, those people who had been forced to embrace other faiths due to unavoidable circumstances.

Shuddhi as a Means to Strengthen Hinduism

The word Shuddhi simply means purification. At first, the term was used to apply to efforts by Arya Samajists and others to reconvert Hindus who had become Christians or Muslims. Traditionally a Hindu who converts to Christianity or Islam becomes an outcaste, and there is no mechanism whereby that individual might be restored to caste upon reconverting. Arya Samajists were among the first reformers to try to change the situation, to develop a system through which Hindu converts to other religions could become Hindu again. The motivation behind this initiative was not just sympathy for individual outcastes. Arya Samajists understood Hinduism to be hobbled by its own exclusiveness. While Christianity and Islam were able to proselytize and draw others into their community, Hinduism could not even take back reconverted Hindus much less accept converts. From 1884 to 1894 at least eighteen local Arya Samaj chapters sponsored Shuddhi ceremonies; whereby Hindus who had converted to other religions were accepted back into the Hindu fold.

The real expansion of Shuddhi came when it was used to make the Untouchables into caste Hindus. On 3rd June 1900 a large number of low caste Rahtias from the Jalandhar area were declared to be no longer Untouchable through a Shuddhi ceremony sponsored by the Lahore Arya Samaj. By the 1911 census three to four thousand Rahtias had become "purified" caste Hindus. From 1903 the Sialkot Arya Samaj worked with the Untouchable Meghs. By 1911 there were 30,000 Arya Meghs. The programme with the Meghs was not limited to the Shuddhi ceremony. The Sialkot Samaj also supported the establishment of an industrial training school and grammar schools for the "purified" Meghs. The Arya Samaj believed that political agitation was futile because a nation, which considered millions of human beings as untouchables, had no business to talk of liberty and democracy. The Vedic magazine of the Samaj argued that Indians were subjected to foreign rule because of their moral weaknesses and that without the necessary religious and social reforms, political subjection of Indians was bound to continue and that the expulsion of the English could only result in a change of masters for Indians. Even the intellectual giant, Lala Hardayal had observed that the future of Hindu race and Hindustan rest on Hindu Raj, Hindu Sangathan, Shuddhi and conquest and Shuddhi of Afghan and the Frontier, otherwise it is useless to win Swaraj. The Congress under Gandhiji created a lot of awareness among the masses, the need for the removal of Untouchability resulting in the passing of legislation to abolish it. Similarly the Congress could had have taken a positive stand towards Shuddhi to consolidate the Hindu society.

THE PARTITION: 1947

Mountbatten Plan

The actual division between the two new dominions was done according to what has come to be known as the *3 June Plan* or *Mountbatten Plan*. The border between India and Pakistan was determined by a British Government-commissioned report usually referred to as the Radcliffe Line after the London lawyer, Sir Cyril Radcliffe, who wrote it. Pakistan came into being with two non-contiguous enclaves, East Pakistan (today Bangladesh) and West Pakistan, separated geographically by India. India was formed out of the majority Hindu regions of the colony, and Pakistan from the majority Muslim areas.

On 18 July 1947, the British Parliament passed the Indian Independence Act that finalized the partition arrangement. The Government of India Act 1935 was adapted to provide a legal framework for the two new dominions. Following partition, Pakistan was added as a new member of the United Nations. The union formed from the combination of the Hindu states assumed the name *India* which automatically granted it the seat of British

India (a UN member since 1945) as a successor state. The 625 Princely States were given a choice of which country to join.

Geography of the partition: the Radcliffe Line

The Punjab – the region of the five rivers east of Indus: Jhelum, Chenab, Ravi, Beas, and Sutlej – consists of interfluvial *doabs,* or tracts of land lying between two confluent rivers.

These are the *Sind-Sagar* doab (between Indus and Jhelum), the *Jech* doab (Jhelum/Chenab), the *Rechna* doab (Chenab/Ravi), the *Bari* doab (Ravi/Beas), and the *Bist* doab (Beas/Sutlej). In early 1947, in the months leading up to the deliberations of the Punjab Boundary Commission, the main disputed areas appeared to be in the *Bari* and *Bist* doabs, although some areas in the *Rechna* doab were claimed by the Congress and Sikhs. In the *Bari* doab, the districts of Gurdaspur, Amritsar, Lahore, and Montgomery (Sahiwal) were all disputed.

All districts (other than Amritsar, which was 46.5% Muslim) had Muslim majorities; albeit, in Gurdaspur, the Muslim majority, at 51.1%, was slender. At a smaller area-scale, only three *tehsils* (sub-units of a district) in the *Bari* doab had non-Muslim majorities. These were: Pathankot (in the extreme north of Gurdaspur, which was not in dispute), and Amritsar and Tarn Taran in Amritsar district. In addition, there were four Muslim-majority tehsils east of Beas-Sutlej (with two where Muslims outnumbered Hindus and Sikhs together).

Before the Boundary Commission began formal hearings, governments were set up for the East and the West Punjab regions. Their territories were provisionally divided by "notional division" based on simple district majorities. In both the Punjab and Bengal, the Boundary Commission consisted of two Muslim and two non-Muslim judges with Sir Cyril Radcliffe as a common chairman.

The mission of the Punjab commission was worded generally as: "To demarcate the boundaries of the two parts of the Punjab, on the basis of ascertaining the contiguous majority areas of Muslims and non-Muslims. In doing so, it will take into account other factors."

Each side (the Muslims and the Congress/Sikhs) presented its claim through counsel with no liberty to bargain. The judges too had no mandate to compromise and on all major issues they "divided two and two, leaving Sir Cyril Radcliffe the invidious task of making the actual decisions."

Independence and population exchanges

Massive population exchanges occurred between the two newly-formed states in the months immediately following Partition. Once the lines were established, about 14.5 million people crossed the borders to what they hoped was the relative safety of religious majority. Based on 1951 Census of displaced persons, 7,226,000 Muslims went to Pakistan from India while 7,249,000 Hindus and Sikhs moved to India from Pakistan immediately after partition.

About 11.2 million or 78% of the population transfer took place in the west, with Punjab accounting for most of it; 5.3 million Muslims moved from India to West Punjab in Pakistan, 3.4 million Hindus and Sikhs moved from Pakistan to East Punjab in India; elsewhere in the west 1.2 million moved in each direction to and from Sind. However, the net flow of Muslims since partition is from Pakistan to India. More Muslims in Pakistan have chosen to come and stay in India than Muslims in India have chosen to move to Pakistan.

The newly formed governments were completely unequipped to deal with migrations of such staggering magnitude, and massive violence and slaughter occurred on both sides of the border. Estimates of the number of deaths range around roughly 500,000, with low estimates at 200,000 and high estimates at 1,000,000.

Punjab

The Indian state of Punjab was created in 1947, when the Partition of India split the former Raj province of Punjab between India and Pakistan. The mostly Muslim western part of the province became Pakistan's Punjab Province; the mostly Sikh and Hindu eastern part became India's Punjab state. Many Hindus and Sikhs lived in the west, and many Muslims lived in the east, and so the partition saw many people displaced and much intercommunal violence. Lahore and Amritsar were at the centre of the problem, the British were not sure where to place them-make them part of India or Pakistan. The British decided to give Lahore to Pakistan, whilst Amritsar became part of India. Areas in west Punjab such as Lahore, Rawalpindi, Multan, Gujart, had a large Sikh population and many of the residents were attacked or killed by radical Muslims. On the other side in East Punjab cities such as Amritsar, Ludhiana, and Gurdaspur had a majority Muslim population in which many of them were wiped out by Sikh guerrillas who launched an all out war against the Muslims.

Bengal

The province of Bengal was divided into the two separate entities of West Bengal belonging to India, and East Bengal belonging to Pakistan. East Bengal was renamed East Pakistan in 1955, and later became the independent nation of Bangladesh after the Bangladesh Liberation War of 1971. While Muslim majority districts of Murshidabad was given to India, Hindu majority district Khulna and the Buddhist majority Chittagong division was given to Pakistan by the award.

Sindh

Hindu Sindhis were expected to stay in Sindh following Partition, as there were good relations between Hindu and Muslim Sindhis. At the time of Partition there were 1,400,000 Hindu Sindhis, though most were concentrated in the cities such as Hyderabad, Karachi, Shikarpur, and Sukkur. However, because of an uncertain future in a Muslim country, a sense of better opportunities in India, and most of all a sudden influx of Muslim refugees from Gujarat, Uttar Pradesh, Bihar, Rajputana (Rajasthan) and other parts of India, many Sindhi Hindus decided to leave for India.

Problems were further aggravated when incidents of violence instigated by Indian Muslim refugees broke out in Karachi and Hyderabad. According to the census of India 1951, nearly 776,000 Sindhi Hindus moved into India. Unlike the Punjabi Hindus and Sikhs, Sindhi Hindus did not have to witness any massive scale rioting; however, their entire province had gone to Pakistan thus they felt like a homeless community. Despite this migration, a significant Sindhi Hindu population still resides in Pakistan's Sindh province where they number at around 2.28 million as per Pakistan's 1998 census while the Sindhi Hindus in India as per 2001 census of India were at 2.57 million.

Kashmir conflict

The Princely state of Kashmir and Jammu had a majority Muslim population in the Kashmir valley and a majority Hindu population in Jammu and sparse population elsewhere. The Maharaja of Jammu and Kashmir acceded to India at the outbreak of violence. This Kashmir conflict lead to the 1947 war between India and Pakistan in that region.

Perspectives

The Partition was a highly controversial arrangement, and remains a cause of much tension on the subcontinent today. The British Viceroy, Lord Mountbatten of Burma has not only been accused of rushing the process through, but also is alleged to have influenced the Radcliffe Line in India's favour since everyone agreed India would be a more desirable country for most. However, the commission took so long to decide on a final boundary that the two nations were granted their independence even before there was a defined boundary between them. Even then, the members were so distraught at their handiwork (and its results) that they refused compensation for their time on the commission.

Some critics allege that British haste led to the cruelties of the Partition. Because independence was declared *prior* to the actual Partition, it was up to the new governments of India and Pakistan to keep public order. No large population movements were contemplated; the plan called for safeguards for minorities on both sides of the new border. It was an impossible task, at which both states failed. There was a complete breakdown of law and order; many died in riots, massacre, or just from the hardships of their flight to safety. What ensued was one of the largest population movements in recorded history. According to Richard Symonds, "at the lowest estimate, half a million people perished and twelve million became homeless"

However, some argue that the British were forced to expedite the Partition by events on the ground. Law and order had broken down many times before Partition, with much bloodshed on both sides. A massive civil war was looming by the time Mountbatten became Viceroy.

After World War II, Britain had limited resources, perhaps insufficient to the task of keeping order. Another viewpoint is that while Mountbatten may have been too hasty he had no real options left and achieved the best he could under difficult circumstances. Historian Lawrence James concurs that in 1947 Mountbatten was left with no option but to cut and run. The alternative seemed to be involvement in a potentially bloody civil war from which it would be difficult to get out.

Conservative elements in England consider the partition of India to be the moment that the British Empire ceased to be a world power, following Curzon's dictum that "While we hold on to India, we are a first-rate power. If we lose India, we will decline to a third-rate power."

Delhi Punjabi refugees

An estimated 25 million Hindus, Muslims and Sikhs (1947–present) crossed the newly drawn borders to reach their new homelands. These estimates are based on comparisons of decadal censuses from 1941 and 1951 with adjustments for normal population growth in the areas of migration. In northern India-undivided Punjab and North Western Frontier Province (NWFP)-nearly 12 million were forced to move from as early as March 1947 following the Rawalpindi violence.

Delhi received the largest number of refugees for a single city-the population of Delhi grew rapidly in 1947 from under 1 million (917.939) to a little less than 2 million (1.744.072) between the period 1941-1951. The refugees were housed in various historical and military locations such as the Old Fort Purana Qila), Red Fort (Red Fort), and military barracks in Kingsway (around the present Delhi university). The latter became the site of one of the largest refugee camps in northern India with more than 35,000 refugees at any given time besides Kurukshetra camp near Panipat.

The camp sites were later converted into permanent housing through extensive building projects undertaken by the Government of India from 1948 onwards. A number of housing colonies in Delhi came up around this period like Lajpat Nagar, Rajinder Nagar, Nizamuddin, Punjabi Bagh, Rehgar Pura, Jungpura and Kingsway Camp.

A number of schemes such as the provision of education, employment opportunities, easy loans to start businesses, were provided for the refugees at all-India level. The Delhi refugees, however, were able to make use of these facilities much better than their counterparts elsewhere.

Refugees settled in India

Many Sikhs and Hindu Punjabis settled in the Indian parts of Punjab and Delhi. Hindus migrating from East Pakistan (now Bangladesh) settled across Eastern India and Northeastern India, many ending up in close-by states like West Bengal, Assam, and Tripura. Some migrants were sent to the Andaman islands. Hindu Sindhis found themselves without a homeland. The responsibility of rehabilitating them was borne by their government. Refugee camps were set up for Hindu Sindhis.

Many refugees overcame the trauma of poverty, though the loss of a homeland has had a deeper and lasting effect on their Sindhi culture. In late 2004, the Sindhi diaspora vociferously opposed a Public Interest Litigation in the Supreme Court of India which asked the Government of India to delete the word "Sindh" from the Indian National Anthem (written by Rabindranath Tagore prior to the partition) on the grounds that it infringed upon the sovereignty of Pakistan.

Refugees settled in Pakistan

In the aftermath of partition, a huge population exchange occurred between the two newly-formed states. About 14.5 million people crossed the borders, including 7,226,000 Muslims came to Pakistan from India while 7,249,000 Hindus and Sikhs moved to India from Pakistan. About 5.5 million settled in Punjab Pakistan and around 1.5 million settled in Sindh.

Most of those refugees who settled in Punjab Pakistan they came from Indian Punjab, Haryana, Himachal Pradesh, Jammu and Kashmir and Rajasthan. Most of those refugees who arrived in Sindh came from northern and central urban centers of India, Uttar Pradesh, Bihar, Madhya Pradesh, Gujarat and Rajasthan via Wahga and Munabao border, however a limited number of muhajirs also arrived by air and on ships. People who wished to go to India from all over Sindh awaited their departure to India by ship at the Swaminarayan temple in Karachi and were visited by Muhammad Ali Jinnah, the founder of Pakistan.

The majority of Urdu speaking refugees who migrated after the independence were settled in the port city of Karachi in southern Sindh and in the cities of Hyderabad, Sukkur, Nawabshah and Mirpurkhas. As well the above many Urdu-speakers settled in the cities of Punjab mainly in Lahore, Multan, Bahawalpur and Rawalpindi, the number of migrants in Sindh was placed at over 540,000 of whom two-third were urban. In case of Karachi, from a population of around 400,000 in 1947, it turned into more than 1.3 million in 1953.

MOUNTBATTEN'S PLAN OF PARTITION

After difficult negotiations a federal solution was proposed. Despite initial agreement, both sides eventually rejected the plan. An interim government with representatives of all the Indian parties was proposed and implemented. However, it soon collapsed through lack of agreement. While the Muslim League consented to join the interim government the Indian National Congress refused.

By the end of 1946 communal violence was escalating and the British began to fear that India would descend into civil war. The British government's representative, Lord Wavell, put forward a breakdown plan as a safeguard in the event of political deadlock. Wavell, however, believed that once the disadvantages of the Pakistan scheme were exposed, Jinnah would see the advantages of working for the best possible terms inside a united India. He wrote: 'Unfortunately the fact that Pakistan, when soberly and realistically examined, is found to be a very unattractive proposition, will place the Moslems in a very disadvantageous position for making satisfactory terms with India for a Federal Union.' This view was based on a report, which claimed that a future Pakistan would have no manufacturing or industrial areas of importance: no ports, except Karachi, or rail centres. It was also argued that the connection between East and West Pakistan would be difficult to defend and maintain. The report concluded:

'It is hard to resist the conclusion that taking all considerations into account the splitting up of India will be the reverse of beneficial as far as the livelihood of its people is concerned'. Lord Mountbatten replaced Lord Wavell as Viceroy of India in 1947.

Mountbatten's first proposed solution for the Indian subcontinent, known as the 'May Plan', was rejected by Congress leader Jawaharlal Nehru on the grounds it would cause the 'balkanisation of India'. The following month the 'May Plan' was substituted for the 'June Plan', in which provinces would have to choose between India and Pakistan. Bengal and Punjab both voted for partition.

On 3 June 1947, Lord Mountbatten announced his plan. The salient features were:-

1. Mountbatten's formula was to divide India but retain maximum unity. The country would be partitioned but so would Punjab and Bengal, so that the limited Pakistan that emerged would meet both the Congress and League's position to some extent. The League's position on Pakistan was conceded to the extent that it would be created, but the Congress position on unity would be taken into account to make Pakistan as small as possible. Whether it was ruling out independence for the princes or unity for Bengal or Hyderabad's joining up with Pakistan instead of India, Mountbatten firmly supported Congress on these issues.
2. The Mountbatten Plan sought to effect an early transfer of power on the basis of Dominion status to two successor states, India and Pakistan. For Britain, Dominion Status offered a chance of keeping India in the commonwealth for India's economic strength and defence potential were

deemed sounder and Britain had a greater value of trade and investment there.

3. The rationale for the early date for transfer of power was securing Congress agreement to Dominion status. The additional benefit was that the British could escape responsibility for the rapidly deteriorating communal situation.
4. A referendum was to be held in NWEP to ascertain whether the people in the area wanted to join India or not. The princely states would have the option of joining either of the two dominions or to remain independent. The Provinces of Assam, Punjab and Bengal were also to be divided. A boundary commission was to be set up to determine the boundaries of these states.

Reasons for the Acceptance of "Partition" by the Congress

By accepting the Mountbatten Plan/Partition, the Congress was only accepting what had become inevitable because of the long-term failure of the Congress to draw in the Muslim masses into the national movement and stem the surging waves of Muslim communalism, which, especially since 1937, had been beating with increasing fury.

The Congress leaders felt by June, 1947 that only an immediate transfer of power could forestall the spread of Direct Action and communal disturbances. Sardar Patel rightly said, "a united India even if it was smaller in size was better than a disorganised and troubled and weak bigger India."

PARTITION AND INDEPENDENCE OF INDIA

In 1900, India was part of the British Empire; but by the end of 1947, India had achieved independence. For most of the Nineteenth Century, India was ruled by the British. India was considered the jewel in the crown of the British Empire. Queen Victoria had been made Empress of India and the British had a major military presence in India.

Indian nationals had no say in central government and even at a local level, their influence on policy and decision making was minimal. In 1885, educated middle class nationals had founded the Indian National Conference (INC). Their aim was to get a much greater say in the way India was governed.

In response to this development, the Morley-Minto reforms were introduced in 1909. Morley was the Secretary of State for India and Lord Morley was Viceroy of India. Their reforms lead to each province in India having its own governor and Indian nationals were allowed to sit on the councils which advised these governors. After 1918, nationalism within India intensified. This was probably due to 2 reasons:

1. Many educated nationals in India were far from satisfied with the Morley-Minto reforms. White Englishmen still dominated India and there had been no real decrease in their power or increase in national power. The INC (Indian National Council) wanted a lot more.
2. Woodrow Wilson had stimulated the minds of many people with his belief in national self-determination – i.e. that people from a country had a right to govern themselves. The whole concept of national self-determination undermined the basic idea of the British Empire – that the British governed this empire (or people appointed by the British to do the same). For national self-determination to fully work, India would have to be governed by the Indians living there.

As early as 1917, Britain had toyed with the idea of giving India a measure of self-government: "the gradual development of self-governing institutions with a view to the progressive realisation of responsible government in India as an integral part of the British Empire".

In 1919, the Government of India Act was introduced. This introduced a national parliament with two houses for India. About 5 million of the wealthiest Indians were given the right to vote (a very small percentage of the total population)

Within the provincial governments, ministers of education, health and public works could now be Indian nationals A commission would be held in 1929, to see if India was ready for more concessions/reforms. However, the British controlled all central government and within the provincial governments, the British kept control of the key posts of tax and law and order.

Many Tory MP's in Britain were against the whole idea of giving anything whatsoever to India in terms of self-government.

They had two complaints about the whole idea:

1. If you gave India some form of self-rule, where would it end?
2. Would it start the process that would lead to the break-up of the British Empire?

The reforms were introduced very slowly and their spread throughout such a large country was equally as slow. This angered many as there was a general belief that the British were deliberately stalling on introducing these reforms to ensure their continued supremacy in India. Riots did break out and the most infamous was at Amritsar in the Punjab where 379 unarmed protesters were shot dead by British soldiers based there. 1200 were injured. This incident shocked many in India but what caused equal outrage was the British reaction to Amritsar – the officer commanding British troops at Amritsar, General Dyer, was simply allowed to resign his commission after an inquiry criticised his leadership during the riot. Many national Indians felt that he, and others in the army, had got away very lightly. The more radical Indians felt that the British government had all but sanctioned murder.

As a result of Amritsar, many Indians rushed to join the INC and it very quickly became the party of the masses. The most vocal opponent of the idea of some form of self-rule for India was Lord Birkenhead whole was Secretary of State for India from 1924 to 1928. With such an opponent, any move to self-rule was very difficult at best, and probably impossible in reality.

In India, the 1920's saw the emergence of three men who were to have a huge impact on the future of India:

- Jawaharlal Nehru
- Mahatma Gandhi
- Muhammed Jinnah.

Gandhi persuaded many of his followers to use nonviolent protests. They had sit-down strikes, they refused to work, they refused to pay their taxes etc. If the British reacted in a heavy-handed manner, it only made the British look worse; essentially, the British would come across as bullies enforcing their rule on the bullied. However, there were those in India who wanted to use more extreme measures.

Part of the 1919 Government of India Act stated that a commission would be established after 10 years to assess whether India could/should have more self-rule. This first met in 1928 – the Simon Commission. This commission reported in 1930. There were no Indians on the commission. It proposed self-government for the provinces but nothing else. This was unacceptable for the INC, which wanted dominion status, granted immediately.

During the time the Simon Commission reported, Gandhi started his second civil disobedience campaign. This included Gandhi deliberately breaking the law. The law in India stated that only the government could manufacture salt. After a 250-mile march to the sea, Gandhi started to produce his own salt. This produced a violent clash with the British authorities and Gandhi was arrested.

At this time, a sympathetic Viceroy to India had been appointed – Lord Irwin. He believed that India should have dominion status – and he publicly expressed this idea. Irwin pushed for the issue to be discussed. He organised two Round Table conferences in 1930 and 1931. They were both held in London.

The first conference failed as no INC members were present. Most were in Indian prisons. Irwin pushed for their release and he persuaded Gandhi to travel to Britain to take part in the second conference. Despite this development, the conference achieved little as it broke down over an issue that was to haunt India in future years – religion. Those present at the second conference, argued and failed to agree over what the representation of Muslims would be in an independent Indian parliament.

In 1935, the Government of India Act was introduced. Britain, at this time, had a National Government and progress was made over India purely because Stanley Baldwin, the Tory leader, and Ramsey-MacDonald, the Labour leader, agreed on a joint course of action. Winston Churchill was bitterly opposed to it. The Act introduced:

An elected Indian assembly to have a say in everything in India except defence and foreign affairs. The eleven provincial assemblies were to have effective full control over local affairs. The nationalists in India were not satisfied with this as the act did not introduce dominion status and white dominions were allowed to control their own defence and foreign policies. Also the princes who still ruled areas of India still refused to co-operate with the provincial assemblies so the second strand of the Act would have been meaningless.

The act's major failing was that it ignored the religious rivalry between the Muslims and Hindus. Nearly two-thirds of India's population were Hindus and the Muslims feared that in an independent and democratic India they would be treated unfairly. In the 1937 provincial elections, the Hindus, who dominated the Congress Party under Nehru, won eight out of the eleven provinces.

The Muslim League under Jinnah demanded a separate state of their own to be called Pakistan. Both Gandhi and the Congress Party were determined to preserve Indian unity. Such a rivalry between the Hindus and Muslims could only bode ill for the future of India. World War Two shelved the Indian issue – albeit temporarily. The Indians provided valuable military help in the fight against Japan especially in the campaign in Burma. The British promised dominion status for India once the war had ended.

In 1945, the newly elected Labour government headed by Clement Attlee wanted to push ahead with solving what was seen as the "Indian Problem". However, the religious rivalry in India was coming to a head and made any potential solution very complex.

Attempts to draw up a compromise constitution that was acceptable to both Muslims and Hindus failed. The British plan was to allow the provincial governments extensive powers whilst central government would only have limited powers. The Labour government put its faith in the hope that most Muslims lived in one or two provinces and that the governments in these provinces would reflect this in their decision making. If this plan worked, the need for a separate Muslim state would not be needed. The plan was accepted in principle but the details for it were not.

The Governor-General of India, Lord Wavell, invited Nehru to form an interim government in August 1946. Wavell hoped that the details of such a government could be sorted out later– but he hoped that the creation of an actual government headed by Indian nationals would be supported by all.

The Hindu Nehru included two Muslims in his cabinet but this did not succeed in stopping violence. Jinnah became convinced that Nehru could not be trusted and he called on Muslims to take "direct action" to get an independent Muslim state. Violence spread and over 5000 people were killed in Calcutta. India descended into civil war.

Early in 1947, Atlee announced that Britain would leave India no later than June 1948. A new Viceroy was appointed– Lord Mountbatten – and he concluded that peace could only be achieved if partition was introduced. The Hindu Congress agreed with him.

Mountbatten became convinced that any delay would increase violence and he pushed forward the date for Britain leaving India to August 1947. In August 1947, the Indian Independence Act was signed. This separated the Muslim majority areas (in the northwest and northeast regions of India) from India to create the independent state of Pakistan. This new state was split in two, the two parts being 1000 miles apart. The act was not easy to put into action.

Some people found themselves on the wrong side of frontiers especially in the mixed provinces of the Punjab and Bengal. Millions moved to the new frontiers – Hindus in what was to be the new Pakistan moved to India while Muslims in India moved to Pakistan. Where the two moving groups met, violence occurred especially in the volatile Punjab province where it is though 250,000 people were murdered in religious clashes. By the end of 1947, it seemed as if the violence was on the wane but in January 1948, a Hindu assassinated Gandhi. In a gesture that summed up the whole problem of India, the Hindu detested Gandhi's tolerance towards Muslims. However, the murder of Gandhi shocked so many people, that ironically it ushered in a period of stability.

TRUE HISTORY OF INDEPENDENCE AND PARTITION OF INDIA

Common impression in India and the world is that Atlee and Labour Party were good and wanted to give independence to India after WW II, but due to differences among Indian leaders, they had to divide the country. This belief is based on British version and is totally false. History books written in Britain, US, and even in India are based on this version. The truth is England did NOT want their raj to end in India. Atlee, Cripps, Labour Party and Churchill wanted British raj to continue in India. The British propagated this version to hide their guilt. One million Indians were killed and 12 million were forced to migrate leaving their homes where they had lived for centuries due to British plan to partition India. This false version of Indian history is very injurious to India. It is high time that we learn our true history, so that we can defend ourselves and will not repeat old mistakes. Independence was not due to good will of England but due to balance of military force.

To understand the history of 1946-1948 period, it is necessary to know a few ideas. Mao said that political power comes from the barrel of a gun. This has been always true in the past, is true even now and will remain so in future. Idealism has no place in politics, which concerns with power-how to get it and how to use it after getting it. An imperial power rules by the policy of "divide and rule". Previously an imperial power ruled the subject country directly and exploited it. As this became unpopular, imperialism changed its form into neo-imperialism. Divide and rule became "divide and dominate." The imperial power does not rule directly but through appointed ruler and exploits the subject country. The US developed this method of neo-imperialism in the 19th century in South America. The South American countries were politically and internationally free. The invisible empire was economic. It exploited and dominated. The invisible empire is not resented, as people do not see it, as is the case with political domination.

Gandhiji used to describe the British policy of divide and rule as monkey justice from an Aesop's fable. This fable is about two cats, which were fighting for the just division of a loaf of bread and went to a monkey to divide it justly between them. The monkey deliberately divided the bread into two unequal pieces. When the cat with smaller piece objected, the monkey took a big bite from the bigger piece, so that it became smaller. The other cat objected now and the monkey kept on taking bites from the bigger piece, till the cats found that the monkey had eaten all the bread while pretending to divide it equally.

When Viceroy Linlithgow's replacement was considered in 1943, Prime Minister Churchill wanted his trusted lieutenant, Eden as Viceroy. Churchill told Eden on April 21, 1943 that "what a calamity it would be to win the war and lose India." Eden opposed the idea because he felt once he was out in India; he could not be considered Churchill's successor. Churchill agreed with Eden on this point and after lot of arguments dropped the idea. Churchill selected General Wavell in stead in June 1943 to hold the status quo in India till war end. Then Wavell was Commander-in Chief of British Indian Army. This shows the British had no intention of leaving India. Labour Minister in Labour government wanted Libya for Britain in the discussion of disposal of Italian colonies in the meeting of big powers, even though the British government had declared earlier that Britain did not want any new colony after the war,

When Viceroy Wavell went to London, he met Bevin and Alexander on December 21, 1945. He writes that Bevin like everyone else hated the idea of leaving India, but Bevin had no alternative to suggest. Bevin said that America was very much worried about India and did not want England to leave India. Wavell replied that US had changed its policy, now they could hardly expect British to face another Palestine in India, because it suited American commercial interest that Britain should remain in India. All this proves that the British and even US did not want the raj to end in India.

There were many reasons put together why Britain had to give India independence. Gandhiji's Satyagrah movements in 1920s and 1930s, the widespread Quit India movement in 1942, formation of Indian National Army by Subhas Chandra Bose in South East Asia, trial of I.N.A officers, then mutiny of Indian navy and air force, sending of Indian army to Indo-China and Indonesia to take surrender for Japan, expansion of Indian army to 2.5 lacs to fight expected Japanese invasion of India made Wavell realize that he could not trust the loyalty of Indian army and England could not rule India militarily.

To control India militarily, British policy had been to have one British soldier to two Indians in the Indian Army. This changed due to wartime expansion from 210,000 troops to 2.5 million, making Indian Army preponderantly Hindu with number of British troops remaining at 70,000. Moreover England had become very weak economically and militarily after war end. Only one year after it's declaration of war against Germany in September 1939, it found it had spent most of its gold and dollar reserves. It had to depend on the US for money and arms to carry on the war. Britain's worldwide empire was based on naval supremacy. After the war the British Navy was not the strongest. Atom bomb appeared as a weapon of war, but Britain had no atom bombs. Naval ships could be destroyed by aeroplanes.

Hence Wavell made a blue print of Pakistan in December 1945 and sent it to Secretary of State for India in a most secret letter. This letter has been now made public. The letter reveals that partition was necessary to protect British interests in Asia and NOT Muslim interests as believed in India and Pakistan. Aim was to protect Near East from Soviet expansion to Indian Ocean and oil wells there. The English had been working on creation of Pakistan since 1888.

The Cabinet Delegation was sent to India in March 1946 ostensibly to help Indians to become free but really to make Indians agree to Partition. To further this aim, the English made Jinnah start communal riots to prove that Hindus and Muslims cannot live together and the country had to be divided. One million lives were lost in communal riots during 1946-1947. Though the British were powerless to control India, they had enough power to create trouble before leaving. Indian navy was much weaker than Royal Navy, which could blockade India and prevent import of many necessary items.

To defeat Congress demand for a free united India, they threatened that if Congress did not agree to partition they would leave India in more than 500 pieces. Sardar Patel had become in charge of Home in the provisional government in September 1946. He read all secret government papers and found how the British were intriguing to make India very weak before departure.

He decided that it was better to accept India in two parts rather than in more than 500. In December 1946, he made V.P. Menon make a blue print of partition, which was different from Wavell's partition plan. It was this plan, which was ultimately adopted in August 1947.

Patel talked to Nehru about his idea, but Nehru said that Gandhiji would never agree to this plan. Gandhiji had realized the harm to India from partition and declared that partition would take place over his dead body. Gandhiji was willing to have a civil war to prevent partition.

Patel told Nehru that he would make Gandhiji agree to his plan. Both went to Gandhiji and told him about Patel's idea. Gandhiji asked them if they had become afraid due to loss of lives in raging communal riots in India. Both Patel and Nehru replied that they were not scared, but facts had to be faced. And that it would be better to accept partition. Gandhiji agreed to partition on condition that it would be a partition between two brothers. The wily English defeated Gandhiji's wish by creating Kashmir problem so that the two nations would keep fighting. Patel explained later in November 1947 the logic for acceptance of partition. He said that with Partition 80 % of India would be free. India will develop economically and militarily and then take the other 20%.

Partition took place on August 14 and 15, 1947. All top civil and military officers were British in Pakistan. They made a plan for Pakistan to attack Kashmir, which had not decided which

Dominion to accede, with some tribesmen and Pakistan Army men in mufti to invade Kashmir on October 20. This made Maharaja and National Conference of Shiekh Abdullah ask for India's help. After accepting accession, Indian army was sent to prevent the Pak invaders from occupation of Kashmir. As the fighting was going on, Mountbatten asked Congress leaders not to attack Pakistan but to complain to UN. Gandhiji, Nehru and Patel were against Mountbatten's suggestion, but Nehru had to agree as Britain reduced supply of arms and petrol to India to put pressure to agree to go to UN. As expected, UN, dominated by US and England did not declare Pakistan as an aggressor, but appointed a mediator (i.e. justice monkey). Pakistan was never declared an aggressor and it continues to occupy parts of Kashmir.

To say that Jinnah created Pakistan is a joke. Jinnah had no gun to get political power. Jinnah was ignorant and he allowed the British to use him as a stooge to divide the country. Later Jinnah himself realized his mistake and wanted India and Pakistan to unite just before his death. Jinnah may be called second Mir Jafar.

PARTITION AND PRECEDING EVENTS

After World War II the British were in a hurry to leave India. The elections of winter 1945-46 were thus in point of fact about the future political shape of an independent subcontinent. Congress sought a mandate to keep India united while the Muslim League stood for a separate Pakistan. Emotive and sensationalist slogans such as 'Pakistan Ka Naara Kaya? La Illaha Il Lillah (What is the Slogan of Pakistan? It is that there is no God but Allah)' and 'Muslim Hai to League Mein Aa' (if you are a Muslim then join the Muslim League) were raised. Hindus and Sikhs were demonised as infidels and exploiters. Muslims who opposed the Muslim League were portrayed as renegades to Islam. In some cases fatwas (religious rulings) were issued to the effect that such persons should be denied a proper Islamic burial. On the other hand, support was solicited from Sunnis, Shias, the Ahmadis, Muslim Communists and anyone who was registered in the census records as a Muslim. The election results vindicated the contradictory claims of both parties. Congress secured 905 general seats out of a total of 1,585 while the gains of the Muslim League were even more impressive. It won 440 seats out of a total of 495 reserved for Muslims. It is to be noted that Muslims in the Hindu-majority provinces also voted massively in favour of the Muslim League.

The Cabinet Mission of 1946 sent by the post-war Labour Government of Clement Atlee failed to convince the two rival parties to agree upon a formula of power sharing within a united India. The factor that sealed the fate of unity was the eruption of large-scale communal violence following Jawaharlal Nehru's ill-considered press statement of 10 July 1946 in Bombay declaring that Congress would enter the Constituent Assembly' completely unfettered by agreements and free to meet all situations as they arise'.

On 29 July 1946, Jinnah gave the call to direct action to Muslims to protest the alleged anti-minority attitude of Nehru. On 16 August 1946, communal massacres, initiated by hotheads despatched by the Muslim League chief minister of Bengal, Hussain Shaheed Suhrawardy, took place in Calcutta, which left thousands of people, mostly Hindus, dead and homeless. The Hindus retaliated with great ferocity. More Muslims died in the counter-attack. The Calcutta killings proved a contagion, and communal riots broke out in many parts of India. The real explosion, however, originated a few months later in the key Punjab province, where the Muslim (57.1 per cent), Hindu (27.8 per cent) and Sikh (13.2 per cent) groups maintained an uneasy peace until the beginning of 1947. In the third week of January 1947, the Muslim League started its 'direct action' in Punjab against the non-Muslim League government of Khizr Hayat Tiwana.

On 3 March, the Sikh Akali Dal leader, Master Tara Singh, gave what in effect was a call for an all-out confrontation with Muslims. It resulted in immediate clashes between Hindu-Sikh and Muslim demonstrators. The first large-scale, organised communal clashes took place in the Rawalpindi area. On the night of 6-7 March, Muslim gangs attacked a number of Sikh and Hindu villages, the campaign continuing until 13 March. It left more than

2000 mainly Sikh and Hindu men, women and children dead. Muslim League cadres were identified as the culprits behind it.

At that point, the Sikh leaders demanded that Punjab be also divided on communal lines if Pakistan was granted to the Muslims. On 6-8 March, the All-India National Congress Committee passed a resolution demanding the division of Punjab into two provinces so that 'the predominantly Muslim part may be separated from the predominantly non-Muslim part'. Congress also demanded the partition of Bengal. The British Government announced the partitions of India, Bengal and Punjab on 3 June 1947. Congress, the Muslim League, representatives of the Sikhs and the various other minor religious and caste groups negotiated the actual demarcation of the Pakistan-India border before the Bengal and Punjab Boundary Commissions.

These deliberations served as the basis for the Radcliffe Award of 17 August 1947 (Pakistan and India had already become independent on 14 and 15 August, respectively). The Radcliffe Award did not satisfy any of the major contestants, and has subsequently been criticised and even condemned by various disgruntled actors.

The riots and pogroms, which accompanied Partition, were most harrowing in the Punjab and effectively led to the first successful post-war experiment in massive ethnic cleansing in the world. At that critical moment Muslim League, the Sikh Akali Dal, RSS and Congress cadres became vicious killers. However, some 30-35 million Muslims stayed on in other parts of India while in East Pakistan some 23 per cent of the population continued to be Hindu. Some half million Hindus stayed behind in Sindh in West Pakistan (since December 1971 the only part which constitutes Pakistan).

INDIA

The failure to keep India united left the Congress ideal of a composite Indian nation in shambles. Millions of Hindu and Sikh refugees were devastated by that traumatic experience. Many objected to the Muslim presence and wanted Muslims driven away to Pakistan. At that critical movement, Gandhi, Nehru and many other stalwarts of the freedom struggle became a bulwark against the forces of reaction and revenge, and although attacks on Muslims continued for some time in many parts of India, they were small-scale occurrences.

When discussion began on the constitution, the notion of a modern individual-rights-oriented civic and composite nation prevailed. The Hindu ethno-nationalist lobby argued in favour of a Hindu cultural hegemony in terms of national identity, but was overruled. It can be asserted, however, that the trauma of Partition made everybody in the Congress High Command overly sensitive to the question of unity.

The Constitution and Education System

The high point of the Nehruvian model was the enshrinement of universal values and norms in the Indian Constitution, which came into force on 26 January 1950. Its declarations on human rights and freedoms were quite radical. Universal citizenship was granted. Public office was open to all citizens. Some 23 percent of jobs (i.e. the ratio of those groups in the Hindu population) were later reserved by law for the so-called untouchable castes and tribes. In 1955 the Untouchability (Offences) Act, was passed. It criminalised the practice of untouchability. The constitution therefore clearly sanctioned a secular-democratic model of the polity. Although various amendments were subsequently made, the basic structure has remained unchanged.

The rational-modernising elite chose the educational system to gradually foster a democratic national identity. Liberal and Marxist scholars (many of Muslim origin) dominated until recently prestigious Indian social science and humanities university faculties and institutes. Their interpretation of the freedom movement was largely imbued with the emancipatory ethos of the European Enlightenment. Not surprisingly, the Hindu communal organisations and parties were very critical of such a foundation of Indian nationalism. The current BJP-led government seems to have decided to promote an educational agenda that will project a pro-Hindu bias in the production of knowledge and education. At the provincial level, such changes have already been introduced, typically identifying former Muslim rulers as responsible for all the ills of society.

Hindu Nationalism and the Growth of Hostility to Minorities

Congress had completely sidelined rightwing Hindu ethno-nationalists during the freedom struggle and alienated them from the state in the early years. Consequently they had to devise strategies to advance the project of Hindutva from outside the state. The loss of life and property and expulsion from their ancestral homes left in Pakistan were blamed on the Congress's willingness to concede Partition.

Muslims as a whole were held responsible for the vivisection of the motherland. Such propaganda did boost the fortunes of the rightwing parties somewhat. For example, in 1943 the total membership of the RSS was only 76,000. In 1948 it had soared to 600,000. In electoral terms, however, such gains did not mean that a major challenge to Congress could be mounted. Rather, initially a major set back resulted from the involvement of the RSS in the assassination of Gandhi.

The Hindu ethno-nationalists were infuriated over Gandhi's insistence that the Indian government pay 550 million rupees to Pakistan as compensation for losses incurred during Partition. Accordingly, he began a fast unto death to put pressure on the government. On 31 January Nathu Ram Godse, a member of the RSS, murdered Gandhi. Nehru decided to deal firmly with the Hindu ethno-nationalists. The RSS was banned, although it reappeared in 1952 in the form of Jana Sangha.

In the 1960s some other avenues for a Hindu political revival were tried. The Vishwa Hindu Parishad (VHP) was founded in 1964 ostensibly as a cultural movement purporting to inculcate pride among Hindus in their great culture and civilisation. Initially the VHP identified the proselytising activities of Christian missionaries as a major threat. It is intriguing to note that the VHP movement was sustained with considerable assistance from the Hindu diaspora, especially the large Indian/Hindu population of North America consisting of successful professionals and other upwardly mobile groups. Support from the UK has also been significant. The VHP and its various student and labour affiliates have been able to acquire political clout and infiltrate the state machinery and important cultural and media institutions. However, the most significant boost to Hindu great nation chauvinism came initially from another quarter: the Congress government led by Mrs Indira Gandhi.

In December 1971 India defeated Pakistan in the latter's eastern wing, where a rebellion had been going on since March of that year. In 1974 India exploded a nuclear device. Mrs Gandhi began to be hailed as a great stateswoman. Sycophants began to raise slogans such as 'India is Indira and Indira is India'. However, in 1974 popular strikes, demonstrations and agitations broke out in protest against price rises, unemployment and bad government. The government retaliated by suspending many of the normal parliamentary practices and civil liberties. The Hindu ethno-nationalists made capital out of the situation by joining the democratic opposition. On 5 April 1980, some of them came together and founded the Bharatiya Janata Party (BJP).

A shift in the Congress electoral strategy could also be noticed. Instead of relying upon its traditional supporters, the so-called vote-banks comprising the various social and religious minorities such as the Dalits and Muslims, Mrs Gandhi began to cultivate the more traditional upper caste voters. In the 1980s, the BJP, RSS, and the rabidly anti-Muslim Shiv Sena in Mahrashtra and several other such parties and organisations began to evolve a martial discourse based on the mythical Mahabharta Epic and other heroic tales with a view to instilling militancy and a sense of collective nationalism. The idea of Hindutva or Hindu nation, first propounded by Sarvarkar in the 1920s, was revived. It asserted that only Hindus were trustworthy and loyal citizens of India; and further, that Nehruvian secularism had been harmful to Hindus, while it pampered the minorities. In particular, hostility was directed against the Muslims, who constitute some 13 per cent of the total Indian population.

It is important to note that the vast majority of Indian Muslims are converts from the poorest sections of Hindu society. They have been the main sufferers of the Partition Syndrome. They are grossly underrepresented in education and employment. Discrimination is therefore institutionalised in practice if not in theory. It is, however, their portrayal as a fifth column and therefore a security threat that makes them most vulnerable to hostile propaganda. Thus, even the liberal mass media gave sensational coverage to a report that some Dalits had converted to Islam in Tamil Nadu in 1981. Exaggerated reports of Arab money donated to Islamic organisations and the alleged rapid growth rate of the Muslim population also figured prominently in media discussions.

The galloping Hindu cultural revival struck terror among the minorities. Anti-Muslim attacks became larger, more frequent, and more gruesome. The xenophobia and paranoia, which typifies such a pathological frame of mind, proved to be a self-fulfilling prophecy. However, Muslims did not mount the first challenge. It was the Sikhs of Punjab who were attracted to the idea of a separate Sikh state, Khalistan. The Khalistanis argued that Partition gave India to the Hindus and Pakistan to the Muslims therefore Sikhs should be given Khalistan. The Khalistan conflict came to a head in June 1984 when Mrs Gandhi ordered the Indian army to flush out the Sikh leader Sant Jarnail Singh Bhindranwale and his militants who had been occupying the holiest Sikh shrine, the Golden Temple at Amritsar since 1982. The military action was successful but it cost a great deal in human lives. On 31 October 1984, Mrs Gandhi was assassinated by two of her Sikh bodyguards. Immediately Hindu gangs began to hunt down Sikhs all over India. In the capital Delhi alone at least 3,000 Sikhs were butchered.

The Sikhs had barely been crushed when another major separatist movement emerged in the predominantly Muslim-majority Indian-administered Kashmir. India and Pakistan had inherited the Kashmir dispute at the time of Partition. Its resurgence proved even more difficult for India to bring under control.

The Kashmir conflict continues to claim lives almost every day and India has not been able to bring the situation under control despite extreme repression and the deployment of hundreds of thousands of soldiers and security forces. India's worries have been compounded further by the re-emergence of separatist insurgency among a number of different Christian tribal peoples in the smaller north-eastern border states (provinces of India). The Indian government and mass media have been alleging that the Pakistani secret services, especially the Inter-Services-Intelligence (ISI) help the Sikh, Kashmiri and other separatist movements in India with training, arms and other facilities. From time to time some Indian Muslim is arrested on charges of working for the ISI. This undoubtedly helps portray all Muslims as pro-Pakistan and a subversive factor in Indian society.

While the anti-minority polices of the Hindu right have been steadily growing, a major worry for the BJP, which seeks power through the electoral process, has been the alienation of a significant number of Dalits and the so-called Other Backward Castes (OBCs), a rather large segment of peasant and other castes, which occupy a position between the upper castes and Dalits. The BJP had been seeking ways and means of enveloping such social strata into its fold of Hindu cultural nationalism. An emotive cause or symbol was found in the long, drawn-out dispute between Hindus and Muslims over the site of the Babri mosque in Ayodhya. It was alleged that the god Rama had been born there and a temple existed on that spot before the mosque was built in 1528.

Consequently in the 1980s the BJP, VHP and other communal entities launched a campaign to dismantle the mosque. The Bajrang Dal (established in 1984), a youth wing of the VHP, employed mainly for agitation purposes and demonstrations, played the leading role in mobilising mass action and other activities in favour of the campaign. In early December 1992, the BJP and its supporters the VHP, Bajrang Dal, Shiv Sena and other fanatical groups finally arrived in Ayodhya after a long countrywide march in which thousands of people joined, including OBCs and other traditionally alienated sections of Hindu society.

The mob easily overpowered the rather small police force, climbed onto the top of the mosque and demolished it in a few hours. The Congress government under Narashima Rao seemed to have let the event take place mainly for opportunistic electoral reasons. The demolition of the mosque was accompanied by mob attacks on Muslims all over India and several thousand were killed. Suddenly India was in the midst of perhaps the most serious communal conflict since the partition. There was a fierce reaction in Pakistan and the old temples in Punjab were razed and some Hindus were also killed. The Hindu ethno-nationalists have plans to destroy some 3000 other mosques built allegedly on Hindu temples and holy places. Building the Ram Mandir is part of the BJP's election manifesto. The BJP has subsequently been increasing its electoral support and is currently the biggest party in a coalition government of 25 parties. Thus far it lacks parliamentary support for realising such a project. In fact moderate sections of the BJP have been trying to woo the Muslim vote bank and have made some gains. However, the Shiv Sena leader, Bal Thackerey, has recently demanded that Muslims should be disenfranchised.

The 20 million-strong Christian community had most of the time escaped the type of animosity faced by Muslims since they had played no role in bringing about the division of India. Some conversions to Christianity had continued to take place, mainly among the aborigines. Attacks upon churches and mission-run schools had been taking place, but after Sonia Gandhi (Italian-Catholic by birth) became the leader of the Congress Party in the late 1990s, the Hindu Right has been peddling a Christian conspiracy to annexe India. The last couple of years have witnessed a dramatic increase in church burning, killing of Christians and a countrywide campaign against missionaries. Thus on the night of 22 and 23 January 1999, the Australian missionary Graham Stuart Staines and his two sons were burnt alive in Monouharpur in Orrissa. Finally, the most enduring cleavages in Hindu society remain as deep as before: those between the twice-born upper castes, the assertive OBC groups and the Dalits. Attacks against Dalits continue to take place frequently all over India.

PAKISTAN

A notorious ambiguity about the purposes for which Pakistan was created was it to be simply a national state of Muslims or a theocratic Islamic state based on Sharia (dogmatic Islamic law)? characterises its travails with national identity.. Jinnah had never provided any clear answer to this question. Pakistan can therefore be described as an unimagined nation. The elite that came to power in Pakistan lacked political vision and preparedness. It did not allow democracy to be institutionalised. Recurrent military-bureaucratic take-overs and a host of bizarre decisions contributed to the fostering of a pathological political culture at all levels of state and society. Such a tendency was aggravated by the traumatic loss of East Pakistan in late 1971 through a popular local rebellion backed by an Indian military intervention.

The Constitutional and Legal Structure

However, the first authoritative statement made on 11 August 1947, that is only three days before independence, in the Pakistan Constituent Assembly by Jinnah deviated from the main thrust of the Muslim League's propaganda in favour of cultural nationalism. To the utter surprise of many, he made the following observation in a long address:

> You are free; you are free to go to your temples, you are free to go to your mosques or to any other place of worship in this State of Pakistan. You may belong to any religion or caste or creed that has nothing to do with the business of the States. We are starting with this fundamental principle that we are all citizens and equal citizens of one States I think we should keep that in front of us as our ideal and you will find that in due course Hindus would cease to be Hindus and Muslims would cease to be Muslims, not in the religious sense, because that is the personal faith of each individual, but in the political sense as citizens of the State.

This patently secular and territorial idea of nation contradicted the rationale for the creation of Pakistan as a state for a cultural nation. The controversy that it caused has been generating ever more confusion as time goes by. While the fundamentalists usually dismiss it as irrelevant and an aberration, mainstream Muslim modernists argue that he was actually operating within an ideal Islamic framework of tolerance and justice for non-Muslims within an Islamic state. Marginalised secularists, leftists and oppressed minorities, however, raise it to the level of a sacred covenant that his successors have allegedly broken.

It seems that Jinnah's wording reflected his usual political sagacity rather than a firm ideological position. Communal violence was at its worst at that time. The Radcliffe Award was about to be announced and one could guess that it would result in population movement on a gigantic scale. The speech probably purported to discourage mass migration, uprooting and further communal violence.

However, it is doubtful whether in the wake of the communal riots such a prescription enjoyed any real credibility in Muslim-Pakistani society, Jinnah's prestige and authority notwithstanding. In this regard, it is significant to bear in mind that Jinnah never again reiterated such a commitment although he lived for another year. After his death on 11 September 1948, the idea of a secular state never again received much attention in mainstream Pakistani politics. Rather, Islamic idiom became a central feature of official rhetoric.

One can even argue that once the initial euphoria was over and a framework for national identity and nation building had to be found, the Pakistani leadership felt constrained to distinguish itself from India. There were undoubtedly other issues to be dealt with by the government of Prime Minister Liaqat Ali Khan (d. 1951) but maintaining distinctiveness from Congress and secular India must have been an important consideration. Thus the Objectives Resolution moved in the Pakistan Constituent Assembly by Prime Minister Liaqat Ali Khan on 7 March 1949 proclaimed the novel idea that sovereignty over the entire universe belonged to God. Democracy was to be practised, but within 'Islamic limits'. The minorities were assured that their legitimate interests would be safeguarded, and that provisions would be made for them in accordance with Islam freely to profess and practise their religions and cultures. Although such proclamations sounded like innocuous 'boasts', in the longer run they proved to be constraints that facilitated the politics of exclusion of different religious minorities and deviant sects from the category of nation.

Thus the first constitution of Pakistan adopted in 1956 contained a commitment to bringing all laws into conformity with Islam. In 1973 the third constitution was adopted. Unlike the first two constitutions that only required the president of the republic to be a Muslim, the third also required the prime minister to be a Muslim. It further obliged them to take an oath testifying their belief in the finality of Prophet Muhammad's mission.

The Educational System

The invention of a distinct historical past for the so-called Muslim nation of India justifying its separate existence within the boundaries of Pakistan has been felt to be necessary for conferring legitimacy and authenticity on it. Attempts to imagine such a nation have unsurprisingly resulted in distortion and exaggeration of facts on a massive scale, resulting in mythogenesis.

The main concern has been to foster a Pakistani-Islamic identity defined negatively, as a contrast to India. In his book The Murder of History a leading Pakistani educationalist and historian Prof. K.K. Aziz has scrutinised 66 textbooks used for teaching history, Pakistan studies and social studies in Pakistani schools, colleges and universities. Pakistan studies deal largely with the Muslim nationalist/separatist movement. It is a compulsory subject from 1st grade up to university and not only all students of humanities and social sciences but also scientists, doctors and engineers must gain a pass.

The author alleges that Islamisation by the government of General Zia-ul-Haq vitiated the general academic environment in Pakistan. He cites extensively factual errors, logical fallacies, inconsistencies, falsifications, mythologisations and crass propaganda from books used both in the Urdu and English-medium schools and colleges.

The military and the long military rules are presented in positive terms while hostility towards India, Hinduism and Hindus is their hallmark. For example, Congress is described as a Hindu party. That there were many Muslims among its members and that some held leading positions is not reported. India is described as the state of Hindus, although there are as many Muslims or more living in India as in Pakistan. Furthermore, a grossly exaggerated role is assigned to Muslims in the anti-colonial struggle. The Muslim League is declared as the party of the Muslim masses that successfully resisted both British colonialism and Hindu domination. Only Muslims are mentioned as victims of the partition riots and massacres, which are alleged to have been begun by Hindus and Sikhs. Any comment on the loss of lives among Hindus and Sikhs during that period is conspicuous by its absence. He sums up this approach in the following words:

It is declared that the Muslims of India made 'tremendous' sacrifices to win their freedom. The fact is that, apart from the brief years of 1858-60 and 1920-22, Muslims suffered little hardship between 1857-1947. It is forgotten by everyone that the Muslim League's search for protection and safeguards (in the early years) and its struggle for an independent state (in the later years) were strictly constitutional efforts, peaceful campaigns and political fights, conducted through parliamentary debates and negotiations No Muslim League leaders languished in prisons. No Muslim masses faced British bullets. The many people who died or suffered horribly in 1947 were running away from their homes because their life was in danger, not because they were fighting for the creation of Pakistan. They were casualties of communal riots, not of anti-British warfare.

He comments further, 'A sane educational system does not train students in hate. Whatever the justification for it or the compulsions of patriotism, hatred corrupts the mind, more so if it is still tender, and retards its healthy growth'.

Islamisation, Confessionalism and Hostility to Minorities

States founded on religious and ethnic nationalism invariably discriminate against atypical minorities. Ethnocracies can be a more apt description of such states, even when they practice democracy. Israel is a case in point. However, Pakistan has the rather unenviable distinction of extending the logic of confessionalism to its ultimate limits. In Pakistan, not only non-Muslims but also deviant sects within the broader category of Muslims who were mobilised in support of the 1945-46 elections have been alienated over time. Also, women as a whole have been victims of the so-called Islamisation process.

In 1953, violent anti-Ahmadiyya riots took place in Punjab in which several hundred lives were lost and considerable Ahmadiyya property was destroyed. The masterminds behind those riots were politicians from the ruling Muslim League seeking to challenge the ruling faction within the party. In 1974, the Islamic socialist Zulfikar Ali Bhutto played the anti-Ahmadiyya card again in the hope of extending his populist constituency into the stronghold of the doctrinal-minded Islamic parties of Pakistan. Consequently, when General Muhammad Zia-ul-Haq seized the reigns of power in July 1977 by toppling Zulfikar Ali Bhutto in a bloodless coup, a long tradition of relying on Islam to define national identity and the rights of citizens was already in place.

Upon coming to power in 1977, General Zia announced an ambitious programme to Islamise Pakistan. He expressed his political philosophy in a succinct manner : 'I have a mission, given by God, to bring Islamic order to Pakistan'. His main source of inspiration for an Islamic order was the ideas of the arch fundamentalist Abul Ala Maududi. The latter had set up headquarters in Lahore after Partition, from where he had been propagating his idea of a totalitarian Islamic state. The pre-Partition tradition of exploiting Islamic slogans to rouse Muslim fears against Hindus had been converted into a Machiavellian art by Pakistani politicians that involved damning their opponents as renegades to Islam and enemies of Pakistan. The various governments used it to slur the opposition's call for democracy and elections, while the various fundamentalist parties and factions pushed all governments into a corner with allegations of insincerity in their commitment to Islam. An Islamist political discourse evolved incrementally, each addition supplanting modernistic vagaries with puritan certainty. It bore the hallmarks of Maududism.

Thus in 1979, the government announced the imposition of the Hudud Ordinance, i.e. traditional Islamic punishments for the offences of adultery, false accusation of adultery, drinking alcohol, theft, and highway robbery. In 1984, a new Law of Evidence was adopted which reduced the worth of the evidence give by a female witness in a court of law to half the value of that given by a male witness. It was also a period when Islamic scholars notorious for their misogynist views appeared on television to advocate strict segregation between men and women and the confinement of the latter to the private sphere. In subsequent years the incidence of 'honour killings' has increased sharply. The victims are wives and daughters killed by their own families for allegedly defiling the family honour by demanding divorce or refusing to marry a man chosen for them by their elders. The courts have generally been very lenient to the culprits.

Also in 1984, many new restrictions were imposed on the Ahmadiyya group. They were prohibited from using Islamic nomenclature in their religious and social activities and may no longer call their places of worship mosques. In 1985, separate electorates were reintroduced (they were abolished in 1956), whereby non-Muslims were to constitute a separate body of voters, being thus entitled only to elect non-Muslim legislators to the various assemblies. Consequently their right to take part in normal law-making is severely restricted. It was followed by the adoption of the Blasphemy Law in 1986. It reads as follows:

Use of derogatory remarks etc. in respect of the Holy Prophet: Whether by words, either spoken or written, or by visible representations, or by any imputation, innuendo or insinuation, directly or indirectly, defiles the sacred name of the Holy Prophet (peace by upon him) shall be punishable with death, or imprisonment for life, and shall be liable to fine.

General Zia died in a plane crash in August 1988. The elected governments of Benazir Bhutto (1988-90, 1994-96) and Nawaz Sharif (1990-93; 1997-99) did not dare question the validity of the laws passed during the time of General Zia. It seems that once a law has been adopted in the name of Islam no politician is willing to attempt to rescind it.

In October 1997 retired Lahore High Court judge Arif Iqbal Bhatti was shot down by unidentified members of extremist religious groups. His death was believed to be linked to his role in the acquittal in 1995 of two Christians, Salamat Masih and Rehman Masih, charged with blasphemy. The Pakistan Human Rights Commission has been providing details of the increasing terrorisation of minorities. Charges of blasphemy have been framed against many Ahmadis and Christians. Forced conversions of Hindus have also been reported. The military government of General Pervez Musharraf, which came to power through a coup d'état on 12 October 1999, initially presented a progressive position on Islam, but it had quickly to withdraw from such a position under pressure from the extremists.

Shia-Sunni Terrorism and the Emergence of the Jihadis

During Gen. Zia's regime Sunni-Shia doctrinal differences erupted into open conflict. The difficulties were compounded further when in the late 1980s powerful external actors began to cultivate their lobbies in Pakistan. Thus Saudi Arabia and Iran were believed to be sending large sums of money, books, leaflets, audio and video cassette-tapes and other propaganda material to Pakistan. Such propaganda offensives were backed by the inflow of firearms and other weapons. Sunni and Shia militias began to menace and terrorise society; the assassinations of several rival Sunni and Shia ulama and regular gun battles and bomb explosions have been taking place in Pakistan in recent years.

An international Islamic guerrilla movement comprising Sunni militants, aptly described as Jihadis (holy warriors), has been establishing its headquarters in the northern Pakistani city of Peshawar in recent years. The Jihadis have declared war on India and want to liberate Kashmir through violent means.

The United States is another enemy, as are Israel, secular Turkey and the central Asian republics. In some pronouncements, all non-Muslims have been declared enemies of Islam. The coming into power of the arch-fundamentalist Talebans in neighbouring Afghanistan has once again revived the old pan-Islamic project of Chowdhary Rahmat Ali.

In a recent interview, a leading American South-Asia expert Selig Harrison claimed that General Zia's involvement in Afghanistan was meant to promote a pan-Islamic superstate in the region. He also alleged that such a scheme has powerful backers in the Pakistani military establishment. It can be assumed that Iran (because of its deviant Shia Islam), Turkey (secular) and the central Asian republics (also secular) will have no interest in such a project. Instead what is more likely is that the totalitarian, obscurantist, anti-modernist, medieval type of state and society created in Afghanistan could envelope Pakistan.

Separatist Movements

Although the Muslim League was successful in presenting a broad Muslim unity against Congress, after Partition it quickly dissipated and the centre became a stronghold of mainly Punjabi-Urdu-speaking groups. Recently the equation has been changed and it is a Punjabi-Pukhtun ruling axis which dominates Pakistan. Separatist movements have emerged several times. The Pukhtun nationalists seeking to create a separate Pukhtunistan in the north-western province of Pakistan were contained by a policy of carrot and stick during the 1950s and 1960s. The people of the former East Pakistan seceded to form their independent state of Bangladesh in 1971. It cost, however, between 1.5 and 3 million lives. The Pakistan army especially targeted the Hindus. A bloody guerrilla war raged in Baluchistan during the early 1970s, which was defeated by forceful military action. However, a virulent ethnic conflict that has claimed several thousand lives has been going on in the Sindh province, mainly as a confrontation between the native Sindhi-speakers and the Urdu-speaking refugees (both primarily Sunni Muslims) who settled in the urban areas of that province after Partition. Military action has been undertaken several times to restore law and order. In addition, hundreds of thousands of Afghan refugees have settled in Karachi, where armed militias run lucrative businesses in drugs and arms smuggling.

4

Tibet and the Border Partition

The 1940s saw huge change in South Asia with the Partition of India in 1947 (resulting in the establishment of the two new states of India and Pakistan), and the establishment of the People's Republic of China (PRC) in 1949. One of the most basic policies for the new Indian government was that of maintaining cordial relations with China, reviving its ancient friendly ties. India was among the first nations to grant diplomatic recognition to the newly created PRC.

At the time, Chinese officials issued no condemnation of Nehru's claims or made any opposition to Nehru's open declarations of control over Aksai Chin. In 1956, Chinese Premier Zhou Enlai stated that he had no claims over Indian controlled territory. He later argued that Aksai Chin was already under Chinese jurisdiction, implying that there was therefore no contradiction with his earlier statement, since China did not regard the region as "Indian controlled", and that since the British hand-over, China had regarded the McCartney MacDonald Line as the relevant border. Zhou later argued that as the boundary was undemarcated and had never been defined by treaty between any Chinese or Indian government, the Indian government could not unilaterally define Aksai Chin's borders.

In 1950, the Chinese People's Liberation Army annexed Tibet and later the Chinese extended their influence by building a road in 1956–67 and placing border posts in Aksai Chin. India found out after the road was completed, protested against these moves and decided to look for a diplomatic solution to ensure a stable Sino-Indian border. To resolve any doubts about the Indian position, Prime Minister Jawaharlal Nehru declared in parliament that India regarded the McMahon Line as its official border. The Chinese expressed no concern at this statement, and in 1951 and 1952, the government of China asserted that there were no frontier issues to be taken up with India.

In 1954, Prime Minister Nehru wrote a memo calling for India's borders to be clearly defined and demarcated; in line with previous Indian philosophy, Indian maps showed a border that, in some places, lay north of the McMahon Line. Chinese Premier Zhou Enlai, in November 1956, again repeated Chinese assurances that the People's Republic had no claims on Indian territory, although official Chinese maps showed 120,000 square kilometres (46,000 sq mi) of territory claimed by India as Chinese. CIA documents created at the time revealed that Nehru had ignored Burmese premier Ba Swe when he warned Nehru to be cautious when dealing with Zhou. They also allege that Zhou purposefully told Nehru that there were no border issues with India.

In 1954, China and India negotiated the Five Principles of Peaceful Coexistence, by which the two nations agreed to abide in settling their disputes. India presented a frontier map which was accepted by China, and the Indian government under Prime Minister Nehru promoted the slogan *Hindi-Chini bhai-bhai* (Indians and Chinese are brothers).

According to Georgia Tech political analystJohn W Garver, Nehru's policy on Tibet was to create a strong Sino-Indian partnership which would be catalysed through agreement and compromise on Tibet. Garver believes that Nehru's previous actions had given him confidence that China would be ready to form an "Asian Axis" with India. This apparent progress in relations suffered a major setback when, in 1959, Nehru accommodated the Tibetan religious leader at the time, the 14th Dalai Lama, who fled Lhasa after a failed Tibetan uprising against Chinese rule. The Chairman of the Chinese Communist Party, Mao Zedong, was enraged and asked the Xinhua News Agency to produce reports on Indian expansionists operating in Tibet.

Border incidents continued through this period. In August 1959, the People's Liberation Army took an Indian prisoner at Longju, which had an ambiguous position in the McMahon Line, and two months later in Aksai Chin, a clash led to the death of nine Indian frontier policemen.

On 2 October, Soviet Premier Nikita Khrushchev defended Nehru in a meeting with Mao. This action reinforced China's impression that the Soviet Union, the United States and India all had expansionist designs on China. The People's Liberation Army went so far as to prepare a self-defence counterattack plan. Negotiations were restarted between the nations, but no progress was made.

As a consequence of their non-recognition of the McMahon Line, China's maps showed both the North East Frontier Area (NEFA) and Aksai Chin to be Chinese territory. In 1960, Zhou Enlai unofficially suggested that India drop its claims to Aksai Chin in return for a Chinese withdrawal of claims over NEFA. Adhering to his stated position, Nehru believed that China did not have a legitimate claim over either of these territories, and thus was not ready to concede them. This adamant stance was perceived in China as Indian opposition to Chinese rule in Tibet. Nehru declined to conduct any negotiations on the boundary until Chinese troops withdrew from Aksai Chin, a position supported by the international community.

India produced numerous reports on the negotiations, and translated Chinese reports into English to help inform the international debate. China believed that India was simply securing its claim lines in order to continue its "grand plans in Tibet". India's stance that China withdraw from Aksai Chin caused continual deterioration of the diplomatic situation to the point that internal forces were pressuring Nehru to take a military stance against China.

THE FORWARD POLICY

At the beginning of 1961, Nehru appointed General B. M. Kaul as army Chief of General Staff, but he refused to increase military spending and prepare for a possible war. According to James

Barnard Calvin of the U.S. Navy, in 1959, India started sending Indian troops and border patrols into disputed areas. This program created both skirmishes and deteriorating relations between India and China. The aim of this policy was to create outposts behind advancing Chinese troops to interdict their supplies, forcing them north of the disputed line. There were eventually 60 such outposts, including 43 north of the McMahon Line, to which India claimed sovereignty. China viewed this as further confirmation of Indian expansionist plans directed towards Tibet. According to the Indian official history, implementation of the Forward Policy was intended to provide evidence of Indian occupation in the previously unoccupied region through which Chinese troops had been patrolling. Kaul was confident, through contact with Indian Intelligence and CIA information, that China would not react with force. Indeed, at first the PLA simply withdrew, but eventually Chinese forces began to counter-encircle the Indian positions which clearly encroached into the north of McMahon Line. This led to a tit-for-tat Indian reaction, with each force attempting to outmanoeuver the other. However, despite the escalating nature of the dispute, the two forces withheld from engaging each other directly.

Chinese attention was diverted for a time by the military activity of the Nationalists on Taiwan, but on 23 June the U.S. assured China that a Nationalist invasion would not be permitted. China's heavy artillery facing Taiwan could then be moved to Tibet. It took China six to eight months to gather the resources needed for the war, according to Anil Athale, author of the official Indian history. The Chinese sent a large quantity of non-military supplies to Tibet through the Indian port of Calcutta.

Early Incidents

Various border conflicts and "military incidents" between India and China flared up throughout the summer and autumn of 1962. In May, the Indian Air Force was told not to plan for close air support, although it was assessed as being a feasible way to counter the unfavourable ratio of Chinese to Indian troops. In June, a skirmish caused the deaths of dozens of Chinese troops.

The Indian Intelligence Bureau received information about a Chinese buildup along the border which could be a precursor to war.

During June–July 1962, Indian military planners began advocating "probing actions" against the Chinese, and accordingly, moved mountain troops forward to cut off Chinese supply lines. According to Patterson, the Indian motives were threefold:

1. Test Chinese resolve and intentions regarding India.
2. Test whether India would enjoy Soviet backing in the event of a Sino-Indian war.
3. Create sympathy for India within the U.S., with whom relations had deteriorated after the Indian annexation of Goa.

On 10 July 1962, 350 Chinese troops surrounded an Indian occupied post in Chushul (north of the McMahon Line) but withdrew after a heated argument via loudspeaker. On 22 July, the Forward Policy was extended to allow Indian troops to push back Chinese troops already established in disputed territory. Whereas Indian troops were previously ordered to fire only in self-defence, all post commanders were now given discretion to open fire upon Chinese forces if threatened. In August, the Chinese military improved its combat readiness along the McMahon Line and began stockpiling ammunition, weapons and gasoline.

Given his foreknowledge of the coming Cuban Missile Crisis, Mao Zedong was able to persuade Nikita Khrushchev to reverse the Russian policy of backing India, at least temporarily. In mid-October, the Communist organ *Pravda* encouraged peace between India and China. When the Cuban Missile Crisis ended and Mao's rhetoric changed, however, Russia reversed course.

CONFRONTATION AT THAG LA

In June 1962, Indian forces established an outpost at Dhola, on the southern slopes of the Thag La Ridge. Dhola lay north of the McMahon Line but south of the ridges along which India interpreted the McMahon Line to run. In August, China issued diplomatic protests and began occupying positions at the top of

Thag La. On 8 September, a 60-strong PLA unit descended to the south side of the ridge and occupied positions that dominated one of the Indian posts at Dhola. Fire was not exchanged, but Nehru said to the media that the Indian Army had instructions to "free our territory" and the troops had been given discretion to use force. On 11 September, it was decided that "all forward posts and patrols were given permission to fire on any armed Chinese who entered Indian territory".

However, the operation to occupy Thag La was flawed in that Nehru's directives were unclear and it got underway very slowly because of this. In addition to this, each man had to carry 35 kilograms (77 lb) over the long trek and this severely slowed down the reaction. By the time the Indian battalion reached the point of conflict, Chinese units controlled both banks of the Namka Chu River. On 20 September, Chinese troops threw grenades at Indian troops and a firefight developed, triggering a long series of skirmishes for the rest of September. Some Indian troops, including Brigadier Dalvi who commanded the forces at Thag La, were also concerned that the territory they were fighting for was not strictly territory that "we should have been convinced was ours". According to Neville Maxwell, even members of the Indian defence ministry were categorically concerned with the validity of the fighting in Thag La.

On 3 October, a week before the start of the war, Zhou Enlai visited Nehru in New Delhi promising there would be no war. On 4 October, Kaul assigned some troops to secure regions south of the Thag La Ridge. Kaul decided to first secure Yumtso La, a strategically important position, before re-entering the lost Dhola post. Kaul had then realised that the attack would be desperate and the Indian government tried to stop an escalation into all-out war. Indian troops marching to Thag La had suffered in the previously unexperienced conditions; two Gurkha soldiers died of pulmonary edema. On 10 October, an Indian Punjabi patrol of 50 troops to Yumtso La were met by an emplaced Chinese position of some 1,000 soldiers. Indian troops were in no position for battle, as Yumtso La was 16,000 feet (4,900 m) above sea level and Kaul did not plan on having artillery support for the troops. The Chinese troops opened fire on the Indians under their belief that they were north of the McMahon Line. The Indians were surrounded by Chinese positions which used mortar fire. However, they managed to hold off the first Chinese assault, inflicting heavy casualties.

At this point, the Indian troops were in a position to push the Chinese back with mortar and machine gun fire. However, Brigadier Dalvi opted not to fire, as it would mean decimating the Rajput who were still in the area of the Chinese regrouping. They helplessly watched the Chinese ready themselves for a second assault. In the second Chinese assault, the Indians began their retreat, realising the situation was hopeless. The Indian patrol suffered 25 casualties, and the Chinese 33. The Chinese troops held their fire as the Indians retreated, and then buried the Indian dead with military honours, as witnessed by the retreating soldiers. This was the first occurrence of heavy fighting in the war.

This attack had grave implications for India and Nehru tried to solve the issue, but by 18 October, it was clear that the Chinese were preparing for an attack on India, with massive troop buildups on the border. A long line of mules and porters had also been observed supporting the buildup and reinforcement of positions south of the Thag La Ridge.

IMPACT OF INDIA-CHINA BORDER ISSUE ON SOUTH ASIA

The issue of boundary demarcation between India and China together with the developments in Tibet not only affected the bilateral relationship but also completely changed the geopolitical situation of the entire South Asian region. The strained relations between China and the Soviet Union starting from 1957 on the one hand and the perceived Indo-Soviet closed relationship on the other compelled China to foster a strategic friendship with Pakistan based on common animosity towards India.

There were no cultural, historical, political and ideological commonalities or mutual economic interests between the two to come closure. The urgency to set up strategic relationship was evident from the fact that the two governments concluded the boundary negotiations just in seventy five days. This agreement suddenly pushed the Sino-Pakistan relationship to a higher level. The defence cooperation and nuclear and missile technology support that followed in next four decades between two countries speak volume about the closeness of the relationship.

The Chinese assistance to Pakistan in 1965 and 1971 Indo-Pakistan wars and support to Pakistan in past on Kashmir dispute are linked to China-India border dispute and Tibet issue. Further China's defence cooperation with India's neighbours like Bangla Desh and Myanmar and its support to insurgents in India's north eastern region till 1970s, were cause of concern for India.

NEW APPROACH TO BORDER SETTLEMENT

India and China have held fifteen rounds of talks at official level to resolve the border issue since mid 1980s with little progress. Clarification of the line of actual control has not been yet been completed. Only the maps in respect of the middle sector, which is least disputed, could be exchanged so far in about twenty years since the talks started.

The change in international situation, globalization of economy and national aspirations of the people of the two countries compelled the two states to reassess the over all bilateral relationship in the new situation. After recognizing the security and economic imperatives of each others the two states decided to develop a cooperative relationship for mutual benefit in a realistic way. Under this new approach the two countries, in 2003, separated the issue of border demarcation from the question of overall development of bilateral relations and assigned it priority by appointing Special Representatives to explore the settlement from the political perspective of the overall bilateral relationship.

The special representatives after holding several rounds of dialogues concluded an agreement on the 'Parameters and Guiding Principles for the Settlement of the India-China Boundary Question' in April 2005. This agreement provides that the two sides would abide by and implement the agreement on the maintenance of peace and tranquility along the Line of Actual Control in the India-China border areas, signed in 1993 and 1996 and seek a fair, reasonable and mutually acceptable solution of the boundary issue through peaceful and friendly consultations taking into account, *inter alia,* historical evidence, national sentiments, practical difficulties and reasonable concerns and sensitivities of both sides, and the actual state of border areas.

Important aspect of the agreement is that in reaching a boundary settlement, the two sides shall safeguard due interests of their settled populations in the border areas, which implies that no population transfer would take place. At the same time India and China have affirmed that the two countries are not threat to each other and neither side shall use or threaten to use force against the other in an endeavor to create a better friendly environment.

INDIA BHUTAN CHINA STRATEGIC TRIANGLE

India Bhutan and China are part of a strategic triangle in the Eastern Himalayas with the inverted apex jutting in the form of the all important Chumbi Valley in Yadong (Yatung) county of Tibetan Autonomous Region (TAR). Given proximity of the Chumbi Valley to India's jugular to the North East the 20 kms wide Siliguri corridor, the two arms of the triangle resting on Indian state of Sikkim in the West and Bhutan in the East assume importance. Chinese plans to extend the Qinghai Tibet railway to Xigaze and Yadong close to the Sino Indian border have added to concerns in India with tardy communication links on the Eastern frontier. Given the strategic significance, India has been able to maintain balance primarily through the Indo Bhutan Treaty of Friendship first signed in 1949 and revised on mutually agreed terms in 2007.

Thus two arms of the triangle could be said under Indian control and influence, even as China holds the base. This equation may be upset in case China is able to gain greater access to the Bhutanese arm of the triangle with a reset of the Sino Bhutan boundary, negotiations for which are underway. Given the difficult terrain on the Western arm of the Chumbi Valley and scope for expansion is primarily in the East. These fears were attenuated with the first ever summit held between the prime ministers of Bhutan and China in Rio recently. An over view of the relationships would therefore be in order and is covered as per succeeding paragraphs. Indo Bhutan Treaty of Friendship in 2007 has led to greater diplomatic freedom to Thimpu opening prospects of engagement across the board. The most significant change in 2007 was mutual reaffirmation of sovereignty and territorial integrity in the preamble of the Treaty which was not there in the 1949 text. More over Article 2 of the 1949 Treaty stated that Bhutan will be guided by the advice of India on external relations.

The Article read, "The Government of India undertakes to exercise no interference in the internal administration of Bhutan. On its part, the Government of Bhutan agrees to be guided by the advice of the Government of India in regard to its external relations". This has been reviewed of the 2007 Treaty reads, "__the Government of the Kingdom of Bhutan and the Government of the Republic of India shall cooperate closely with each other on issues relating to their national interests. Neither Government shall allow the use of its territory for activities harmful to the national security and interest of the other". The sum total of implications of the change is greater freedom of choice to Bhutan in management of sovereignty and external relations.

This background is essential to understand the nuances of the first ever bilateral held between the Chinese Prime Minister Wen Jiabao and Bhutan's Prime Minister, Jigmi Y. Thinley on the side lines of the Rio Conference on Sustainable Development in June 2012. While Bhutan has been expanding foreign relations over the years and in 2011 chaired South Asian Association of Regional Cooperation (SAARC), there was no formal diplomatic relations or summit level contact with Beijing.

Having greater autonomy post 2007 Treaty, it is inevitable that there would be greater traction for Bhutan to establish diplomatic relations with China the only nation other than India with which it shares a land border. Proposal for diplomatic relations was first discussed between the two countries in 1998 during the 12th Round of border talks.

Significantly, Bhutan and India are the only two countries with which China has not resolved land borders. There are two areas of dispute, one falling in North West Bhutan covering 269 sq km and the other Central Bhutan covering 495 sq km. The North

West area comprises Doklam (89 sq km), Sinchulumpa (42 Sq km), and Shakhatoe (138 Sq km) in Samste, Haa and Paro districts and Central parts the Pasamlung and the Jakarlung valley in the Wangdue Phodrang district. The 1998 agreement between Bhutan and China entitled, "Maintain Peace and Tranquility on the Bhutan-China Border Areas," provides the framework for stability on the border. However despite this there have been reports of intrusions by Chinese troops in Bhutanese territory. In November 2007 some reports indicate dismantling of unmanned posts in the Dolam Valley. Bhutan's media reported a number of intrusions in 2009.

At the same time Bhutan and China have held 19 rounds of talks on the boundary dispute so far the last one being held in January 2010 after a gap of four years where a joint field survey was agreed upon. This was to be carried out of disputed areas in Doklam, Charithang, Sinchulumpa and Dramana in Bhutan's North West and Pasamlung and the Jakarlung valley in the Wangdue Phodrang district in Central Bhutan. It is reasonably well established by now that China is looking for a package deal with Bhutan seeking areas in the North West while establishing Bhutan's claims in the Central region. This offer was first made in the sixth round of talks held in August 1990. Chinese quid pro quo does not take into account that the territory is a part of the sovereign state of Bhutan and strategic interests seem to be pushing Beijing to offer a package to the southern neighbor. Herein lies the rub where India's interests come in given proximity of the North West areas to the Chumbi Valley. In case Bhutan seeks to appease China to move the trajectory of relations forward, it would most certainly cause concern in Delhi and may even be objected to.

In the light of this legacy the Wen Jiabao – Thinley meet seems to be an opening gambit by both sides to test the waters on how far they can push the envelope without India blocking the package deal altogether. Premier Wen Jiabao as per a report by the AFP stated, "China is willing... to establish formal relations with Bhutan, resolve the border issue between the two nations at an early date, strengthen exchanges in all areas and advance Sino-Bhutanese relations to a new stage." A report in the Hindu of 27 June also quoted Mr. Wen saying that China was "willing to complete border demarcation with Bhutan at an early date." Mr. Thinley was quoted by Xinhua the official Chinese news agency to have expressed that Bhutan wishes to forge formal diplomatic ties with China as soon as possible. Bhutan has also sought China's support in elections to the non permanent seat in the United Nations Security Council being vacated by India in 2013.

South Asia experts from Chinese think tanks, China Institutes of Contemporary International Relations (CICIR) and Chinese Academy of Social Sciences (CASS) as quoted by the Hindu in a report on 26 June 2012 have been quick to speculate that Bhutan would not have taken these initiatives without India's express, "approval or agreement."

The official web site of the Cabinet Secretariat of the Royal Government of Bhutan however makes muted remarks on the bilateral summit and states, "The meeting [Wen Jiabao-Thinley] carries great historic significance as it marks the first meeting between the heads of the two governments. They discussed bilateral issues of mutual interest and multilateral cooperation including Bhutan's bid for a non permanent seat on UN Security Council for the term 2013-2014, elections for which are to be held in fall this year". No mention was made of either diplomatic relations or boundary issue.

Bhutanese writer, Kuenzang Choden writing in web site The Bhutanese on 22 June 2012, quotes Media Attache of Bhutan Prime Minister's office to refute any initiative by Prime Minister Thinley to propose establishment of diplomatic relations with China. He states, "local Chinese media had misreported that Bhutan and China will establish diplomatic ties." Kuenzang further goes on to quote a Foreign Ministry official who sought to remain anonymous indicating, "It is unlikely that Bhutan and China will have diplomatic relations soon. There are certain policies when it comes to the Permanent five of the United Nations Security Council."

There are obviously different versions being floated of deliberation during the summit. Has the Chinese media gone overboard in flagging the initiative for bilateral relations and resolution of boundary issue will not be clear but without a push from the officials accompanying the Prime Minister these reports are unlikely to have been published. Has Bhutan gone ahead with the move after approval from New Delhi as some Indian media reports and Chinese scholars seem to suggest or the Prime Minister of Bhutan has been misquoted by the Chinese media as Bhutanese authorities are indicating or this is an unilateral initiative by Thimpu, hence the foreign office cover up is not clear so far.

Suffice to say that first summit level contact between Bhutan and China has been established and the engagement will be taken forward to establish diplomatic relations and possibly even resolve the boundary issue in times to come. The trajectory may not be easy to determine at this juncture nor the time frame predictable. Settlement of boundary however is unlikely to happen soon. Given importance of the Chumbi Valley India is unlikely to agree to any concessions by Bhutan that leads to exchange of territory in this area providing further elbow room to China. Fears expressed by reports in the Indian media may therefore may be unfounded.

On the other hand Chinese keenness to extend the railway line to Yadung and secure the Bhutanese arm of the Chumbi Valley triangle may be as much due to fears of India cutting off the salient jutting threateningly towards the Siliguri corridor. This will overcome the vulnerability of the Siliguri Corridor providing it additional depth. This could be one explanation for given the operational challenges of launching a major thrust through the Chumbi Valley to cut off the Siliguri corridor and India's build up of forces on the Eastern front, Chinese offensive in the area will be posed major operational challenges.

What ever it be, given mutual apprehensions, strategic stability in the India Bhutan China triangle would require statesmanship of a high order. This will depend on how the political and military leadership of the three countries and especially New Delhi and Beijing are able to manage the same ensuring Thimpu's sovereignty and autonomy. The Indian government has done well not to over react to media reports and would be seeking full details of Chinese interaction from Bhutan to chart out a future course of action. This will no doubt be done keeping in view larger national interests of managing relations with China amicably yet not compromising on basic national security interests, thus implying any attempt to extend the Eastern arm of the inverted apex of the Chumbi Valley will be fiercely resisted by New Delhi.

HISTORY OF BHUTAN-INDIA RELATIONSHIPS

While Bhutan shares borders with both China and India, its relationships with the two are not of equal length and depth. It is a lot closer to India, and the two share intimate bonds in the areas of foreign affairs, economy, trade, education and technology, and national defence and security.

Bhutan used to build its foreign relations completely around India. The two signed the Treaty of Perpetual Peace and Friendship Between the Government of India and the Government of Bhutan in Darjeeling, India on August 8, 1949.

The treaty does not mention Bhutan's status as a sovereign state. Article 2 says that, "The Government of India undertakes to exercise no interference in the internal administration of Bhutan. On its part the Government of Bhutan agrees to be guided by the advice of the Government of India in regard to its external relations."

This means that Bhutan needs to seek "advice" from India in foreign relations in exchange for India's recognition.

Bhutan is heavily dependent on India for financial assistance and foreign relations. India agrees to provide 500,000 INR to Bhutan every year, which is much higher than the 200,000 INR a year from Britain, and also offers to return the 32 square mile of land at Dewangiri to Bhutan as a friendly gesture.

India and Bhutan established formal diplomatic ties on August 8, 1978, but support from India came long before that, as India has been showering Bhutan with financial and technical assistance since 1960s, helping Bhutan set up highways as well as water and power stations.

Bhutan has always supported India on the international scene, taking the side with India in the United Nations, SAARC, and other international conventions. Examples include Bhutan's support for India to become a permanent member of the United Nations

Security Council. The Bhutanese Minister of Foreign Affairs Lyonpo Khandu Wangchuk, on the 59th United Nations Conference in September 2004, explicitly expressed Bhutan's support for India and Japan to become permanent members of the United Nations Security Council.

India is Bhutan's leading provider of economic assistance. The majority of investment in Bhutan's successive five-year economic development projects (hereinafter "five-year projects") comes from India. Under the suggestion of India Prime Minister Jawaharlal Nehru, Bhutan launched the first five-year project in 1961. The first and the second five-year projects were completely funded by India. The third to eighth saw India providing 90% to 27.6% of the funds. India recently agreed to subsidize Bhutan's ninth five-year project.

India is Bhutan's biggest trade partner in terms of import and export. Take year 2001 as an example, Bhutan's export to India in that year amounts to 4.7 billion Bhutanese ngultrums (including electricity), accounting for 94% of Bhutan's total export.

Bhutan's import from India in that year amounts to 7 billion Bhutanese ngultrums, accounting for 77% of Bhutan's total export.

Each year, India provides scholarship to 50 Bhutanese students studying medicine, law, engineering, computer science, science, humanities, and business at universities in India.

Bhutan has two higher education institutions, namely the Royal University of Bhutan (established in June 2003) and Sherubtse College, which shares close relationships with University of Delhi in India. Many Indian teachers work at Sherubtse College. A lot of Bhutanese students study at India at their own expenses.

As for national defence and security, in July 1960 the Indian army dispatched the first Indian Military Training Team commander and some 10 officers to Bhutan. In May 1961, the Indian army sent a training team to Bhutan on scouting missions. So far the training team has set up 1 military academy and 2 hospitals in Bhutan in addition to its base. Bhutan is safe under India's protective umbrella as India is responsible for Bhutan's security, provides training for Bhutan's security troops, covers all of Bhutan's military expenses, and offers military equipment to Bhutan.

Bhutan and India have also joined hands in clearing anti-government organizations in India. There is a 380-kilometer border between Bhutan and Assam and West Bengal in India. Indian rebel troops have occupied southern borders of Bhutan for a long time, causing a headache for India and Bhutan.

There are tens of various anti-government armed forces in northeast India, some have existed for half a century, and some are in their teens. These armed forces resort to the use of force to pursue greater extent of autonomy and even independence in their regions.

The India government tried to solve the problem with negotiations, with little progress. The three largest anti-government forces in India are United Liberation Front of Asom (ULFA), National Democratic Front of Bodos (NDFB), and Kamtapur Liberation Organization (KLO), all declared illegal by the India government.

The ULFA, founded in 1979, is the largest of the three, and pursues independence of Assam just like the NDFB, whereas the KLO are basically people of the Kamtapur tribe seeking to establish their own homes in West Bengal.

The ULFA survived large-scale attack from Indian troops in 1990s and some of its members went on to team up with nearby anti-government forces to set up a base in southern Bhutan. According to statistics, these rebel groups have set up 19 or 20 bases in Bhutan.

They use the strategies of attack and retreat, crossing the India-Bhutan border and attacking targets in India, causing a serious headache for the India government. For 6 years, the Bhutan government has repeatedly asked the two anti-government forces to leave Bhutan and even held talks with them, but has been able to find a peaceful resolution.

Continuing pressure from the India government made Bhutan send troops in December 2003 to clear out the rebel forces, destroying some 30 bases and subjecting more than a hundred

Bhutanese citizens who assisted the rebel groups to legal punishment. The rebel groups scattered everywhere and sought assistance from other countries, and were turned down by China. India, fearing that the rebels would seek asylum in places like Bangladesh and Myanmar and that Pakistan would supply them with weapons and training, resorted to diplomatic channels to put pressure on these countries.

Bhutan's attack on rebels was well received by the India government, which immediately extended an invitation to the King of Bhutan to be the guest of honour in the Republic Day celebrations on January 26, 2005. Both India and Bhutan have their own worries for the moment.

India fears that rebels would remain in Bhutan or scatter elsewhere and still pose threat to India's security. India also fears that Nepali refugees in Bhutan would join the rebels and make them stronger. Bhutan worries that Mao rebels in Nepal would join the Indian rebels. India and Bhutan constantly discuss their worries to think of ways to protect themselves from the rebels.

DPT AND INDO-BHUTAN RELATIONS

DPT's foreign policy direction hinged consistently on the unquestionable and inextinguishable reality that India would always be the cornerstone of Bhutan's foreign policy matrix.

The DPT government, therefore, did everything possible to expand, deepen, elevate and secure Bhutan-India relations in the past five years. This was evident from the fact that Jigmi Y Thinley visited India nine times in five years, more than any other Bhutanese leader before him, with the exception of Their Majesties. In fact, Jigmi Y Thinley's first overseas visit as prime minister of democratic Bhutan was to India, barely a month after assuming office. His last official overseas visit, when leaving office, was also to India, in February 2013.

Jigmi Y Thinley interacted with Indian leaders at all levels from a wide social and political spectrum during his tenure as prime minister. His visit to Bihar resulted in the granting of two acres of land by the Bihar government to Bhutan at Rajghir, Bodhgaya, to build a Bhutanese temple and guesthouse. He also met the chief minister of Andhra Pradesh, and was in Madhya Pradesh in the capacity of chief guest at a Buddhist University.

He hosted the chief minister of Assam in Bhutan and met Mamata Banerjee, the West Bengal chief minister. Further, he was invited by the government of India to deliver the prestigious Hiren Mukherjee memorial address to the Lok Sabha. He was also the keynote speaker at PAN IIT congress of the prestigious IIT, besides meeting Indian corporate leaders twice in Mumbai and Kolkata. Similarly, other Bhutanese cabinet ministers met Indian leaders, including the prime minister, in India, as well as at every international fora outside of India.

The visit of Indian leaders to Bhutan was also unprecedented during the tenure of the DPT government. The Indian prime minister, Dr Manmohan Singh, came to Bhutan twice, first on a state visit and second for the 16th SAARC summit hosted for the first time in Bhutan. The opposition leader, Susma Swaraj, also visited Bhutan, besides parliamentarians and leaders from all political walks.

It looks highly implausible that, after such intense and friendly interactions between the two governments and nation states in the past five years, that India should harbour any doubt and suspicion at all of the royal government's commitment to Bhutan-India relations.

If it is indeed true that India is still offended by the routine, harmless and friendly overture extended by Bhutan under the DPT government to China, as it did to so many other countries and heads of government at the Rio Earth summit, and is choosing to implicate DPT (and consequently Bhutan) with culpability at such a crucial point in the elections, I must confess that I am totally baffled and confounded.

Politicisation and Brinkmanship

Bhutan-India relations came to the fore as an issue during the 90-day election period. In fact, it intensified as campaign fodder after the primary round of elections, which gave the DPT a clear advantage and majority over the other party. The appearance of two articles, subsequently in the Times of India, whipping up an old issue, came like a bolt out of the blue. Our friends in India, unwittingly ensnared in this game of political brinksmanship, must remember that such inadvertent, mercenary and gravely injurious attitudes and moves do not bode well at all for Bhutan-India friendship in the long run.

For the discerning Bhutanese, alarm bells should start ringing, given the timing of the withdrawal of subsidies and other very strange posturing from certain quarters and individuals here in the country. The interest groups are resorting to desperate pressure tactics to leverage New Delhi's influence in Bhutan to not only induce, but perhaps blatantly rig, the electoral outcome.

5

Competing Historical Narratives of Partition

British India was divided into the two countries of India and Pakistan after an unsuccessful attempt to find a compromise solution to keep the country together. The long, bitter and acrimonious debates, marred by communal tensions and occasional riots, left more than divided countries; it left a trail of divided legacies. Indians and Pakistanis have viewed differently the creation of their two (now three) countries and the events that led to them.

There was an almost unanimity in Pakistan that the partition was a good thing for Indian Muslims. The only regret was that the new country was deprived of the half of Punjab and Bengal which Pakistan thought rightfully belonged to it. There was a general consensus that, in a united India, the minority Muslim community could not expect to be fairly treated by the Hindu majority, which was thought to be ahead of Muslims in the fields of education and business and to hold deep grudges against Muslims who had ruled over them in popular imagination for a thousand years. Pakistanis believed that their country owed its creation almost entirely to the brilliant stewardship of its great leader Mohammad Ali Jinnah, appropriately named the Qaid-e-Azam, who single-handedly outwitted the "wily and cunning" Hindu leadership masquerading under a supposedly inclusive Indian National Congress

In India, unlike Pakistan, the Partition of the country was regarded as a 'bad' and even a catastrophic event Even today, Mr.

Jaswant Singh, uses the more emotive term 'vivisection' to describe the division of the country in his new book, "Jinnah: India, Partition, Independence". While the Congress leadership took full credit for gaining independence from the British, it was not prepared to accept the responsibility for the partition of the country. Just like the Pakistanis, it was quite happy to put the responsibility for dividing the country on the uncompromising leadership of the communal Muslim League. Jinnah, who was the hero in Pakistan for single handedly achieving a new country, became the villain of the story in India for the same accomplishment.

But unlike Pakistan, there was no unanimity on who to blame for the creation of Pakistan. Unlike the Congress leadership, a large number of Hindus and Sikhs were not willing to put the sole blame on Jinnah and also held the Congress leadership responsible for succumbing to Jinnah's demand. Ironically, the object of their rage was not Patel or Nehru who led the negotiations with Jinnah, but Mahatma Gandhi who had alone stood against the idea of the Partition till the very end. People had implicit faith in Gandhi's repeated assurance that he would never let the country to be divided and felt betrayed by him. Gandhi was also targeted by them as he was viewed as doing too much to save the properties and lives of the Muslims who stayed back in India while ignoring the plight of the suffering Hindus and Sikhs stranded in Pakistan. This rage and hatred towards Gandhi ultimately led to his assassination by an angry Hindu, soon after independence.

The outgoing British rulers came in for criticism from both sides. Indians blamed them for continuing with their 'divide and rule' policy which they had employed during their colonial rule. They alleged that the British wanted to create Pakistan so that they could continue to influence events in the subcontinent after their departure through their new creation, i.e., Pakistan. Pakistanis blamed Nehru's influence over the last British Viceroy, Lord Mountbatten, for depriving them of the whole of Bengal and Punjab, as well as the district of Gurdaspur without which India would have had no access to the state of Jammu and Kashmir. They were even more certain of this influence after Nehru's affair with Lady Mountbatten became public. Pakistanis also blamed

Nehru's influence on Mountbatten for the undue haste in giving independence, giving little time for a successful transition of Pakistan into a new country, so that it would come begging to be taken back in India.

The two countries continued with their cherished notions of heroes and villains for more than a decade. These notions were first disturbed by Maulana Abul Kalam Azad's autobiographical accounts in his landmark book, "India Wins Freedom". Maulana Azad was a prominent leader of India's freedom movement and had the distinction of being the longest serving president of the Indian National Congress, including the crucial seven-year period of 1939-1946. The book was first published in 1959 although he instructed that some parts of the book would remain sealed for a period of 30 years, which were released in 1989. Azad was a towering and respected figure among Indian Muslims whose commitment to a united India was unquestioned. Although he was ridiculed in Pakistan as a Congress show boy, he was nevertheless highly respected there as an eminent scholar of Islam. Therefore, what he said carried a high degree of credibility.

The publication of the book caused a lot of controversy in India. It was critical not only of Jinnah but also of Patel and Nehru in the role that they played in the division of the country. According to him, Gandhi was the only Congress leader who remained opposed to the division of the country to the end. Azad was particularly critical of Nehru in issuing an explosive press statement following the accord reached with Jinnah over the Cabinet Mission Plan (CMP) in 1946. In that statement issued after encountering strong opposition to the CMP from the left wing of the Congress Party whose champion Nehru was, Nehru said that the Congress will not be fettered by the CMP in the proposed Constituent Assembly. The statement gave an opportunity to Jinnah to back out of his acceptance of the CMP, with which he too was not fully satisfied. Because of this statement of Nehru, Azad regretted leaving the Presidency of the Congress Party just before the CMP negotiations. What may be surprising to many is that he also regretted anointing Nehru as his successor instead of Patel who was the preferred choice of Gandhi and most Congressmen. He thought that Patel would never have made the kind of unthoughtful statement that Nehru did under pressure from his socialist supporters.

The book, or at least the part blaming Indian leaders, was well received in the progressive sections of Pakistan. While there had been a consensus in Pakistan about the role of Jinnah in achieving their country, there was no such consensus about what kind of legacy he represented. This was largely because of the fact that Jinnah had not clearly defined his vision of Pakistan, perhaps to keep together the disparate elements that he had collected under his Pakistan tent. In his famous speech to the Constituent Assembly on August 11, 1946, he did articulate a vision of Pakistan where non-muslims would be equal citizens, but there were other references in some of his speeches which could be interpreted as a support of a society based on Islamic principles. From the very beginning of Pakistan, religious forces were in ascendancy and powerful enough to delete the "objectionable" phrases from Jinnah's 11th August speech from public domain. Azad's book could be used by progressive Pakistanis to show that Jinnah was more interested in safeguarding the interests of the Muslim community than in creating a state ruled by Islamic laws.

Azad's book was followed by various other books by Indian and Pakistani writers which tried to rehabilitate Jinnah as a secular, as opposed to a communal leader. The most prominent of these was Ayesha Jalal's "The Sole Spokesperson". Jalal took the position that Jinnah never wanted to create a separate state of Pakistan and merely used this demand as a bargaining chip to wrest concessions for the Muslim minority in a united India. He ended up obtaining a country that he did not want because of the obduracy of the Congress leaders who refused the reasonable accommodation that Jinnah was looking for.

The rehabilitation of Jinnah as an Indian nationalist has continued, especially by some right wing politicians in India, albeit with considerable controversy. The first right wing politician to praise Jinnah was the President of the Bhartiya Janata Party, Lal Krishna Advani who praised Jinnah's August 1947 speech as one by a truly secular leader. And now, another BJP leader, Jaswant

Singh, has come out with a scholarly book which seems to place the primary responsibility on Patel and Nehru for the 'vivisection' of the country. Very few people have yet read the book, but based on excerpts and his interviews, it is clear that he thinks highly of Jinnah and considers him as one of the great sons of India.

There is a considerable amount of fog that clouds the history of the crucial years that led to India and Pakistan's independence. It is encouraging to note that scholarly work has started to objectively analyse those events without the passions and emotions that marked the earlier historiography in the two countries. One hopes that Jaswant's work will be followed by others, using all the evidence that has become available through declassification of various documents relating to that period.

It is generally believed that but for Nehru's unthoughtful press statement, India would have still been one united country and we all would have avoided the bitterness of cold war of the past six decades, including three wars. Mualana Azad called it a 'Himalayan blunder' in his book. This was also my belief for a long time. However, I have now come to believe that the universe unfolded as it should have. The CMP was a cleverly worded compromise document; like all such documents, it was drafted so as the opposite parties could spin its meaning to suit their constituents. This is exactly what they did. Nehru said that he was not bound literally by all its clauses; Muslim League leaders said that this was a transitionary arrangement which would lead to their cherished dream of a separate state. Even without different interpretations and objectives, the interim government of united India was dysfunctional as Congress and Muslim League ministers, especially Patel and Liaqat Ali, could never agree on any thing. One can imagine the havoc that would have been created if the CMP had been accepted with different objectives by its signatories. Nehru would have felt unfettered by the CMP and the Muslim League would have opposed it tooth and nail. The resulting impasse would have resulted in frequent calls for 'Direct Action'. The country would have been turned into a magnified version of Lebanon and the bloodshed of 1947 would have paled in comparison to the holocaust that would have resulted.

The two countries have since gone their separate paths trying to seek their preferred destinies. Nehru and his Congress were able to develop a constitution to create a secular, democratic republic to meet the needs of a diverse country. By and large, Indians are quite satisfied with that constitution. Pakistanis, too, do not regret their separate country and are quite content with religion based nationhood.

Sixty two years after the two countries became independent, it is now time to move on. The generations that fought the old battles are gone and have been replaced by new generations which are free from the baggage of the old history. If the two countries can resolve their outstanding bilateral issues, they may some time in the future, agree to have a common economic and political institutions a la European Union. This would, in essence, recreate essentially what was envisaged in the Cabinet Mission Plan.

INDIA AND PAKISTAN: PARTITION LESSONS

The sixtieth anniversary of the independence of Pakistan and India on 14-15 August 2007 has prompted official celebration in both countries, as well as an ocean of commemorative coverage in the world's media. The terrible violence that accompanied the birthpangs of the two states from the ashes of empire is an inevitable theme in much commentary. What is being less addressed amid the profusion of human stories - and what this article considers - is whether the problems of communal division in the subcontinent were or are best addressed by the partition of territory.

Ravinder Kaur teaches at the University of Roskilde, Denmark. She is the editor of *Religion, Violence and Political Mobilisation in South Asia* (Sage, 2005) and author of *Since 1947: Partition Narratives among Punjabi Migrants of Delhi* (Oxford University Press, 2007) The bare details of 1947 and its legacy are stark. The territorial partition that created modern India and Pakistan involved the internal division of Punjab and Bengal provinces, which - in unimaginable conditions of collapse of authority, flight, and massacre - resulted in the forced movement of 20 million people (Hindus and Sikhs to India and Muslims to Pakistan) and approximately 1.5 million deaths.

This partition created both a harvest of bitterness and the basis for further conflict. In 1970-71, Pakistan itself was further divided as East Pakistan became the new state of Bangladesh, a process attended by an enormous human tragedy of war and famine. The four armed conflicts between the inheritors of the British Indian partition (1947, 1965, 1971, and 1998) are only the most dangerous moments in a pattern of near-permanent regional hostilities which has also been marked by low-intensity conflict in Kashmir, disputes over terrorism, and an escalating nuclear-weapons rivalry.

The question raised by the "great partition" bridges the divides between 1947 and 2007, and between India-Pakistan and many other global regions - most notably, today, Iraq. In this sense the particular history of the subcontinent is only one stage in a much larger story, one which continues to have potent implications across much of the world.

The Age of Unmixing

The practice of territorial and demographic rearrangements arose in the context of the early-to-mid-20th-century era of world wars and decolonisation in Asia and Africa. As territorial boundaries in Europe were challenged and peoples in other continents began to break free from the European colonial stranglehold, the political map of the world unravelled. In either case, political elites discovered a new solution: amid flux, fix. the best solution found was to fix territorial boundaries of a changing world. Thus the borders of old and new nation-states in Europe were dug deeper, while fresh borders for the emerging nation-states in Asia and Africa were invented to accommodate expressions of national will and demands for self-determination.

Also in open Democracy on India, Pakistan, and history: Maruf Khwaja, "India and Pakistan: states of mind, contests of perception" (23 January 2002)

Rajeev Bhargava, "The political psychology of Hindu nationalism" (5 November 2003)

Maruf Khwaja, "Becoming Pakistani" (19 August 2004)

Rajeev Bhargava, "India's model: faith, secularism and democracy" (3 November 2004)

Muzamil Jaleel, "Kashmir's bus-ride to history" (18 April 2005)
Sadat Hasan Manto, "Toba Tek Singh" (5 January 2007)

Territories had always changed hands, but what was new was the wholesale transfer of populations inhabiting those territories. A growing idea after the "great war" of 1914-18 was that conflicts arise among ethnically heterogeneous populations, and that the best way of resolving and preventing ethnic conflicts was to engineer the "unmixing of populations". The desired unmixing was achieved (for example) in the exchange of population between Greeks and Turks in 1923, and the expulsion of ethnic Germans from east-central Europe in 1944-49.

Behind the aim of achieving an internally homogenous population in a given nation-state was a view of peoples as a national collective whose membership was defined by ethnic-religious affiliation. This implied less tolerance to ethnic-religious groups that did not fit easily into the national imaginary: only when the defined communities could be fixed in their own territories would violence cease.

The Fruit of Division

It was against this background, when international opinion was already in favour of territorial rearrangements and population transfers, that the partition of British India took place in 1947. As the tripartite negotiations over power- sharing between the Indian National Congress, the Muslim League and the British colonial government began to fail, partition came to be seen as the most realistic option. At the same time, outside leading circles "partition" was little more than a vague, unfathomable - even harmless - word that cropped up occasionally in the speeches of political leadership. That they would be forced one day to leave their homes and livelihoods amidst raging violence, was yet inconceivable to millions of ordinary people.

This feeling of disbelief is best summarised in the words of an officer in charge of refugee rehabilitation in Punjab, who said: "we in India were only vaguely familiar with the word 'refugee' and used to wonder why people should be compelled to leave homes. Even *our* refugees [my italics] expressed surprise at the strange phenomenon of exchange of population and were heard saying we used to hear about the change of rulers but for the first time the ruled are also changing places".

The partition of 1947 was far more than an abstract line across administrative maps; it sought to create separate enclaves for different religious communities. In August 1947, when the "Radcliffe award" partitioning Punjab and Bengal was announced, millions of Hindus, Muslims and Sikhs now found that they no longer "belonged" to the place they were born in and had lived in forever. The advocates of territorial separation (most prominently according to the "two-nation theory" of Pakistan's founder, Muhammad Ali Jinnah) saw borders as the natural, physical expression of communal differences: that the new borders would exacerbate and reinforce these perceived differences was not considered.

Since the early summer of 1947, the abstract notion of "not-belonging" had become real when private armies belonging to the Muslim League's national guard), the Sikh *Akal Fauj* and the Hindu-nationalist *Rashtriya Swayamsevak Sangh* (RSS) began orchestrating major attacks on minority groups in their area of influence. The formal creation of borders in August meant that what was considered a temporary movement by many people to avoid violence months before had now became absolute and permanent.

From that point, the trickle of refugee movement turned into a deluge as millions began seeking safety in areas across the border where their community was in a majority. Hindus and Sikhs now "belonged" to India, and Muslims to Pakistan. The chaos of the early days abated as the two states began a planned exchange of population amidst continuing violence.

This period in Indian-Pakistani history is often visualised through archival photos of packed "refugee special" trains with people clambered on the rooftops, epic refugee walking-caravans, and women and children in bullock-carts escaping to safety with their meagre belongings. The personal memories of those affected, especially those who witnessed mass violence, are often saturated by scattered limbs, the inescapable stench of dead bodies, extreme sexual violence against women, and of people who took their own lives amid unbearable grief.

Such heartbreaking memories and images are testimony to the unconsolable pain of partition. They also contrast vividly with the single most striking image I encountered during six years of research into violence and identity in the region for my book *Since 1947: Partition Narratives among Punjabi Migrants of Delhi* (Oxford University Press, 2007). It was a photo published in several Delhi newspapers during the nuclear stand-off of 1998, when popular media discourse was spiced with comment about how the Indian nuclear-tipped warheads could reach all the way to Lahore and Islamabad. Hindus and Sikhs dancing in patriotic celebration of India's momentary advantage over Pakistan in the race for regional military supremacy. What intrigued me was that the revellers were the descendants of Hindu and Sikh refugees from Pakistan; in hard logic, they were cheering the capacity to annihilate the land of their parents and grandparents. Such nationalist intoxication too is the fruit of partition.

The Echo of History

The enduring hostility between India and Pakistan at official level - notwithstanding the efforts of many to seek to cross the divide - is at the very least a warning to those who argue for territorial partition as a solvent of violent antagonism. Iraq is the foremost contemporary example. Since 2005, the idea of partitioning Iraq into three regions - *Shia, Sunni* and Kurdish - has gained momentum in direct proportion to the intensification of sectarian violence. A number of policy-makers and commentators in the United States and Britain - among them Peter Galbraith, Joseph Biden, Leslie H Gelb, Richard Betts and Simon Jenkins - have endorsed this idea in one form or another (other analysts, such as **open Democracy** authors Zaid Al-Ali and Reidar Visser, have argued powerfully against it). The general notion is that the internecine violence between *Shia, Sunni* and Kurds would cease once each group has gained political control and territorial sovereignty in a tripartite Iraq; partition is regrettable but inevitable, and the earlier the world accepts it, the better.

The idea of partition may in large part emanate from the good intention of seeking to end violence and chaos in Iraq - though in some cases, a post-imperial "divide and rule" instinct may also be at work. But what is more important than the motive is the logic and the human implications of the proposal to divide people according to an accident of birth. The lesson of India-Pakistan in 1947 for the world is: don't make new borders between people, but work to make borders irrelevant.

Indian Muslim leader and Pakistan's first governor-general. Mohammed Ali Jinnah, a Muslim Indian politician, played the leading role in the formation of the nation of Pakistan. Born in Karachi, Jinnah initially pursued a business career in London but soon switched to studying law at Lincoln's Inn and eventually became a barrister in Mumbai (then Bombay). Hiscareer in politics began when he helped Parsi Dadabhai Naoroji win a seat in the Indian legislature. He joined the Indian National Congress in 1906 and in 1913 became a member of the Muslim League, working to increase cooperation between Hindus and Muslims. Jinnah contributed significantly to drafting the Congress-League Lucknow Pact of 1916.

6

'New Front' of China on Indo-Nepal Partition

The Chinese clamour over Arunachal Pradesh has raised many eyebrows in India. Even as the meeting between Prime Minister Manmohan Singh and Chinese Premier Wen Jiabao in Thailand on Saturday was being looked at as an effort to cool down the tension between the neighbouring countries, the Dragon nation has opened another anti-India front. This time in Nepal. Silently but speedily China is spreading its wings in the erstwhile Hindu kingdom, mainly to unleash anti-India propaganda. Besides acquiring some major construction projects in Nepal, the Chinese are also making their presence felt by opening language centres in Nepali cities on the Indo-Nepal border. These centres are teaching Chinese language. But, what raises suspicions on Chinese intentions is the fact that these centres are open only for Nepali citizens.

The surge in Chinese activities in the neighbour country is a matter of concern for India which is already fighting terrorism being pushed into the country from Pakistan. It's a known fact that China often uses Nepal as a buffer state against India. After the Indo-China war of 1962, the Dragon country has made constant efforts to increase its influence in Nepal. Though it did not succeed much till Nepal was under the rule of monarchy, the fall of monarchy and growing Maoist grip over Nepal has given a fillip to Chinese plans.

A clear indicator of this is the construction of Sikta barrage in Agaiya village of Banke district (Nepal). Its construction was delayed for almost three decades owing to Indian protest. But, once Maoists held sway over the Nepali government, the construction was given a go-ahead in 2006. Moreover, the contract for the project was given to Chinese firm — Sinehydro. In fact, a team of 40 Chinese engineers is engaged in the construction of the Sikta barrage in Agaiya district of Nepal. The district touches the Indian district of Shravasti. The distance from Indian border to the barrage is barely 14 kilometres. The possibility of Chinese infiltration in important zones of war on Indian border areas due to the presence of Chinese engineers cannot be ruled out.

Also, after the completion of the barrage the flow of river Rapti towards India will be diverted towards Nepal which will create acute water shortage in Indian area. Efforts have also been started to divert the flow of rivers flowing towards Indian area from Parchu lake located in Chinese area adjoining the state which may lead to floods in the borders districts of India during monsoon. Not only this, if the and Sikta barrage ever breaks down due to technical reasons it will severely impact the security arrangements made on the India border.

China, thus, seems to be working on these two projects under well-planned policy to tease India. Similarly, China has established the office of 'Maitri Sangh' in Nepal adjoining Indian border territory. Meanwhile, a 10-member team comprising five Chinese and five Tibetan national recently visited Nepalganj headquarters of Banke district (Nepal). The team toured the Indo-Nepal border and secretly clicked photographs of the Rupaidiha main gate located on Indo-Nepal border. The Indian intelligence agencies, however, learnt about this when the team had already left for Kathmandu. Assistant army Nayak Devendra of Shashtra Seema Bal (SSB), when contacted, told TOI that he will report the incident to his senior officers.

Nepal's Prime Minister Mr. Madhav Kumar Nepal and Chairman of the Nepalese Congress (NC) Party Girija Prasad Koirala have assured China that Nepali soil will not be allowed to be used against China under any circumstances. Talking with the Chinese delegation led by politburo member of the Chinese Communist Party, Mr. Zhang Gaoli, separately, September 1, 2009, the two veteran politicians of Nepal, according to the high placed sources, did try to convince China towards Nepal's firm stand on 'One China Policy'. However, Beijing is not that fool to believe such parroted/repetitive assurance of Nepali politician, say Kathmandu based analyst.

"The lame duck government has not even asked official clarifications from those lawmakers from the Madhesh parties who had assured the Tibetan community in exile in India that they will raise the issue of 'Free Tibet' in Nepal's Constituent Assembly (CA) during their last meet with Dalai Lama in Dharmasala of Himanchal Pradesh, India", laments a Kathmandu based analyst who preferred anonymity. 'The recent meet of the Nepal law makers has raised suspicion in the minds of the Beijing authorities as regards the Nepalese structured stance that she remains firm on "One China Policy' of Nepal. And Beijing understands the Nepali intentions well. According to PM's political advisor Mr. Raghujee Panta, PM's upcoming visit to China, Constitution drafting process and ongoing peace process were also discussed during the meet.

NEPAL AS NEW 'STRATEGIC PARTNER' OF CHINA

In China's foreign policy towards Nepal since the Maoist ascendance to power. China had earlier adopted a policy of 'non-intervention' in the internal matters of Nepal and largely stayed out of Nepalese internal politics. However, the demise of the monarchy and the ascendance of political parties have forced China to reshape its Nepal policy. Moreover, frequent protests by Tibetans in recent months alerted the Chinese to the possibility of the China-Tibet border being misused.

Consequently, China has sought to engage Nepalese political actors at all levels, primarily to secure the border with Nepal. With the Maoists in power, China also hopes to use its ideological commonalities to suppress the Tibetan movement in Nepal. When the Maoists emerged victorious in the April 2008 elections, China adopted a wait and watch policy because it was unsure of their intentions. After all, the Maoists were backed by India and were catapulted to the political centre stage only after a comprehensive peace agreement in which India had played a substantial behind the scenes role. However, media reports reveal that after several interactions with Maoists leaders.

China has begun to feel quite comfortable with the Maoist-led government. The Maoists' ideological linkages with China and their keenness to neutralize India's influence in the region have also made them an obvious choice for engagement. It has been reported that in interactions with Chinese the Maoist leaders gave the impression that the future of democracy in Nepal could be guided by the example of the Communist Party of China. Indeed, there are many in Nepal who argue that persistence with the Maoist tag in the party name despite joining competitive politics indicates that the party may work towards a single party system in the future, given that dictatorship of the proletariat has prime of place in the Maoist lexicon. In fact, some hardline leaders of the party have suggested a people's republic similar to that of China on a number of occasions even after Maoists joined the political mainstream.

These ideas might have encouraged China to attempt to consolidate its position in Nepal by continuously engaging the Maoists at the political, economic, military and social levels, and thus secure its strategic interests in the region. In fact, twelve high-level Chinese delegations, including two military teams, visited Nepal in the course of 2008-2009. During these visits, China has repeatedly assured economic, technological and military aid to Nepal. The Maoist-led government was also asked to adopt a 'One-China' policy, not to allow Nepalese land for anti-China activities, take strong action against Tibetan refugees and grant special facilities for Chinese investments in strategic sectors. Beijing has also initiated Track-II diplomacy with Nepal and invited Nepalese scholars to undertake visits to Chinese think tanks.

Some of the important visits from China to Nepal were:

- 25 February 2009: Assistant Chinese Foreign Minister Hu Zhengyue led a 14-member delegation.
- 19 February 2009: Liu Hongcai, Vice Minister of the International Department of the central committee of the

CPC led a delegation to take part in the inaugural ceremony of the 8th convention of the UML in Butwal.

- 10 February 2009: A high level Peoples' Liberation Army (PLA) delegation, one of the largest delegations in two months, arrived in Nepal.
- 06 December 2008: Lieutenant General Ma Xiaotian, deputy chief of General Staff of the PLA headed a ten-member delegation. China agreed to provide US $2.61 million worth of security assistance to Nepal.
- 01 December 2008: China's Foreign Minister Yang Jiechi visited Nepal.
- 24 July 2008: Chinese Vice-Minister for Foreign Affairs, Wu Dawei, visited Nepal. He pledged a grant assistance of 100 million yuan as economic and technical cooperation.
- 04 March 2008: Assistant Minister for Foreign Affairs of China, He Yafei, undertook a three-day visit to Nepal.

Nepal's engagements with China have also increased manifold with the visit of delegations both at State and non-state levels. Apart from visits at the official levels, private visits by political leaders, journalists and academicians are also sponsored by China as part of public diplomacy. During these visits Chinese authorities have reportedly assured all kinds of support to the Maoist government in its efforts aimed at laying the foundation for a 'New Nepal'. For the Nepalese Maoists, growing Chinese engagement is a win-win situation in line with their 'policy of equidistance', which has been deliberately adopted to counter-balance India's influence in Nepal.

The increasing level of bilateral engagement also indicates that China is wooing Nepal as a new strategic partner. This has been confirmed by the statements made by various Chinese officials. For example, on 16 February 2009, Chinese Foreign Minister Yang Jiechi said in Beijing that China would prefer to work with Nepal on the basis of a strategic partnership. In fact, Vice Minister of International Department of the Central Committee of Communist Party of China, Liu Hongcai said in Kathmandu in February 2009 that "we oppose any move to interfere in the internal affairs of

Nepal by any force." Similarly, on November 04, 2008, Liu Hong Chai, International Bureau Chief of the Chinese Communist Party, stated that "China will not tolerate any meddling from any other country in the internal affairs of Nepal-our traditional and ancient neighbour."

China has also submitted to Kathmandu a draft Sino-Nepal friendship treaty. The draft states that China will not attack Nepal and would respect Nepal's sovereignty and territorial integrity. Nepal would recognize 'One China' policy and not allow its territory to be used for "anti-China" activities. The draft treaty in fact looks more like a strategic one that is tilted highly in favour of Chinese security concerns. China needs this agreement because it does not have confidence in the democratic arrangements and future governments in Nepal, and wishes to consolidate its position while the Maoists are in power.

China has penetrated the Nepalese political system by gaining the confidence of hardline communist leaders both in the CPN-UML and the CPN-Maoist. China is also known to have played a major role in facilitating the alliance between the CPN-UML and the Maoists. Prior to Jhala Nath Khanal becoming UML Chief, a four-member Chinese delegation visited Kathmandu on May 10, 2008 and met Khanal and other Maoist leaders. A senior delegation from the Communist Party of China led by vice Minister Liu Hongcai was also in Kathmandu in February 2009 to attend the inaugural ceremony of the 8th national convention of the UML. The victory of Khanal as chairman of the UML, who is close to Prime Minister Prachanda, has been crucial for the survival of the Maoist-led coalition government. The nature of Chinese engagements in Nepal goes beyond the political domain. They might also be aimed at influencing the process of drafting of the new constitution to ensure that China's long-term interests are served, particularly in hydropower and other strategically important projects. China has also assured Nepal help in the modernization and integration of registered Maoist guerrillas into the Nepal Army.

Considering the strategic and economic interests Beijing has in Nepal, in terms of energy from hydro projects and as a transit country between China and India, China may expand its state level engagements by entering into long-term agreements at various levels. The proposed new friendship treaty marks the beginning of this process. Moreover, the treaty may enhance the bargaining power of the Maoist government vis-à-vis India to resolve some of the long standing disputes between the two countries.

Any foreign presence in Nepal is a concern for India. Given the centuries-old socio-cultural and economic ties between India and Nepal, recent Chinese insistence on closing the Indo-Nepal open border is a matter of concern for both countries. The Indo-Nepal relationship was acknowledged as "unassailable" during the official visit of Nepalese Prime Minister, Puspa Kamal Dahal to New Delhi in September 2008. But an 'equidistance policy' can only come at the expense of India-Nepal relations.-

THE COLLISION OF THE SINO-INDIAN WAR

In many ways, how China and India relate to each other indicates where they see themselves in the international system. Firstly, however, it is necessary to have an understanding of the events leading up to and following the 1962 Sino-Indian War, as this continues to affect the contemporary Sino-Indian relationship.

The major causes of conflict between China and India – namely, the disputed border and the issue of Tibet, including the fourteenth Dalai Lama's ongoing residency in India – have their roots in the political dealings that went on in the late 1800s and early 1900s between British India, pre-Communist China and feudal Tibet. The major question was whether treaties signed by British India and Tibet demarcating the border – known as the McMahon Line – were valid, given that, according to the Chinese, Tibet was part of China and had no authority to act unilaterally. Disagreements of this nature and the exact location of the border persisted throughout the early twentieth century, further complicated by Indian independence in 1947 (which removed British backing and so altered the balance of power in the region in favour of China) and the Chinese 'liberation' of Tibet in 1950.

1954, marked with a visit to India Chinese by Premier Zhou Enlai in June, and a reciprocal visit by Indian Prime Minister

Jawaharlal Nehru to China in October, was a high point in the relationship; it was during the latter visit that the term 'Hindi-Chini bhai-bhai' (Indians and Chinese are brothers) was coined, and denoted a period of rapprochement after decades of strife over the disputed India-Tibet border.

This new-found friendship in theory forged a renewed basis for discussions over the disputed border, though this was tested only two years later. There were (and still are) two contested areas: the north-eastern stretch, which was known under the British as the North-East Frontier Agency (NEFA) and since 1986 has been the Indian state of Arunachal Pradesh (claimed by the Chinese as Southern Tibet), and the western region of Aksai Chin (claimed by the Indians and currently administered by the Chinese), which borders the Indian state of Jammu and Kashmir.

Although up until the mid-50s most of the border tensions had existed over the eastern stretch – and specifically the disputed border known as the McMahon Line – the western region became the focus when in 1956 the Chinese constructed a highway from Xinjiang province to Tibet through the Aksai Chin to allow the rapid movement of troops between the two restive provinces. In spite of disputing the occupation of the territory, India did not actually administer the Aksai Chin in any way, and consequently after the building of the road the region effectively passed into Chinese hands. Nevertheless, the Aksai Chin continued to be a volatile area – not helped by the fact that the rest of Jammu and Kashmir was the subject of an ongoing and often violent dispute between India and Pakistan – and subsequently provided one of the flashpoints for the 1962 Sino-Indian war.

Matters were further complicated with the Lhasa Revolt of March 1959, an uprising of Tibetans which culminated in the fleeing of the fourteenth Dalai Lama (and subsequently thousands of Tibetan refugees) to India and the systematic crushing of the resistance by Chinese forces. In the northern autumn Chinese and Indian troops clashed along the McMahon Line border. An attempt at resolving the border issue was made during a visit by Premier Zhou Enlai to Delhi from19-25 April 1960, but "the talks...did not resolve the differences that had arisen and the two Prime Ministers decided that officials of the two Governments should examine the factual material in the possession of the two Governments in support of their stands" (Ministry of External Affairs, 1961:1). The committee met three times throughout 1960, with both sides producing reports of the discussions for their respective governments.

The contents of these reports illustrate how intractable the border problem was and indeed still is, with the two sides unable to agree even on the basic tenor of the talks, such as whether the border had ever been officially delimited (no, according to China; yes, according to India). Consequently no resolution was reached at the 1960 talks which, with hindsight, were really the last opportunity to effect an agreement before relations broke down completely.

The Sino-Indian War began on 8 September 1962 when the Chinese crossed into NEFA (now Arunachal Pradesh) and attacked an Indian border post, alleging that the Indians had already violated the McMahon Line. This was the first time the conflict flared along the McMahon Line, though there had been some fighting around the Aksai Chin region, inflamed by Sino-Pakistani border talks which the Indians alleged were aimed at undermining their position in Kashmir. These skirmishes continued throughout September and into October.

On 20 October the Chinese launched a full-scale offensive all along the frontier, from Ladakh to NEFA, arguing that it was a pre-emptive strike against Indian aggression. This was significant because it moved the conflict beyond the disputed areas and into Indian territory, essentially becoming an invasion of India. The Indian force was fatally under-prepared and crumbled before the Chinese onslaught.

The fighting lasted for just over a month, with the Chinese declaring a unilateral ceasefire on 21 November. Statistics released by the Indian government on 29 October had between 2000 and 2500 Indian soldiers killed during the first week of fighting, with 1102 held prisoner, 291 wounded and 5174 missing and presumed dead. On 8 November the Chinese proposed a ceasefire agreement whereby both parties would withdraw twenty kilometres behind the positions held on 7 November, 1959. This meant that the Chinese would withdraw back behind the McMahon Line, but they would maintain control of Indian-claimed territory in Ladakh, including the strategically important Aksai Chin road linking Xinjiang and Tibet. This was initially rejected by the Indians, but after another fortnight of fierce fighting the Chinese surprised everyone by announcing a unilateral ceasefire and the withdrawal of troops from 1 December to the 7 November 1959 positions. The Chinese also added that, provided the Indian government took corresponding measures, the two parties could meet to discuss troop withdrawal and an end to hostilities. Militarily weakened, and with the rest of the world supporting all measures to solve the conflict, India was in no position to argue.

In December 1962 six non-aligned nations (Ceylon, Burma, Cambodia, Indonesia, the United Arab Republic and Ghana) met in Colombo to try to broker a formal peace deal, but their lack of condemnation of the Chinese invasion incensed India. India nevertheless accepted the Colombo proposals, but China rejected them, insisting on a "unilateral implementation" of its 21 November 1962 statement; consequently the talks broke down and nothing was resolved, even in subsequent bilateral meetings.

Sino-Indian relations did not begin to normalise until the mid-1970s; a turning point was the resumption of ambassadorial relations in 1976. Although the two countries retained non-official diplomatic relations throughout the 1960s (with missions headed by a *charge d'affairs* rather than an ambassador), interaction was minimal. In fact, Gautam Das describes the period between 1962-76 as a period of "cold peace" rather than cold war, and notes that "Sino-Indian relations after 1962 are, in substance if not chronology, Sino-Indian relations after 1976 [because very little of note happened in the intervening period]".

Rapprochement continued after the resumption of diplomatic relations, albeit with a few hiccups, but it wasn't until 1988 that the turning point came with Indian Prime Minister Rajiv Gandhi's visit to Beijing. This made him the first Indian Prime Minister to visit China since Nehru in 1954 and marked the end of the impasse on the border issue which had lasted for most of the 1980s; the two sides agreed to maintain peace and stability along the Line of Actual Control (LAC) in Arunachal Pradesh (roughly equivalent to the McMahon Line), and they also agreed to set up a Joint Working Group (JWG) to help defuse the border issue. In addition, India agreed to curtail the anti-China actions of Tibetans in India. According to Das, "the decade that followed the Rajiv Gandhi visit up to the 1998 Indian nuclear explosions (Pokhran-II) has been the most cordial phase of Sino-Indian relations after 1962".

These warm relations continued during the mid-1990s, and were further consolidated by Chinese President Jiang Zemin's visit to India in 1996, where four mutual cooperation agreements were signed, and it appeared that a breakthrough in the tensions had finally occurred.

Unfortunately, this series of small steps forward was followed by a giant leap backwards in 1998. During a visit of the People's Liberation Army (PLA) Senior General Fu Quanyou to New Delhi, the Indian Defence Minister, George Fernandes, publicly stated that he believed China was continuing to carry out border incursions into Indian territory, and later accused China of being India's number one security threat, greater even than Pakistan. This was immediately followed by India's second ever nuclear tests, known as Pokhran II (ibid). The fact that the tests occurred before Fu had even arrived back in Beijing caused a huge loss of face for the Chinese, because they felt that after a decade of overtures to the Indians they had been callously rebuffed and humiliated.

Nevertheless, the overall Chinese reaction to the tests was initially quite controlled, and might have remained so, had India not justified the tests by claiming they were in response to the 'China threat'.

This was articulated in a letter from Indian Prime Minister Vajpayee to US President Bill Clinton, which was printed in the *New York Times* on 13 May (ibid). This was seen as "unwarranted and provocative", and the fact that the issue was given such a public airing caused another immense loss of face for the Chinese; consequently they reacted angrily, cancelling the next meeting of the Joint Working Group on the border issue.

This issue of the 'China threat' still permeates relations today, with more than one Chinese interviewee claiming that the Indian military deliberately promotes China as a threat in order to get increased defence spending, and that 1998 was one of the clearest examples of this (Author interviews with Wang Dehua and anonymous interviewee, 2010).

After the low point of the 1998 tests, relations began once again to normalise, in spite of a brief hiccup over Tibet when 14-year-old Ugyen Thinley Dorje, the 17th Karmapa Lama of the Kagyupa sect of Tibetan Buddhism, fled China for Dharamsala in January 2000.

Nevertheless, in February 2000 India and China concluded an agreement for China's accession to the World Trade Organisation; in March India participated in the first ever Sino-Indian security dialogue in Beijing, and the Joint Working Group sessions resumed in April of the same year. In 2003 an incursion by Chinese troops into Indian territory occurred in Arunachal Pradesh, shortly after Indian Prime Minister Vajpayee's visit to Beijing; Vajpayee put this down to "differences in perceptions" regarding the Line of Actual Control, but some politicians and analysts took it much more seriously. This incident shows that in spite of another gradual thawing of relations, the border question still remains a highly contentious issue in the Sino-Indian relationship. Furthermore, in addition to ongoing Indian concerns about the Sino-Pakistani relationship, China is also disturbed about the growing relationship between India and the USA, fearing that such an alliance will upset the balance of power in the region.

Seen in the light of history, the most recent incidents to affect the Sino-Indian relationship – the 2008 Tibet protests and the subsequent disruption of the Olympic torch relay (including in Delhi); and the border skirmishes and associated negative media coverage throughout 2009 – are unlikely to cause permanent damage to the relationship.

They do, however, highlight the fact that the border issue is still unresolved, and most analysts agree that the Sino-Indian relationship will not be able to move forward in any meaningful way until this question is answered. As well as being rooted in political reality, however, a large element of the Sino-Indian conflict also stems from misplaced perceptions, both of each other's motives and of their own place in the world order.

The concept of 'Chindia' is popular at present but it is based on flawed logic. Although the geo-civilisational aspects, where cultural practices flowed freely across what is now Central Asia to India and China and back again, cannot be denied, China and India are also distinct civilisations with their own histories and cultures and to conflate them is to understate the importance of this in shaping their distinctive governments and policies.

It also minimises the very real animosity which remains between them and deeply influences not only the Sino-Indian relationship but also how they see themselves and how they relate to the wider international community. On a political and strategic front, India and China have followed extremely different developmental trajectories with different outcomes and they also have different aims for their status in the international system. These differences in aims, policy and strategic thought can be seen to be playing out in Central Asia at present.

The 'Chindia' concept is for the most part a Western construct developed as a response to the 'China threat' perception and tied into the former US and ASEAN policy of containment, in which India would play an important role.

This idea of a mutual rise or equating China and India was seized upon by some in India who were attracted by the idea that India has or will soon have the same type of international economic and political clout as China, even when the present reality suggests otherwise. In fact, India should not seek to emulate China because it is unlikely that such a course of action would succeed; in any case the two countries' systems are extremely different.

Rather, India must forge its own path and decide what kind of a role it wants to play internationally, and how it will achieve this. It must also in the immediate-term concentrate on domestic development and remember that 'national security' cannot just be about the military but must also include human, food, environmental and other types of security as well as poverty reduction.

This seems to be the path which the Indian government is beginning to take and it is likely to be far more successful than any which frames the question of India's development in relation to China. Regarding China, we need to rethink the way we examine it in terms of international relations theory in order to avoid overlooking the real issues in Chinese strategic thought because of a desire to fit Chinese development into an established international relations model.

Finally, scholarship – both in China and India and further afield – needs to be developed so that more scholars are educated in the practices and policies of both countries, and communication is facilitated between China and India scholars the world over, rather than operating simply in closed 'China studies' or 'India studies' spheres. This would not only prove beneficial to promoting stability in the Sino-Indian relationship, but would also go some way to ensuring that the two countries can be viewed as separate but parallel entities rather than as 'Chindia'.

CHINA-SOUTH ASIA POLITICAL RELATIONS: A VIEW FROM NEPAL

"Peaceful co-existence" is the main principle in China-South Asia relations. The fundamentals of this principles are i) mutual equality, ii) non-interference in each other's internal affairs, iii) mutual respect to territorial integrity, iv) cooperation against hegemonism and power politics, and v) mutual accommodation and benefit (Wang Hongwei, 2005). In view of the colonial and feudal background, the main principle and fundamentals of China-South Asia ties are progressive. If one closely examines the natural and spiritual realities that persist between China and South Asia, the main principle and fundamentals of their ties can not truly be more than egalitarian.

China and South Asia are linked by land and water, mountains and rivers. Unlike East Asia and South East Asia and China, Chinese and most of South Asian ties are contiguous, more natural and comprehensive. Mountains pass through and major rivers flow down to China and South Asia from the Tibet Autonomous Region (TAR) of China. Now, it is science and technology that is poised to harness snow and water for larger benefits of the people. In China and South Asia, it has yet remained a geo-political as well as ecological truism that link maintained by mountains and rivers are more stable than opportunistic alliances offered by nuclear power.

Another basic articulation of China-South Asia relations is Buddhism. Gautam Buddha, who was born and had acquired knowledge about the ultimate truth in South Asia, very much lives life-size every where in China. The civilization of China and South Asia thus holds common source of inspiration with a profound degree of continuity. As Buddhism does not stand as an anti-thesis for any other religion, it helps to create an internal capacity to absorb, acculturate and assimilate in both China and South Asia. In short, geo-politically charged neighborhood in an intense natural and spiritual sense is what stands out in China-South Asia relations.

China's politics till the recent past was concentrated on its east coast of the Taiwan Straits. Asia as a whole ranked relatively low in its security agenda since creation of the People's Republic of China. But the Cold War era did not leave China untouched. Tibet in particular conditioned China in formulation of its South Asia policy and to the stability in its frontier regions. The tenets of this policy were: Peace at the south-west border region of China. Efficient signing of border treaty with the neighboring countries was part of this policy to ensure peace along China's long border.

The Tibetan question. This question raised by the external forces had made China acutely sensitive of its national integration and domestic stability. Chinese policy recognized Tibetan separatism as having serious implications for the national integration and domestic stability. It also recognized that the forces supporting the Tibetan separatism were working by proxy, and many aspects of the separatist moves were utterly non-transparent. So trying its best to correctly understand the external as well as internal features of Tibetan question, and appreciating highly those neighboring countries and organizations who did not allow Tibetan separatists to engage in activities and also did not permit outside powers to support such activities on their soil, China's South Asia Policy tried proactively hard to work at the two inter-related fronts at the same time-discouraging the separatist elements and, praising and encouraging those countries and organizations who did not support and did not provide any ground to support the Tibetan separatism.

Independent relations with South Asian states. China was aware of the unequal interstate relations that do not allow development of cordial and trustily ties between them. Difference in size, power and interpretation of agreements had affected relations between states in South Asia. During the Cold War years, the dominating trend in the interstate relations was exploitation and gains at the cost of other, and a tendency to have "sphere of influence." Exchange and cooperation between China and a number of small South Asian states was not liked by India. But China continued to cultivate ties with small South Asian countries independently. It supported independence of these countries, and their independent decision making. After 1962 border war with India, the importance of independence of the countries in South Asia-particularly of those small and non-nuclear power countries-had increased for China. China realized that only unilaterally wishing for cooperation might not be wise and realistic.

Therefore in view of a Chinese analyst, "It is undeniable, ...after the 1962 border war, China's policy toward Nepal might have reflected, to some extent, a strategy in which China supported Nepal, along with other small countries in South Asia, to check India's influence" (Hua Han, 2005). Despite so, China provided unflinching support to late King Birendra's proposal to declare Nepal a "Zone of Peace" in mid 1970s. It was indicative of China's firmer conviction that the indigenous will and ability of neighboring small states in South Asia to independently conduct their foreign and defence affairs together with its independent foreign policy and self-defence strategy was more important and conducive for peace and stability of China's frontier regions than mere lonely Chinese efforts directed at the same. It was this sense of working together which had been the driving force for China to reciprocally commit to the independence of the small South Asian states. Whatever financial, material and military assistance China has provided to these countries were corollary of the said policy.

The United States of America (the US) has ever been at the centre stage whether it was the end of the bi-polar Cold War, 9/11 terrorist attacks and the subsequent US campaign against terrorism, and now the US campaign for democracy. It is the only power which could put troops in Iraq and Afghanistan at the same time and spend enough money to rebuild the economies. Indeed, despite the euphoria for multi-lateralism after the end of Cold War, the South Asian countries were "gravely relying on the assistance and loans provided by the World Bank and developed countries, which in turn resulted in the heavy burden of foreign debts and shortage of foreign exchange reserves and investment capital.

After 9/11, the new strategic development (beginning of the US offensive in Afghanistan) changed the security environment in Asia. US military presence in Uzbekistan and Afghanistan and the new military relationship of the US with Pakistan and India completed the US military involvement in the whole of the Asian continent.

Until then South Asia was a gap between the US involvement in West Asia and East Asia. After the US completed its Asian military expansion by filling the gaps left by collapse of Soviet Union under its "war against terror" planning, it felt a need to address another gap which its own larger military involvement had created. The felt US need was primarily due to genuine domestic concerns. The felt need this time was democracy.

For China and the US "the week that changed the world" in February, 1972 when President Nixon visited China had a clear American objective, and that was "to transform the two-power world of the Cold War into a triangle then to manage the triangle in such a way that we would be closer to each of the contenders than they were to each other, thereby maximizing our options". With the disappearance of the Soviet Union, one of the two-power world, despite the initial instability and uncertainty, the US and China appear to move into a maturing stage, and carry out responsibilities particularly in Asia-Pacific region. The following statements of President Bush and Premier Wen confirm how they viewed their role in relation to each other.

Welcoming Chinese Premier Wen Jiabao at the White House on December 9, 2003, President George Bush of the United States of America described the US and China as "partners in diplomacy working to meet the dangers of 21st century." He further added: "As our two nations work constructively across areas of common interest, we are candid about our disagreements. The growing strength and maturity of our relationship allows us to discuss our differences, whether over economic issues, Taiwan, Tibet, or human rights and religious freedom, in a spirit of mutual understanding and respect." Replying to President Bush on the occasion, Chinese Premier Wen said, "Our cooperation in a wide range of areas such as counterterrorism, economy, trade and international and regional issues has effectively safeguarded our mutual interests and promoted peace, stability and prosperity in the Asia Pacific region and the world at large."

The key policy statements above from President Bush and Premier Wen, beyond any doubt, eloquently establishes the importance of Sino-US relationship for the Asia-Pacific region and the world at large over and above the bilateral ties existing between the two great countries. In the period ahead where agenda for democracy is pushed to the front, China-US ties may loose glitters; and China may face all the blames for being a "communist" state. And specifically in the context of South Asia, where the majority belongs to the poor and level of interstate cooperation is low, it is for the people and states of the South Asia to decide either for China-inspired peace with independence and self-governed development or for the US-inspired peace with global democracy and development. Whatever the choice the people and states of South Asia make, the decision of Thirteenth Dhaka SAARC summit to associate China and Japan with SAARC was indeed a very welcome unprecedented geopolitical development. The constructive role played by the small SAARC members in this decision making will certainly help fruitfully maximize comparative advantage of SAARC member's vis-à-vis the new partners (China and Japan).

South Asian states are poor. One major reason for such a condition is they do not have an effective good neighborly policy between themselves. At times certain state's behaviour suggests that it wants to live without neighbours. Mahatma Gandhi has provided an example of a good neighborly policy. In his words of wisdom, "One who serves his neighbours serves all the world."

Since 1978 when the modernization and reform process started, economic growth in China has averaged 9.5 percent per year which remains a truly astounding rate. Similarly, foreign trade has expanded at an annual rate of 15 percent over the same period. As for foreign investment China was able to attract $53.2 billion in 2002 as against $52.7 billion for the United States of America. Indeed, the economic transformation has been so rapid that even renowned investment banking firms like Golsdman Sachs predict that China could be the world's largest economy by 2050 with a GDP of $44.4 trillion ahead of the US GDP of $35 trillion and India's GDP of $27 trillion in the same period.

To correct some of the economic divide of a market based economy so that no part of the country remains left out in the great process of economic transformation, the Chinese government is allocating increasing resources including new investment funds from better off provinces in building new physical and social infrastructure and new industrial establishments in the western region. As a part of this strategy the Qinghai-Tibet railway is completed at a cost of $3.16 billion. Similarly, road network in Tibet is being expanded and improved with links to important cities in other provinces.

China's rapid economic growth has its neighbours change their perception on China. The shift from a "China threat" to "China opportunity" theory opens the alternative to explore the benefits that can be draw from the gigantic China's market-leading to deeper and inner natural and spiritual bonds with China. As the immediate neighbours, as many South Asian scholars and experts have wisely suggested, the SAARC members states should take full advantage of China's achievement, especially China's "western development program," which can facilitate a closer economic and trade interaction specially between Tibet, Xingjian, Sichuan and Yunnan and neighboring South Asian states. Opening of new transport and trade routes and just completed railway line over "the roof of the world" will provide China's western parts with efficient access to neighboring countries leading to a change in geo-political outlook.

The ultimate test of the South Asian ability will lie with its leaders' determination to practically conduct the principle of peaceful co-existence along with its fundamentals in relationship with China. Hopefully the Himalayan twins as if representing north face and south face of Kailash-China and South Asia-cherish more a vision of working together than a division of sphere of influence.

It was this spirit of working together that had inspired the press release that was issued after the international seminar on SAARC and China. China Study Centre, Nepal organized this seminar on 23 December, 2002 in Kathmandu, the venue of SAARC Secretariat. The press release stated: "Based on the papers presented and comments and observations made during the discussion, the participants of the seminar on SAARC and China ...have come to the following consensus." There is a need for institutionalized dialogue mechanism between SAARC and China. The imperative for good neighbourhood and challenges and opportunities of the 21st century in regard to peace, cooperation and development dictate the needs for bold and speedy action to move forward in this direction. In this connection it is necessary to hold follow-up seminar focusing on the specific of the institutionalized dialogue mechanism between SAARC and China.

The SAARC member states may try to expand and intensify their social and economic interaction with China at sub-regional level. The Track II initiative prepares ground for promoting and complementing official level discussion. It is gratifying to note that Thirteenth SAARC summit at Dhaka in November last has gloriously taken initiative for establishing institutionalized dialogue mechanism between SAARC and China. The SAARC member leaders should be commended for their bold and glorious initiative. It is hoped that they will also ensure speedy actions regarding the paraphernalia of China's institutionalized association with SAARC.

What is expected are upcoming SAARC official meetings at various levels will prepare grounds for the SAARC member states to expand and intensify their social and economic interaction with China at sub-regional level. Various sub-regional groupings within SAARC may find, for example, i) eastern Himalayan resource, ii) western Himalayan resources, iii) transportation links and networks, iv) nature tourism and v) spiritual tourism as important themes for sustainable cooperation to the various sub-regional groups within SAARC. It has been learned that attempts have been made to organize seminars on China and South Asian Relations in Colombo. Such activities are encouraging as they promote and compliment official level discussion on inter-regional collaborative dialogue between China and South Asian states.

It will be extremely good if the SAARC member states attempts to expand and intensify their social and economic interaction with China at sub-regional level. A sub-region (based on sub-geographical level-for example, eastern South Asia, western South Asia, and/or function-for example, culture, natural sources or infrastructure) is recognized as a practical mechanism to promote and strengthen SAARC's over all link with China. As more effective, immediate and direct geo-political link between China and South Asia will be through sub-regional grouping of South Asia; members of the South Asian sub-regional grouping will be more dependent on each other to realize the purpose. Whereas for China, this sort of cooperative arrangement will ensure required stability and peace in the frontier regions, for each South Asian sub-region value will be added to tourism, culture, and physical development which will enhance overall quality of life of its people.

NEPAL-INDIA BORDER DEMARCATION : TWO DECADES

Nepal-India Joint Technical Level Boundary Committee has completed two decades and this is the first day of its twenty-first year. The common Nepalese people are anxious to know whether the bye-gone days of these two decades have been taken as short duration or sufficiently long period.

Incidents and Happenings

So many negative and positive incidents have taken place within the nation during the last two decades of demarcation. In the context of such incidents and happenings, nobody had time to care for the borderline of our nation, even if it is broken, disconnected and disputed by our neighbour.

Mahakali Treaty without Determining the Source of River Mahakali

It is mentioned in the Mahakali Treaty that the Detailed Project Report (DPR) of Pancheswor Integrated Project will be formulated within a period of six months of the signing of the treaty. But six years have elapsed and the DPR is not yet framed. It is due to the controversy in determining the origination of river Kali, whether it is originated from Limpiyadhura or Lipulek Pass or an artificial pond! But the Nepalese authorities don't spare their time to verify the historic documents and then original maps that 372 square kilometer of the national soil has been on the encroachment by our close neighbour.

Exchange of Goodwill Visits

During this period, so many friendly, official and state visits have taken place by the authorities of both countries since the formation of Nepal-India Joint Technical Level Boundary Committee. But the main crux of the border problem is as motionless as it was twenty years ago. Foreign Ministers of both nations have exchanged visits so many times and noteworthy is the last visit of Indian Foreign Minister Jaswant Singh to Nepal. He talked to the media on 12 September '99 that an instruction had been issued to the working group of Nepal-India Technical Level Boundary Committee to complete the work efficiently, scrutinizing the facts of the western sector including Kalapani area.

Controversial Statements

The then Ambassador of India to Nepal KV Rajan made several statements and press releases on the matter of Kalapani issue. However, Mr. Rajan made another statement that he did not say Kalapani is a part of India. On the country he said that India would leave the area of Kalapani then and there, if Nepal could produce authoritative documents (10 June '98).

The Nepalese people in general think that these are controversial statements of the Ambassador of India about Nepal. At the same time, with reference to the inconsistent statement of honourable Ambassador, elites were of the opinion that there must have been underlying fact that not only Kalapani but also further west.

Border Issues on Shade

It may be a fact that we Nepalese do not have time to talk to India. We forget our national issues like border problems during the mourning period. During the assassination of the royal families including our beloved King Birendra and Queen Aishwarya, the whole nation was in sorrowful mood. In other side of the coin, during the preparation of happy SAARC summit, officials would have no time to remember how the Nepalese territory had been encroached upon by one of our neighbours. But the people are aware that there are dialogues, disputes and encroachment in 54 places along Nepal-India borderline, having its area from small patch of land to a large chunk of 372 square km. Some of the examples are Kalapani-Limpiyadhura, Susta, Mechi, Thori, Tanakpur, Pashupatinagar, Sandakpur, Lalapatti, Timbapokhari etc.

In the same way, who cares for border issues during the fighting with arms between Nepalese Policemen and Nepalese Maoists? They don't have time to think about their encroached frontier during the confrontation. Both groups have been engaged in killing and firing each other ignoring that the innocent men and women including children have been killed.........

Difficult Question to Answer

Whatever may be the issues, incidents and happenings during the last twenty years, Nepalese people are curious, to know at what date Nepal-India border demarcation will be completed. In other words, is the twenty years period a long one or a short duration in the context of the demarcation of the two borders? The answer may be easy as well as difficult. It is a difficult question to answer, if we look at the border issues of neighbours of India, other than Nepal. So far as the easy answer is concerned, Nepal and China have completed their boundary business on 20 January 1963, less than three years period, starting from boundary agreement to demarcation and signing on the boundary protocol. In this context, Nepàl-India boundary demarcation is too long for Nepal. However, it may not be too long for India in the perspective of her neighbours. Our political leaders and authorities are too busy to solve their internal and intra-party problems. Government officials are engaged in carrying out the ministerial instructions. The only thing is that the common Nepalese people have to become more active and build up pressure on the government. Government authorities and officials are the machinery who have to play the role to execute it for the preservation and protection of the boundary of the nation.

NEPAL-CHINA BORDER DEMARCATION : TOKEN OF FRIENDSHIP

Nepal and China have a common border of 1,414.88 kilometers presently. Timely and successfully completed Sino-Nepal boundary business is considered as the symbol of friendship in the history of Nepal.

Historic Border Treaties

In the past history of some centuries, there were some confrontations between two countries especially in the economic and trade affairs. In this context, there were border conflicts in some trade and transit points. But agreement and treaties were made from time to time to settle those conflicts amicably.

Developing border agreement and treaty: To develop relations and friendship furthermore between the two countries, Sino-Nepal Boundary Agreement (21 March 1960) was signed by two Prime-Ministers, Bisheshwor Prasad Koirala and Chou En-Lai......... It was regarded as a boundary of peace and friendship towards strengthening peace in Asia and the world.

Boundary Delimitation: In order to execute the treaty, boundary delineation was made on the basis of existing traditional customary line with the technical principles of determining the water-parting line to connect snow-capped high altitude mountain peaks, passing and crossing through mountain passes and spurs, saddles and cols, rivers and rivulets, pastureland and river basin or valleys. The most important aspect adopted was to maintain certain adjustments in accordance with the principles of mutual accommodation on trans-frontier cultivation of lands and trans-frontier pasturing by the inhabitants of certain border areas.

Boundary Demarcation: In the context of the boundary demarcation, some of the maps produced by both sides did not coincide in 35 places on the Sino-Nepal borderline. But it was settled forever in accordance with the principles of equality, mutual benefit, friendship and mutual accommodation. Besides, it was adopted by both the parties; the Five Principles of Peaceful Co-existence and in a spirit of fairness, reasonableness, mutual understanding and most importantly respecting each other as Nepal and China have equal rights and status in the international arena.

Settlement of the Tallest Peak

In connection with the boundary delineation, China had claimed that Sagarmatha (Chomolungma) belonged to her, while Prime-Minister B.P. Koirala visited Beijing on 21 March 1960. But Koirala refused to entertain the claim. Regarding the question of Sagarmatha, two parties exchanged the maps. As a result, the dispute of Sagarmatha was settled while the visiting Prime Minister Chou En-Lai made a statement in Kathmandu that "Sagarmatha belongs to Nepal." This statement was made in a press conference at Singha Darbar Gallery Hall on 28 April 1960 at 10.30 P.M. And it proved as an outcome of the principles of mutual accommodation and real friendship with mutual understanding of the degree of sensitivity and gravity of the problems.

NEPAL-INDIA-CHINA TRI-JUNCTION POINTS, YET TO BE FIXED

But the tri-junction points (zero serial numbers) on both the western and eastern ends of the borderline have not yet been fixed, where Nepalese, Chinese and Indian territories meet. This is due to the fact that the Indian representative was not present during boundary demarcation, though Nepal had intimated and invited India formally. But there was no response from India, as it is reported.......... But nobody knows even the approximate period of the finalization of these triple-points, because it needs the consent of India, as an inevitable fact.

Boundary Protocols

After the completion of the joint boundary demarcation physically on the ground, Boundary Protocol was signed on 20 January 1963 by Chinese Vice-Premier and Foreign Minister Chen Yi and Vice-Chairman of the Nepalese Council of Ministers and Foreign Minister Dr. Tulasi Giri.

Now it is high time to make the fourth protocol, because twelve years have elapsed since the third protocol was signed. Some of the main boundary pillars might have been damaged and disappeared and same is the case with reference pillars or markers due to landslide, flood and snow. So it is necessary to formulate a joint inspection committee to erect the missing pillars and repair the damaged ones. Nepal-China friendship will be further consolidated as good neighbour with the inspection and maintenance of Nepal-China borderline at an interval of a decade. This is the common interest of both the nations. Next, it is expected that Nepal will undertake positively to open two more trade routes at Kimathanka (Dingri) and Mustang (Liji) in the very near future as already agreed by both nations. It will help to promote not only the trade and economic activities but also to strengthen furthermore the cordial friendship between the people of Nepal and China.

NEPAL-INDIA BORDER RELATIONS

Nepal's border with India measures 1,753 kilometers. The boundary between Nepal and India was demarcated only after the Anglo-Nepal War of 1814-16. The border between the two countries is called *Dash Gajja* (ten-yard no-man's land). By and large, this boundary is not a natural boundary separated by rivers or mountains except the Mahakali River that divides the two countries in the west and the Mechi River that divides the country in the east. At certain places, the border even divides the same village. As such, while the home of a person fell in one country, the agricultural land was on the other side of the border.

Interestingly, during the time the border was demarcated between the two countries, many people in Nepal's border region fought against the *Gurkhas* as they did not want to become part of Nepal. It was likely that such a course could have enabled the *Gurkhas* to take revenge against those people. In this context, the British regime had to enter into agreement with the *Gurkhas* and seek a promise that the latter would not take revenge against the border inhabitants in Nepal for their reluctance to merge with Nepal. Ever since then the British regime and the *Gurkhas* did not restrict the movement of people from one country to the other fearing that any restriction on their movement might trigger a backlash.

Ever since the border was demarcated between Nepal and India, there has not been any major problem between the two countries. The two countries have completed 98 per cent of the survey work along their border. Border problems between the two countries exist only in Susta and Kalapani, which the two countries hope to resolve through negotiation. Susta is situated in the Nawalparasi district in west Nepal; while Kalapani is in the far west of Nepal in the Darchula district.

After India achieved independence from the British in 1947, Nepal and India signed the Treaty of Peace and Friendship in 1950. The Treaty committed not only to keep the border open but also to provide national treatment (i.e. the same conditions a country gives to its own citizens) to the people of the other country in business, trade and other economic activities. Clause 6 of the Treaty provided the people of one country the right to conduct industrial and other economic activities in the other. Moreover, Clause 7 allowed the citizens of one country the right of residence, ownership of property, participation in trade and commercial activities, movement and other privileges in the other country. But later on in the letter of exchange of the 1950 Treaty, India conceded Nepal's sensitivity over being a small country and gave it protection with regard to participation of the Indians in economic activities. Because of the open border system, there have been no passport or visa formalities for the Nepalese and Indian people to enter into each other's territory.

But it is strange that visa regulations were imposed by the Nepalese authority even on the people living in the border region of Nepal when they had to travel to the capital city of Kathmandu. This system was in vogue until the mid-1950s.

Encouragingly, the arrangement of the open border system is unique. It proved immensely beneficial to the border inhabitants of Nepal and India as it promoted their traditional ties in religious, cultural, social and economic fields. The arrangement of an open border system with India has been rewarding. It fostered friendly relations, mutual understanding and cultural ties among the border inhabitants of the two countries.

People of one country can cross over the border without any restriction from any point, though 22 checkpoints exist at different places along the border. But foreign nationals require both an entry and exit visa and they must cross over the border through six immigration points, which include Banbasa, Dhangadhi, Nepalgunj, Bhairahawa, Birgunj and Kakarbhitta. With regard to the Nepal-India border, Ravi Nitesh rightly commented, "... It gives the message of peace and mutual trust rather than hate, and restrictions. It is more towards freedom rather than binding a person within a confined political boundary."

Because of ethnic and linguistic similarities, people along the two sides of the Nepal-India border speak Maithili, Hindu, Bhojpuri and Awadhi. Their food habits, dress and way of living are almost the same. This has promoted matrimonial relationships among border inhabitants. Each year thousands of marriages take place among the border inhabitants of the two countries, which has added warmth in their relations.

Often, the border inhabitants of Nepal cross over the border and go to different parts of India on pilgrimages. Likewise, the Indian border inhabitants also visit different religious places in Nepal. For the Nepalese border inhabitants, the popular pilgrimage sites across the border in India are Gaya, Kashi, Prayag, Mathura, Vrindaban, Vaishnodevi, Balaju Tirupatti, Rameshworam and Dwarka. Conversely, the popular pilgrimage site for the Hindus of India in Nepal, include Janakpur, Gadhi Mai, Barahakshetra, Muktinath and Kathmandu.

A number of sites such as Koshi Tappu, Parsa Wildlife Resort, Bardiya and Chitwan National Parks in Nepal's border region with India are tourist attractions. In addition, rafting in rivers and beautiful tea gardens also attract tourists. Many Indian tourists visit Lumbini, the birthplace of Buddha. The thick forest region, rivers, flora and fauna and the hospitable nature of the Nepalese border inhabitants is the source of attraction for the Indian tourists.

Significantly, many of the border inhabitants from Nepal cross over the border and go to India to study in different disciplines such as arts, commerce, science, law, medicine and engineering. Often, the Nepalese border inhabitants go to Siliguri, Darjeeling, Madhubani, Darbhanga, Sitamadhi,

Muzaffarpur, Gorakhpur and other border towns of neighboring Indian states of Bengal, Bihar and Uttar Pradesh for study. This is so because educational institutions in India are of higher quality as compared to those in Nepal. Besides, the Nepalese students are provided national treatment in India as per the provision of the Treaty of Peace and Friendship of 1950 between Nepal and India. They pay the same fees for their education in Indian educational institutions as is paid by the Indian students. If the Nepalese students were charged fees on par with other foreign nationals, it could have drained much of Nepal's scarce foreign exchange. Nevertheless, over the last few years certain educational institutions in India have started charging fees in foreign currencies even from the Nepalese students, which is against the letter and spirit of the Treaty of Peace and Friendship of 1950. Also, some private engineering and medical colleges opened in the border areas in Nepal admit Indian students; for which they are charged higher tuition fees as compared to the Nepalese students.

The border inhabitants of Nepal and India also cross over the border in order to receive health treatment. Often, the Nepalese border inhabitants seek health services on the Indian side of the border in border cities such as Siliguri, Darbhanga (Laheriyasarai), Sitamadhi and Gorakhpur. Some Indian border inhabitants also visit the B.P. Koirala Institute of Health Sciences, Dharan to take advantage of the health treatment facilities. Similarly, many of the patients from across the border in India visit Cancer Hospital at Bharatpur, Eye Hospital at Lahan, and medical colleges in Janakpur, Chisapani and Nepalgunj for treatment. Because of the provision of national treatment to the people of one country into the territory of the other, the border inhabitants do not need to pay extra for health services than what is paid by the locals.

Nepal's open border system with India also provides scope for shelter to political leaders from one country to the other. Whenever there is any political upheaval in one country, people easily escape by crossing over the border. During the time India was ruled by the British, eminent Indian leaders like Jay Prakash Narayan and Ram Manohar Lohiya along with their guerrilla fighters popularly called *Aazad Dasta* escaped to Nepal in the wake of Quit India Movement in 1942. Later on, those leaders were caught by the Nepalese security agencies and then imprisoned at the Hanuman Nagar Jail in the Saptari district. But again with the help of *Aazad Dasta,* the two leaders were freed. Similarly, several other Indian freedom fighters also took shelter in the Nepalese border region during the Quit India Movement.

As and when occasions arise, Nepalese political leaders cross over the border and take shelter in India. During the authoritarian Rana regime that lasted for 104 years until 1951, many Nepalese political leaders took shelter in India. When King Mahendra dissolved the parliament and the duly elected government of Prime Minister B.P. Koirala in 1960, many of the democratic leaders of Nepal took shelter in India. Many of the Tharus, particularly in Jhapa, Chitwan, Nawalparasi, Banke, Bardiya and Kanchanpur districts of Nepal, opted to migrate across the border to India to avoid atrocities at home.

This happened when the hill migrants (people living in the hill/mountain regions of Nepal who migrated to the plain Terai region of the country) managed to take away their property and virtually made them homeless, landless and paupers during the Panchayat regime (1960-1990). Those Tharus who did not migrate and chose to stay in their villages had to live a life of Kamaiya – a kind of life in slavery. Even the state helped a large number of hill migrants to clear the forest so as to enable them to settle in the Terai region, when the local landless and poor people were devoid of any such opportunities.

Even as recently as the Maoist insurgency period (1996-2006), many of the Nepalese crossed over the border to India to escape from the atrocities of the rebel forces and the security agencies with a view to protecting their lives and to seek a livelihood and employment opportunities. The number of people crossing over the border to India through certain border checkpoints shot up to 2,000 per day during the conflict period. From the Nepalgunj sector alone, the number of people crossing over the border from Nepal to India was 300 to 400 per day in November-December 2002, which shot up unprecedentedly to 1,200 during the same period in 2003. There are reports that during the conflict period 24,000 people from the Rajapur areas of the Bardiya district had left their villages *en masse* to settle in the Baharaich and Bachya areas across the border in India.

Before the green revolution in India in the 1970s, many of the agricultural laborers from across the border in India used to come to Nepal for seasonal employment and get themselves engaged in agricultural activities during the plantation and harvesting seasons as there was a great demand for labor in this country. Subsequently, because of the growing employment opportunities within India, the agricultural labors from across the border stopped coming to Nepal. The green revolution in certain parts of India such as in Punjab and Hariyana attracted many of the Nepalese border inhabitants for seasonal employment in that country. Additionally, the Nepalese border inhabitants also visit Delhi, Mumbai and other parts of India to seek employment. The Nepalese are allowed to work in government, semi-government and private sectors in India without any restriction. Earnings by the Nepalese border inhabitants in Indian states have helped reduce poverty at home and raise their standard of living. But there has not been any serious study to estimate the amount of remittance that is coming to the border region of Nepal from India. However, there has been a decline in the tendency of the border inhabitants to go to India because of the growing alternative opportunities of employment in Malaysia, Qatar, Saudi Arabia and other overseas countries.

Many of the farmers living along the border regions buy and sell agricultural and livestock products at the border *hat bazaars* and other market centers in each other's territory. This has generated employment opportunities for many people in the border regions.

Often, the Nepalese border inhabitants buy commodities to meet their daily needs at the neighbouring markets of Bengal, Bihar, Uttar Pradesh and Uttarakhand of India, which include such goods as sugar, food grains, clothes, cooking oil, cement, fertilizers, electrical and electronic goods. The Indian border inhabitants, however, buy such goods in Nepal that originate from third countries like China, Japan, Thailand, Hong Kong, Singapore and Taiwan. There is also unauthorized trade in gold, beetle nuts, and tea from Nepal to India.

Many of the border inhabitants in Nepal often visit market places across the border in India for shopping. Since the border inhabitants are not expected to pay customs for goods procured for personal use, many of them buy goods for their household needs across the border in India. Such goods of daily needs are commonly cheaper in India than in Nepal.

However, the security personnel on both sides of the Nepal-India border often harass the people when they carry with them goods even for their personal use as the volume of such goods is not defined. But many of those who indulge in the smuggling of goods from one side of the border to the other manage to deal with the security personnel by bribing them. The increasing presence of the security personnel on both sides of the Nepal-India border has not put a stop to the smuggling of goods. Rather it discouraged genuine Nepalese border inhabitants from buying goods across the border in India at a cheaper price. It is estimated that the general price of Indian goods in the Nepalese market increased by at least 50 per cent owing to some of these factors.

Despite the growing presence of security forces along both sides of Nepal-India border, unauthorized trade is common almost all through the border points, including in the Kakarbhitta, Biratnager, Janakpur, Birgunj, Bhairahawa and Nepalgunj corridors. Often, the carriers involved in unauthorized trade load goods either on their heads or on bicycles while crossing over the border. The normal commission that the carriers get for this purpose is 10 per cent of the value of the goods.

Interestingly, nearly 55 per cent of the people along the Nepal-India border region conduct border trade for private consumption, 23 per cent for business purposes and the remaining 14 per cent for social functions. About 68 per cent of the border inhabitants use authorized custom checkpoints for border trade, while the remaining one third go for trade through non-custom checkpoints.

There is hardly any estimate made about the volume of border trade between Nepal and India. But it is estimated that each day there is a transaction of around fifty million rupees worth of goods through the Sonauli border between Nepal and India. The total value of informal imports of agricultural products from India to Nepal through the Nepal-India border amounted to Rs. 55 billion in 2012. It is believed that the informal trade through the Nepal-India border is more than what takes place through formal channels. India is the largest trade partner of Nepal and the volume of bilateral trade between the two countries amounted to $4.21 billion in 2010-11. In that year, Nepal's exports to India amounted to $599.7 million, while its imports from India amounted to $3.62 billion.

There is no provision of tariff concessions for the border inhabitants for trade under the existing trade arrangement between Nepal and India, though there is a large volume of unauthorized trade all along the border region of the two countries. Unauthorized trade often results in revenue loss for the governments. Hence, there is a need for duty free border trade as it has the potential to exploit raw materials, capital and human resources existing in the border areas.

Most importantly, the presence of over 361 million people across the border in the neighboring Indian states of Sikkim, West

Bengal, Bihar, Uttar Pradesh and Uttarakhand provide a wider prospect for the development of trade and industries in the Nepalese border region. The border areas of Nepal are best suited for the development of SEZs, which enhance the prospect for the export of goods from Nepal to those Indian states partly due to the proximity factor and partly due to the similarity of taste, preferences and purchasing power.

There are three dry ports in Nepal's border region, including in Biratnagar, Sirsiya (Birgunj) and Bhairahawa, which facilitate trade with third countries. Birgunj dry port is connected to India through rail and it is used for direct transshipment of goods between Birgunj and Kolkata Port of India to facilitate Nepal's trade with third countries. In October 2011, Nepal and India signed the Bilateral Investment Promotion and Protection Agreement (BIPPA) in order to promote investments from India to Nepal in such sectors as fast-track roads, railways, tourism, education, health, agriculture and other infrastructural projects. Nepal's border region could benefit if this agreement is realized.

Some of the recent efforts to upgrade four major custom checkpoints at Birgunj-Raxaul, Biratnagar-Jogbani, Bhairahawa-Sunauli and Nepalgunj-Rupediya might promote trade, commerce and other economic activities in the border regions of Nepal and India. Besides, India has undertaken a project to enable cross-border rail links at five locations at Jalpaiguri-Kakarbhitta, Jogbani-Biratnagar, Jaynager-Bardibas, Nautanwa-Bhairahawa, and Nepalgunj Road-Nepalgunj. India has also undertaken a project whereby it would develop a postal highway from the east to west end of Nepal. Nepal Oil Corporation and Indian Oil Corporation have undertaken the construction of an oil pipeline between Raxaul and Amlekhgunj. In addition, India has completed the East-West Highway Fiber Project in the border region. All such activities might go a long way in promoting the development of the regions on both sides of the Nepal-India border.

Nevertheless, there are reports of criminal and anti-social activities along the border regions such as the circulation of counterfeit currency, robberies, theft, smuggling, drug trafficking, human trafficking and arms smuggling. Many militants from other countries infiltrate India through the porous Nepal-India border. In order to control some of those activities, Nepal has deployed security forces to oversee the border on the Nepalese side. India has also mobilized security personnel in its border region for this purpose.

But this has not helped much to control undesirable activities along the border region. In certain quarters, there is thinking that the controlling or closure of the border is the solution to some of those problems. But it is likely that controlling or closure of the border might help accentuate the feeling of alienation among the border inhabitants, which might have a negative impact on the process of national integration in Nepal. With this respect, Jayant Prasad, the Indian ambassador to Nepal rightly observed that there was no need to erect any barricade in the Nepal-India border area.

NEPAL-CHINA BORDER MANAGEMENT SYSTEM

A controlled border system has been adopted between Nepal and China. This means any Nepali citizen willing to enter China compulsorily needs passport and visa. There was no visa requirement for Nepalis to visit Hong Kong before it was returned to China, but now it is necessary. There are certain designated border crossing points between Nepal and China, only through which a traveller from each country can cross the border. One such point is the one accessed through the Kodari Highway. The list of the Nepali customs and sub-customs offices on the Nepal-China border. These customs offices are located 25/30 kms inside the Nepalese territory from the boundary line. Because they are far too inside the border, they have not proved as effective checkpoints in regulating export-import transactions. Besides, the frontier zone of both countries that covers 20 km each inside from the boundary line has been declared as demilitarised zone by the China-Nepal Boundary Treaty of 21 March 1960. Only the civil police and administrative personnel could be deployed in this zone. This implies that there is no possibility of army's confrontation, as the militaries of both countries cannot meet each other at the same point.

Nepal-China Joint Border Committee

Thus, it is found that between Nepal and China all the procedures for the boundary protocol were completed and signed within two years and ten months of the boundary agreement. During the period the work went on smoothly without interruption, and minor disputes and differences were solved promptly and the task was completed within the given time frame.

Himalayan Range is No Longer Obstacle now

The Himalayan range, elongated east to west as a frontier between Nepal and China, is no longer an obstacle to Nepal's development. Until the last few decades, the Himalayas, including the world's highest mountain, the Mount Everest were like a natural boundary wall for Nepal, and treated as a barrier to building infrastructures in the country. But now, with the invention of a number of new technologies, they are no longer insurmountable even for transportation.

There appears to be a need for opening other various entry points on Nepal-Tibet border with a view to developing in a balanced way the Terai, mid-hills, high hills and the Himalayan region of the kingdom of Nepal...........

What is worth considering is that China has built in its autonomous province of Tibet a highway from Lhasa to Pakistan, accessing through Pakistan's Karakoram Mountains. It is also heard that, within a few years, a railway line will link Chengdu with Lhasa and then with Beijing. The Lhasa-Karakoram Highway runs west-east in Tibet, and it is about 90-170 kms farther north from Nepal's northern boundary line.

The distance from this Highway of most of the entry points on Nepal's northern border is 130 km on average. The estimated distance from the Nepalese points to the nearest Tibetan Motor vehicle road head is roughly as follows:

Nepal China (Tibet) Distance :

- Kimathanka -Dinge (Rongxar) 160 km
- Lambagar -Tingri 170 km

- Lomanthang -Zhongba (Xilin) 90 km
- Musigaon (Dolpa) -Paryang 150 km
- Khaptangchaur (Mugu) -Samsang 100 km
- Larke (Gorkha) -Saga 170 km
- Rasuwagadhi -Kerung 110 km

The opening of these entry points in the Nepalese frontier will make headway for the economic and social development of Nepal's trans-Himalayan region. This has become even more necessary now as China has recently included Nepal in its list of tourist destinations, and Nepal has also accepted the Chinese currency, Yuan into its basket of convertible foreign currencies. The initiative in opening the potential entry points along the northern border will therefore be Nepal's great advantage, and it should materialize as soon as possible.

CHINA-NEPAL TIES ATTAIN NEW HEIGHTS

This March 10, Nepal proved itself unwilling to allow a repeat of the mass Tibetan demonstrations that were held here from March to September 2008. Although the energy and numbers of last year's demonstrations surrounding the anniversary of the failed Tibetan uprising and Dalai Lama's flight into exile were not present this year, Nepalese riot police still took forcible measures to prevent a group of approximately 200 Tibetan demonstrators leaving the Boudha district of Kathmandu. A British activist named Daisy Karen Wood who attempted to dodge police and enter the Chinese Embassy carrying balloons and a Tibetan flag was quickly arrested. Nepal's desire to quickly suppress events that would embarrass China, its massive northern neighbour, comes as no surprise. Ties between the two countries have been increasing in recent months.

Historically, relations between Nepal and China have been relatively good. For centuries Nepal sent tribute bearing missions to China and acknowledged its superior regional force. The tension that did exist originated out of the perceived threat from India and contention over Tibet, which lies just 114 kilometres from Kathmandu. Following China's refusal to give military assistance to Nepal during the Anglo-Nepalese war of 1814-1816, Nepal invaded Tibet in 1854. China quickly intervened and the Treaty of Thapathali was signed between the two countries in 1856. Nepal recognized China's supremacy in the region and agreed to provide assistance if Tibet was ever invaded by a foreign force.

When an armed British mission arrived in Tibet from India in 1905, however, Nepal did not intervene. Having come under the influence of British India after its loss in the Anglo-Nepalese war, Nepal went as far as to tell China that it would assist the Tibetans if they ever declared independence, provided it was within British interests. When the Tibetans used the chaos of the 1911 Revolution to expel the Chinese, Nepal broke ties with China altogether.

Relations were re-established in 1955 when the Chinese began sending soldiers into Tibet. With the British gone from India, Nepal recognized Tibet as a sovereign part of Chinese territory and in 1960, a year after Tibet's failed uprising and the Dalai Lama's flight into exile, the two countries signed the Treaty of Peace and Friendship, cementing strong ties that continue today.

Now the new "Comprehensive Treaty" will bring the two countries even closer. The treaty puts into place agreements that China will not attack Nepal and will respect its sovereignty, while Nepal will solidify its acceptance of the "One China" policy. Under the policy Tibet, Taiwan, and Hong Kong are stated as indisputable parts of Chinese territory, and Nepal will not allow anti-Chinese activities on its soil. Nepal proved its willingness to fulfil such promises in the days surrounding the 50th anniversary of the March 10, 1959, Tibetan Uprising. The day after a visit by Chinese assistant foreign minister Hu Zhengyue, who arrived in Nepal last month leading a 14-member delegation, 27 Tibetans monks were arrested in Kathmandu. Eighteen were released and nine turned over to the United Nations and deported to India. The streets around the two Chinese embassies in Kathmandu were also closed off, declared "protest-free zones", and staffed with police who had orders to arrest anyone demonstrating nearby. Additional arrests of Tibetan activists were carried out and demonstrators were quickly confronted.

China welcomes these closer relations, with the additional support for its "One China" policy and assistance in controlling the more than 20,000 Tibetan refugees living in Nepal. The refugees, if they ever gave up the aging Dalai Lama's method of peaceful negotiation, could use Nepal's difficulty to control its northern border to launch attacks on Chinese forces in Tibet-something which Khampa fighters did with short-lived US Central Intelligence Agency support in the late 1960s and early 1970s. China views the establishing of closer relations with Nepal as an important step in its competition with India for regional influence. "China now seems to view Nepal as a vital bridge toward South Asia as part of strategy of encircling India," said Nepal expert Sanjay Upadya.

However, Nepal's interest in expanding relations with China is more complicated. The country has long sought to balance the interests of India and China, the two regional powers it lies between. Since the signing of the Indo-Nepalese Treaty of 1950, India has come to heavily dominate Nepalese politics. While the treaty acknowledges Nepal's sovereignty, clauses in the agreement give India a greater amount of control over Nepal than the Maoist government would prefer.

It is the overbearing influence of India that has pushed Nepal's Maoist government decisively towards China. The shift has been so strong that Premier Prachanda went as far as to break the long-standing tradition of Nepalese heads of state making their first foreign trip to India, instead visiting China, ostensibly to attend the opening ceremony of the 2008 Summer Olympic Games in Beijing. The move toward China does not necessarily mean that Nepal is breaking ties with India-the government rather seeks to decrease Indian influence. As Nepalese journalist Narendra Prasad Upadhyaana said, "It is not that China is ideal. It is only to neutralize India. Historically, socially, and culturally Nepal is closer to India. On a political level however the Maoist government wants to avoid being controlled by India as much as possible."

This new partnership with China comes at a time of great necessity for Nepal. The country is facing growing insecurity which many experts in Kathmandu believe could escalate into a crisis within the next year. With the decade-long civil war resulting in the overthrow of the monarchy, Nepal is facing the challenges of a newly democratic nation that has innumerable political groups and organizations vying for a tiny amount of resources amid growing insecurity.

The country's police and army have become polarized, with different groups supporting the Maoists, opposition forces, and even the return of the monarchy. A number of journalists have been attacked in the past six months. Amid simmering discontent within the Maoist Army, which refuses to integrate with the regular army and continues to recruit soldiers, the expected flood of returning immigrants from jobs in the Middle East and Malaysia due to the global financial crisis makes Nepal's immediate future seem grim.

Perhaps the most dangerous threat to the country's stability, however, is the deteriorating situation in the southern Terai region. Members of the Tharu indigenous group recently declared a 14-day strike, shut down roads, and engaged in near daily clashes with police that left four people dead.

The Tharus were demanding to be recognized as distinct from the Madhesis, the ethnic group that most indigenous people from the Terai are lumped into. Government negotiation ended the strike only after the situation had become so tense that police were ordered to escort petrol trucks through checkpoints and the price of fruit and vegetables in some Kathmandu markets had nearly doubled.

Though the strike has ended, the Tarai will continue to be an issue for Nepal. The indigenous groups demand that a new constitution divide the country into ethnically based autonomous states, something that could spell disaster as many of the ethnic groups in Nepal do not even acknowledge the others' right to exist. The idea of "ethnic federalism" will not be given up easily though. According to Dr Om Gurung, an indigenous rights leader in Kathmandu, the establishment of ethnically based autonomous federal states was a key promise of the Maoists during the civil war. Recently, however, the government has begun backing away from the promise, and most experts believe that such a system would set the stage for future conflict. Indigenous leaders are adamant, however, that Nepal's diverse nature requires such a system.

Dangerously, after the Maoist victory in the civil war and their subsequent international recognition, organizations in Nepal realized that agitation and violence does indeed work as a means of achieving political goals. With 70 identified armed groups operating across Nepal, most the wings of political organizations, the government and safety of the people are severely threatened. How the indigenous groups will choose to assert themselves if their demands for autonomous states are not met is still unknown.

Unless the government manages to control this growing unrest, the Maoist revolution may in fact prove to have just been the catalyst for a longer struggle for territory, resources, and representation in Nepal that the country will have to face as it struggles over the course of the next year to write a new constitution and make the difficult transition from a country at war to a country at peace.

This is a desire that can be assisted by a closer relationship with China. Over the past years China has proven itself willing to give large amounts of no-strings-attached cash and support for infrastructure building to countries that support its "One China" policy and allow it to expand its growing global influence. This is in contrast with most Western countries which demand that aid goes to specific projects and require greater oversight regarding where the funds end up. While the lack of transparency in Nepal means that much of the aid will be lost due to corruption, there is enough being offered that some effect will be felt by the population.

Along with the $16.4 million donation, after the signing of the "Comprehensive Treaty" China will add an additional 770 kilometres to the Kathmandu-Khasa highway in Tibet, effectively linking Nepal with China's massive internal railway system. Additional roads connecting Tibet and Nepal will be built and Chinese products are increasingly replacing Indian products, something that most Nepalese appreciate because of the lower cost. "China's products are sound to our pockets," said Nepalese journalist Narendra Prasad Upadhyaana.

The additional access to China is also expected to stimulate economic growth in Tibet, something that the Chinese government considers key to making the Tibetans drop their demands for autonomy. Larger groups of tourists coming from Nepal, and Tibetan salt being sold to Nepal, certainly may lessen some of the Tibetans' anger towards China, but it will not quite be the salve that the Chinese government wants it to be. As one Tibetan activist in Kathmandu said, "China does not have human rights. Nepal is following that. They are bending over for China and letting the Chinese control the police and treat the Tibetans here like animals."

The closer relationship with China is also not being viewed favorably by Delhi. Earlier this month several Nepalese opposition politicians left for India, claiming the trip was for health reasons. Their visit coincides with the presence of Nepal's disposed King Gyanendra, who has been in India since last month for a wedding. Although the Indian government allowed the Maoists to overthrow the monarchy, the new preference for China is making India reconsider its support. This is something that the Maoists must have expected. They are, however, reacting nervously to the opposition visit to India. "A new pact is being signed in New Delhi against the Maoist government," said the Janadisha newspaper, a mouthpiece for the Maoist Party. "Delhi is encircling the Maoists," said Nepalese journalist Narendra Prasad Upadhyaana. "India brought them to power and now suddenly they have gone to the Chinese. And India and China still do not have cordial relations."

7

India, Bangladesh Settle Boundary Partition

India and Bangladesh inked a historic pact on Tuesday to exchange 162 enclaves, resolving a 64-year-old boundary demarcation problem. Describing this and a slew of other negotiated agreements, Prime Minister Manmohan Singh - on his maiden visit to Dhaka - said the two countries had "agreed on a new architecture for partnership".

The landmark enclave deal is expected to give a new lease of life to over 50,000 inhabitants of the area who have been struggling to eke out a decent livelihood for decades. The breakthrough was made following discussions on the 162 enclaves (51 in India and 111 in Bangladesh) between Singh and his Dhaka counterpart Sheikh Hasina. Enclaves are defined as pockets of a country's territory surrounded by the other's.

They have been a bone of contention between successive regimes in India and Bangladesh and were created centuries ago when local kings in undivided Bengal and Assam exchanged pieces of land while gambling or playing chess.

The Indian enclaves in Bangladesh are located in four districts - Panchagarh, Lalmonirhat, Kurigram and Nilphamari. All of Bangladesh's enclaves lie in West Bengal's Cooch Behar district. The agreement enables Bangladesh to retain the Dahagram and Angarpota enclaves. According to a recent headcount conducted jointly by both sides, the total population in the enclaves is 51,000.

Officials of the two countries admitted that this number was much lower than the figure estimated earlier.

The headcount revealed that 34,000 people resided in the Indian enclaves in Bangladesh and there were 17,000 inhabitants in the latter's enclaves. The earlier unofficial estimates pegged the population of the 111 Indian enclaves at around 100,400, and that of the 51 Bangladeshi enclaves inside India at 44,000. Interestingly, 56 enclaves are not inhabited, of which 37 are Indian. Some others have a population of less than 10 people.

ALMOST 3,000 acres of Bangladesh's land lies in India and India has around 3,500 acres inside Bangladesh. Union home minister P. Chidambaram had given the lowdown on the pact in the Rajya Sabha recently. He had explained that people living in an enclave "shall be given the right of staying on as nationals of the state" to which the area will be transferred. He had referred to the 1974 agreement between Indira Gandhi and Sheikh Mujibur Rehman.

The pact signed by Singh allows residents of an Indian enclave in Bangladesh to seek local citizenship once the area becomes a part of Bangladesh. Such inhabitants also have the right to return to their original country from which they will be allotted land. Hasina's international affairs adviser Dr Gowher Rizvi said the land boundary issue had remained unresolved since 1947. "There were pressing demands to address it," he explained. People in these enclaves have been asking for rights and facilities as citizens for decades.

Bangladesh's leading English newspaper The Daily Star quoted Abdul Latif Sarkar of Garati enclave in Bangladesh as saying: "People in enclaves live in squalid conditions amid lack of adequate employment opportunity, infrastructure, educational institutions, electricity and medical facilities. Most people are below poverty level." Johir Ali, a dweller of Sreerampur enclave in Bangladesh, struck an optimistic note and told the daily: "With the signing of the bilateral deal, we will get all the facilities as Bangladeshi citizens."

Expressing similar sentiments, Bhitorkuti enclave resident Amzad Hossain said it was his dream to live a free life and hoped that it would materialise soon. The issue of the exchange of enclaves has, however, been opposed by some sections in India. On the eve of Singh's departure for Dhaka, the main Opposition party BJP expressed its apprehension over the arrangement. The party feared that India may give away more territory than it would get.

The BJP also claimed that the UPA government had failed to spell out whether or not those living in the enclaves would be told to cross the border to the country whose citizenship they held. The party wanted to know that if this was not the case, would the territory be demarcated? The deal on the exchange of the enclaves was a part of the larger boundary package that included adversely possessed lands, demarcation of 6.5 km of undefined border, allowing-Bangladeshis to use the Tin Bigha Corridor round the clock and finalisation of strip maps. For the first time, the two countries prepared strip maps of their 4,156-km boundary. These will be useful in settling border-related disputes. A strip map is a non-scaled drawing of a route to include key points along the border and usually incorporates distances, roadside features and town facilities on a simple flip-over style map.

ISSUES BETWEEN INDIA AND BANGLADESH

India and Bangladesh share a unique bond and a special relationship rooted in a common cultural heritage, shared principles and values and forged by common aspirations and sacrifices of its peoples. India is committed to carry forward the mission of strengthening the historic bonds and impart a vision for the future that is durable and sustainable and conducive for the collective prosperity of the region. Bangladesh's geopolitical importance for India is due to three factors. First, Bangladesh's location is a strategic wedge between mainland India and Northeastern seven states of the Indian Union. Each of these states is land-locked and has shorter route to the sea through Bangladesh. Currently, Kolkata port is used by these states for both domestic and imported cargo. Bangladesh is a natural pillar of "Look East Policy". A friendly Bangladesh that ensures no anti-India terror or insurgent activities can be carried out from its soil unlike in the past will substantially assist India in handling security problems in some of its restive north-east States. Importantly, a 'neutral' Bangladesh also ensures containment of an assertive China in this region, including along the strategic sea-lanes of the Bay of Bengal.

Further the navigable rivers in India's Northeast that could connect West Bengal or Orissa ports pass through Bangladesh. The only entry to and exit from the Northeastern region of India is through the Shiliguri Corridor that is close to the Chinese border and within striking distance of Bangladesh. The Shiliguri Corridor is the most sensitive 'choke point' for the Indian Union.

But unfortunately, there exist many contentious issues between the two countries.

Water Dispute

India and Bangladesh share 54 trans-boundary rivers, big and small. In 1996, the sharing of the Ganga waters was successfully agreed upon between the two nations. However, the major area of dispute has been India's construction and operation of the Farakka Barrage. The aim of construction of the Farakka Barrage was to increase the lean period flow of the Bhagirathi-Hooghly branch of Ganga to increase the water depth at the Kolkota port which was threatened by siltation. As irrigation withdrawals increased in Bangladesh, dispute arose between India and Bangladesh over the sharing of the lean season flow at Farakka. The inadequacy of water during the lean season to meet the assessed demands in the two countries is the root cause of the conflict.

The Bangladesh government feels that the reduction in flow caused damage to agriculture, industry and ecology in the basin in Bangladesh. Because of the inability of the concerned governments to come to any lasting agreement over the last few decades on sharing the river water, this problem has grown and now it is also viewed as a case of upstream-downstream dispute.

The other reason for water dispute is Teesta River – which has its source in Sikkim – flows through the northern part of West Bengal in India before entering Bangladesh, where after crosssing through about 45km of irrigable land, merges with the Brahmaputra River (or Jamuna when it enters Bangladesh). In 1983, an ad-hoc water sharing agreement was reached between India and Bangladesh, whereby both countries were allocated 39% and 36%

of the water flow respectively. The new bilateral treaty expands upon this agreement by proposing an equal allocation of the Teesta River. However, the deal fell through when the then newly elected Chief Minister of West Bengal, Ms. Mamata Banerjee, refused to approve the treaty, fearing that the loss of higher volume of water to the lower riparian would cause problems in the northern region of state, especially during drier months.

Construction of the Tipaimukh Dam is another contentious issue between India and Bangladesh. Tipaimukh Dam is a hydel power project proposed on the river Barak in Manipur. Bangladesh's objection is that it would have adverse ecological effects in its eastern Sylhet district. In spite of India's reiteration that no dam would be constructed overlooking Bangladesh's objections, the controversy is far from over. The popular arguments in Bangladesh against the Tipaimukh project are:

- India should not decide what is good for people of Bangladesh without taking them into confidence;
- No study has been undertaken in Bangladesh to assess the impact of the ecosystems that exist and depend on the natural flow of the water in Surma-Kusiyara-Meghna and their tributaries.

India and Bangladesh have agreed on a joint study group to examine the points raised by Bangladesh.

Boundary Dispute

India's land border with Bangladesh as per the Ministry of Defence is 4351 km. running through five states, viz., West Bengal (2217kms), Assam (262 kms), Meghalaya (443kms), Tripura (856 kms) and Mizoram (318 kms), including nearly 781 kms of riverine border. The border traverses through 25 districts.

The border is used as a route for smuggling livestock, food items, medicines and drugs from India to Bangladesh. Moreover, illegal immigrants from Bangladesh cross the border to India in search of improving their lives. Because of a large number of illegal immigrants crossing from Bangladesh into India, a controversial shoot-on-sight policy has been enforced by the Indian border patrols. This policy was initiated with reports of violence between the illegal migrants and Indian soldiers. The border has also witnessed occasional skirmishes between the Indian Border Security Force and the Border Guards Bangladesh, most notably in 2001.

The killing of Bangladeshi nationals by Border Security Force (BSF) has become a major irritant between the two countries in the recent past. It has evoked strong public sentiments in Bangladesh. According to a report of Bangladesh Human Rights Watch organization Odhikar, BSF has, from January 1, 2001 to March 31, 2012, killed 907 Bangladeshis. Bangladesh wants no time lost in stopping these killings.

Further the Agreement on the demarcation of Land Boundary between Bangladesh and India and related matters had been signed in May 1974 between the two great statesmen, Bangabandhu Sheikh Mujibur Rahman, and Smt. Indira Gandhi. This comprehensive agreement was intended to resolve all lingering and vexing problems that history had bequeathed on the two nations. But it has not full filled by both Governments.

During the State visit of the Prime Minister to Bangladesh in September 2011, a "Protocol to the Agreement between the Government of India and the Government of Bangladesh Concerning the Demarcation of the Land Boundary Between India and Bangladesh and Related Matters (LBA)" was signed. It settles the long outstanding land boundary issues related to un-demarcated segment of 6.1 Kms; territories in adverse possession; and exchange of enclaves.

The Cabinet has, on 13 February 2013, approved the draft of a Constitution (Amendment) Bill for implementing the India-Bangladesh Land Boundary Agreement (LBA) 1974 and the Protocol to LBA signed in 2011.

The Protocol envisages that 111 Indian Enclaves in Bangladesh and 51 Bangladesh Enclaves in India, as per the jointly verified cadastral enclave maps, shall be exchanged. As per Article 3 of the LBA 1974, when the Enclaves are transferred, people living in these areas shall be given the right of staying on where they are as nationals of the State to which the areas are transferred.

The delay in implementation of the land boundary agreement signed during the Indian Prime Minister's visit has increased the differences. The Bangladesh Parliament has ratified the agreement, but it awaits ratification by the Indian Parliament. Bangladesh is urging India to take necessary steps at the earliest to make it functional. The reason for the parliamentary delay is the reservation expressed by some sections, mainly people living on the border, who complain that they had not been consulted before signing the treaty. They also argue that implementation of the treaty would have adverse impact on their lives.

MARITIME BORDER

While Bangladesh, having concave coastlines, delimits its sea border southward from the edge of its land boundary, India stretches its claim southeast wards, covering around thousands of miles in the Bay of Bengal. Due to competing claims of the two countries, delimitation of the sea boundary and determining Bangladesh's exclusive economic zones have remained unresolved. Moreover, in terms of determining the continental shelf, the presence of the Andamans and Nicobar Islands puts India, in a favourable position.

Territorial Waters

The issue of demarcating territorial waters led to serious differences between the two countries. Questions of ownership over a new born island known as South Talpatty in Bangladesh and New Moore/ Purbasha in India spotted by a satellite picture in 1975 in the estuary of Haribhanga River on the border of the two countries has been a source of contention since its discovery. In order to settle the above dispute Bangladesh proposed sending a joint Indo Bangladesh team to determine the flow of channels of the river on the basis of existing International Law of the Sea. But the Indian counterpart sent forces to establish claims by stationing naval troops on the island in 1981. After initial resentment by Bangladesh, India agreed to resolve the issue through negotiations. Till now the sovereignty over the island nation remains undecided, and recent reports of the press and media suggests that Bangladesh views India with suspicion in its activities over the disputed piece of landmass on the breast of an international water.

ILLEGAL MIGRATION

Illegal migration is one of the bones of the contention of these two countries, Since the 1971 war of independence that created the state of Bangladesh, millions of Bangladeshi immigrants (the vast majority of them illegal) have poured into neighbouring India. While the Indian government has tried to deport some of these immigrants, the sheer number of them, as well as the porous border between the two countries, has made such an enterprise impossible. It is difficult to assess how many illegal immigrants are currently residing in India. Consider that in 1971, during the civil war in neighboring East Pakistan (the former name of Bangladesh), at least 10-million Bangladeshis poured into West Bengal in India

Illegal migration appears in the eastern and north-eastern parts of the country from neighbouring Bangladesh, threat to India's internal security, from Bangladesh is impacted on communal, political, social and economic tensions and conflicts in several areas of the northeast of India. The most affected states are West Bengal, Assam, Megalaya, Nagaland, Bihar, and Tripura, although migrants "have spread too far off states like Tamil Nadu, Maharashtra, Gujarat, Rajasthan and Delhi." Although the exact figure is not known, it is estimated that there are about 15-20 million Bangladeshis staying illegally in India.

The National Investigation Agency has found links with Pakistan in rackets engaged in printing and smuggling fake currency into India. NIA sources said fake currency was now being smuggled into the border with Bangladesh has gaps at some points and immigrants cross into India on foot through the breaks in the fence. Some also swim across rivers on the border to reach India. The National Investigation Agency has found links with Pakistan in rackets India through its porous border with Bangladesh. Malda district in West Bengal is a key transit point for counterfeiters. Once they reach India, immigrants obtain fake documents through local agents. Political leaders in parts of West

Bengal were also involved in endorsing fake documents such as ration cards for illegal immigrants.

This unfettered illegal migration impacts on national security and socio-economic stability. Intelligence inputs indicate that the Inter Service Intelligence Agency (ISI) of Pakistan is utilizing these migrants as conduits to ferry in terrorists and arms into India. Counterfeit Indian currency with its origins in Bangladesh has flooded border areas, crippling in these parts.

Vote bank politics in Assam is the one of obstacle to control illegal migration from Bangladesh, led to communal violence between indigenous Bodos and Muslims (migrants from Bangladesh) in 2012. The illegal Bangladeshi immigrants have not only changed the demography and disturbed the ecology of the north-east but have also encouraged them to exercise their political rights in India as citizens. It has been one of the key reasons for the rise of insurgent groups in the north-east as some of the insurgent groups like Assam Gana Sangram Parishad started, and got support of the masses, because of the issue of illegal immigration from Bangladesh. At the same time the immigration laws (Illegal Migrants [Determined by Tribunal] (IMDT) Act 1983) followed in Assam has aided illegal immigrants' settling in the north-east easy.

SECURITY CONCERNS

Insurgency has been playing the role in straining relations of India with Bangladesh. Northeast India has been facing insurgency since 1956 due to feelings of ethnic separatism among its inhabitants. ISI is operating from Bangladesh, supporting the insurgents in the North east India. National Liberation of Tripura (NLFT), Liberation Front of Assam(ULFA) and National Democratic Front of Bodoland (NDFM) are major insurgent groups in Northeast India. There are some rumours that ULFA has several lucrative income generating Projects in Bangladesh to sustain its insurgency activities in India.

Drug Trafficking

Bangladesh is increasingly being used as a transit point by drug dealers and the drug mafia, which dispatches heroin and opium from Burma, and other countries of the golden triangle, to different destinations. As a result, Bangladesh's Department of Narcotics Control has come under the scanner several times and invited criticism. Bangladesh has become the prime transit route for trafficking heroin to Europe from Southeast Asia, according to a report from the International Narcotics Control Board (INCB) 2007 annual report. INCB notes that the most common methods and routes for smuggling heroin into Bangladesh are by courier from Pakistan, commercial vehicles and trains from India, and via sea through the Bay of Bengal or overland by truck or public transport from Burma.

Trade and Investment

Bangladesh is an important trading partner for India. The two-way trade in FY 2011-2012 was US$5.242 billion with India's exports to Bangladesh accounting for US$4.743 billion and imports US$0.498 million.

The trade deficit with India is frequently highlighted by Bangladesh as a major contentious issue. Trade deficit for Bangladesh is more than $4 billion. For long, Bangladesh has been urging India to reduce this gap by lifting the tariff barriers as they were a major impediment to the growth of Bangladesh's exports to India. Responding to Bangladesh's concern, in November 2011, India granted duty free access to all products, except 10 tobacco and liquor items from Bangladesh which amounts 30% of Bangladesh export. As much as 98 per cent of Bangladesh products now enjoy zero duty benefits in the Indian market. Bangladesh's exports to India are expected to cross $1 billion in 2012.

However, Bangladesh is now urging India to remove all non-tariff barriers (NBTs) as it views NTBs as the major obstacles to its export growth. Some of these barriers are: laboratory test for every consignment of food products, cosmetics, and leather and textile products; delay in getting test results; imposition of state tax; packaging requirement, anti-dumping and countervailing duties; inadequate infrastructure facilities such as warehousing, trans-shipment yard, parking yard and; connecting roads at land customs stations of India. To encourage exports from Bangladesh,

India must move proactively to provide facilities of customs and testing at the border check posts. Besides, removal of non-tariff barriers should be accompanied by tariff reforms since the opportunity cost of non-tariff barriers is very high. A Consumer Unity & Trust Society (CUTS) International report says: "In 2010, value of unexplored market was more than 48 per cent of total value of India- Bangladesh trade and potential saving, which is a proxy for cost of non-tariff barriers, is more than seven per cent of total value of Indo-Bangla trade".

India is also encouraging investments in Bangladesh. In this regard, a Bilateral Investment Promotion and Protection Agreement have been signed between the two countries. The agreement is expected to increase Indian investment in Bangladesh.

Transit

India has been urging Bangladesh to provide rail and road transit to connect with its north-eastern states. Technically speaking, the issue of transit was resolved in 1972 when both sides agreed on a mutually beneficial arrangement for the use of their waterways, railways and roadways for commerce between two countries and for passage of goods to places in one country through the territory of the other. Inland water transit has been functional, but the rail and road transit is still waiting to be operational.

Bangladesh's initial reluctance to granting India rail and road transit was on the grounds that transit facility once given was difficult to take back and such a facility may encourage terrorism and insurgency.

Other concerns included damage to the roads and bridges in Bangladesh by the increased traffic flow from the Indian side.

The reason for delay was that Bangladesh's infrastructure was not yet prepared to take the load of the increased traffic that will follow with the granting of transit to India. Addressing Bangladesh's concern, India provided a credit line of $1billion to Bangladesh for development of infrastructure projects. But the credit line could not be used to its potential because of the strict conditions India imposed, to the effect that 85 per cent of the raw materials for the road projects has to be procured from India, on the ground that it produces all the materials necessary. Bangladesh has countered by claiming it too has the necessary raw materials. It could earn $44 million per annum for first five years if it grants transit to India. From the sixth year, earnings would be around $500 million, which could rise to $1 billion. Transit would not only boost connectivity between the two countries, but also offer opportunities for regional connectivity and help Bangladesh develop Chittagong port into a regional hub.

The Chittagong port can become a modern busy port like Singapore and China serving the SAARC countries. Huge foreign investment may be attracted by Bangladesh and finally, a throbbing service sector like banks, insurance, hotels, rest houses, petrol pumps etc. may develop around the Transcontinental roads and railways. There is an estimate of direct economic gain from transit fees. It ranges from 500 crore taka to 4,666 crore taka. The mutual transit will also give Bangladesh a much shorter route to China and an initiative to link Chinese province of Yunan with Seven Sisters of India, Myanmar, Thailand and Bangladesh.

Conclusion

India-Bangladesh relations have more than an academic strategic content. In the long run, India's national interests primarily lie towards and beyond its eastern flanks to South East Asia and the new geographical and strategic construct namely Indo-Pacific Asia. India thus needs to strengthen the various regional groupings in this region like the ASEAN and the BIMSTEC (Bay of Bengal Initiative for Multi-Sectoral Technical and Economic Cooperation). Importantly, they should work together to resolve all the issues.

The following steps should be taken to improve relation between India and Bangladesh.

a) Agreement on water sharing should be given priority. Early resolution of the Teesta issue is necessary.

b) India should give prominence to the ratification of land boundary agreement.

c) Security cooperation between the two countries has been good. But there is need for institutionalizing this cooperation so that it does not remain restricted to the tenure of a particular government in either country. In this regard, a beginning could be made by signing the bilateral extradition treaty.

d) Connectivity should be given top most priority. Both the countries should work together to operationalise it.

e) There is need for addressing the issue of illegal migration. In this regard innovative measures should be taken to resolve the problem, being extra careful to ensure that illegal migrants do not acquire voting rights and Indian nationality.

f) People-to-people contact needs to be encouraged; hence liberal visa system should be put in place.

g) Trade relationship has improved significantly between the two countries. India has provided zero duty access of Bangladeshi products thereby addressing the tariff related issue to a great extent. The two countries should now consider an agreement on non-tariff barriers.

h) Indian investment should be encouraged in Bangladesh through visits of trade delegations, trade fairs, and bilateral assurances on protection of the interests of potential investors.

i) Progress can be made by cooperating on common challenges like disaster management, food and energy security.

j) Greater involvement of people and wider public debate on foreign policy issues will discourage conspiracy theories and distrust.

k) A greater level of people-to-people contact should be encouraged.

l) Implement the no-firing policy fully. Ensure accountability to ensure that the image of India as an enemy ceases to exist.

m) Fencing needs to be completed speedily and monitored effectively.This would create misgivings but also ensure that Bangladesh knows that India means business. The state governments and the Indian border forces seem receptive to such an idea

n) India and Bangladesh need to strengthen their military ties. They are being revived after a long gap but much more can be done in terms of increasing visits, contacts at various level as well as by selling military hardware. Apart from initiating joint exercises, India should consider the China model of gifting hardware in the initial instance, and offer technical expertise that Bangladeshi military is in need of. They have to be weaned away from Pakistan and China. There can be no overnight successes but sustained efforts are essential.

ILLEGAL BANGLADESHIS AND BJP-SHIV SENA GOVERNMENT

Since the late 1980s, the Bharatiya Janata Party (BJP) and the Shiv Sena have been the main political parties instrumental in the revival of Hindu nationalism. The 1980s and 1990s saw a time of growing fear on the part of the majority Hindu population that the Muslim minority was increasing its presence in India, challenging Indian sovereignty and controlling the politics of the country.

The right wing political parties feared that demographic change and an increase in the Muslim population as well as the rise of Islamic fundamental groups would make the Hindus of India vulnerable. Combined with the growth of Islamic fundamentalism in Pakistan, the increased violence of the Kashmir insurgency and the displacement of Kashmiris instigated the perception in India that the number of Muslims was growing and they posed a threat to Hindus in India. These factors made it easier for the BJP to enter the political sphere and work with the Sangh Parivar in using the media to play on Hindu insecurity. Further, the BJP successfully characterized the Indian National Congress government as 'pandering' to Muslims and undertook key symbolic mobilizations as a means of fortifying a Hindu identity. This played a part in the rapid rise of the BJP in the 1990s followed by an electoral victory in 1998.

The Sangh Parivar, the force of Hindi chauvinism, has characterised the undocumented migration from Bangladesh in recent decades as 'infiltration'-Muslim migrants as 'infiltrators' as opposed to 'refugees' for Hindu migrants. The issue of illegal migrants from Bangladesh as infiltrators was also raised by the BJP and Sangh Parivar in the 1980s and 90s. In the 1980s, the BJP and associated Hindu nationalist organizations such as the Vishwa Hindu Parishad (VHP) and the Rashtriya Swayamsevak Sangh (RSS) repeatedly drew attention to the cross border movements of Bangladeshis to India.

Ramachandran (1999: 236) documented that on 6 May 1997, former Union Home Minister Indrajit Gupta announced in the Indian Parliament that there were nearly 10 million undocumented immigrants, largely from Bangladesh, residing in India (Times of India, 1997). This was the first official statement by the Government of India regarding the extent of Bangladeshis' migration into the country. In response to that statement, Uma Bharati, a member of the Sangh Parivar, told the House that the 'Indian government had failed to take effective steps to check the entry of Bangladeshi citizens. She sounded the alarm by warning that the undocumented Bangladeshi immigrants would soon demand a separate state from India.

The BJP is widely known for Hindutva -a religion-centric and chauvinistic political ideology that seeks to bring all Hindus under one umbrella through out the 1980s and 1990s. At that time, the party's national leadership was searching for an alternative issue instead of the campaign to construct a Ram temple (a Hindu deity) at Babri Masjid in Ayodhya in order to provoke its supporters. In April 1992, the BJP National Executive passed a resolution claiming that over 15 million Bangladeshis had illegally entered India. The resolution said that, 'the influx constitutes a serious strain on the national economy, a severe stress on the national society and withal a serious threat to the stability and security of the country. And yet the Congress takes no action to stem this flood or push back illegal immigrants, because it views them as its vote bank'. The BJP aimed to use this migrant issue as one of tne main campaign agendas to get support and widen its political base in West Bengal and Northeast Assam in 1992 and 1993 where it had low standing and support as the politics of these two states were dominated by the Communist Party of India (Marxist) and the Indian National Congress respectively.

The BJP was successful in its objectives and received increased media attention at that time. Many central level leaders regarded the migrants' campaign as a long term component of the party's electoral platform. Some even thought it might overtake the Ram temple issue as a national strategy for political mobilization. In 1999, the BJP formed a coalition government under the name National Democratic Alliance (NDA) with support from other political parties including the Shiv Sena with 15 seats in Lok Sabha. The BJP and the Shiv Sena share common ground on the Hindutva issue.

The Shiv Sena is widely known for its communal and chauvinistic ideological campaign which can leave the BJP behind in its anti-Muslim, anti-Pakistan and pro-Hindu rhetoric. They are commonly provocative in their campaigns, claiming that 'the Muslims in India are behaving as if they are Pakistani citizens. It is as if there are two countries within this one. Hindus, open your eyes and see what is going on. Your funeral pyres are burning'. When Mumbai was waterlogged for three days, the Mayor of Mumbai-a member of the Shiv Sena held the illegal Bangladeshi population responsible saying their (Bangladeshi migrants') filth blocked up the gutters. The Shiv Sena's proposed solution to illegal Bangladesh migrants in India had always been to truck them out of India. In 1998, a project conducted in selected Delhi slums by the People's Union for Civil Liberties (PUCL) found that the workers of BJP and Shiv Sena had been active in identifying Bangladeshi Muslims immigrants in selected slums.

In response to the Shiv Sena-BJP campaign on the security threats arising from migrants by Bangladeshis, the Centre for Study of Society and Secularism (CSSS), a non government organization in Mumbai carried out a study in 1995. In 'Immigrants in Bombay: A Fact Finding Report', the findings revealed that the BJP-Shiv Sena estimates about the number of illegal migrants was not merely an exaggeration but almost complete fabrication. The report points out that the BJP-Shiv Sena government attempted to fabricate illusionary danger and generate fear. According to the report, this issue was raised by the BJP to divert people's attention after the demolition of Babri Masjid. The report further argued that the propaganda matched the Shiv Sena's past records of arousing competition against one section of the population by another; their past targets have been Dalits (low caste Hindu) and South Indians to get the Marathi (local people from Maharashtrsa) vote bank in Maharashtra. The report criticized Operation Push Back initiated by the Narashima Rao government in 1992 as 'inhuman, condemnable and unthinkable in this century'. It concluded that the so-called infiltrators did not pose any threat and the perception of danger was a product of Hindutva-led propaganda. The study argued that the migrants were more preoccupied with their day to day subsistence needs and hardly had any time to think about other issues. The report recommended that 'if immigration from Bangladesh is indeed a serious issue for the Indian Government, then problem must be resolved through negotiation with Bangladesh government; deportation of poor Muslims is not the answer'.

The Left Front government of West Bengal (Communist Party of India-Marxist or CPI-M) sharply criticised both the Centre and Maharashtra governments for Operation Push Back and for failing to consult the West Bengal administration before using the state border for deportation. The erstwhile Chief Minister Jyoti Basu described the action as "uncivilised" and claimed many of the arrested people were Bengali-speaking Muslims from West Bengal with legitimate claims to citizenship. The Left Front Government was held responsible for encouraging and approving Bangladeshi migration in order to capture votes and political support in key electoral constituencies. Though the West Bengal government coordinated with the Centre and announced several policies to curb the influx of Bangladeshi migrants, the state government was perceived to have adopted a comparatively sympathetic stand on the migrants themselves by the BJP. Karlekar (2005) criticised the Chief Minister of the CPI-M government of West Bengal Budhadeb Bhattacharya for not taking any measure to close unrecognized madrasas in the border areas that have he claims become centres of anti-India propaganda. The West Bengal government was also considered to be a contributing factor for Bangladeshis to come to West Bengal for its secular values and control on local level administrative structure.

MANAGEMENT OF BANGLADESH INDIA BORDER

A border is something that indicates a limit where one's responsibility ends and another's begin. The term "boundary" is used in similar sense inasmuch as it is one of the most significant manifestations of state territorial sovereignty. It delimits physical space and has proven to be quite a daunting task that can bedevil state relationship. But not so always if both sides understand each other better and are amenable to rational choices.

In the Eurocentric global model of modernity from which no culture in the world has remained untouched and which the Third World leaders have adopted, national borders left by their colonial rulers continue to provide them with challenges that so far many have been unable to resolve satisfactorily specially with their value system as tools. But this should not necessarily be the case. Borders could be sources of conflict as well as peace and prosperity depending on how the issues are tackled. This paper would look into the options that the two neighboring states Bangladesh and India can adopt in order to overcome the impediments that have alternately soured or given boost to their relationship from time to time taking necessary cue from the Eurocentric practices.

Prime Minister Sk. Hasina's planned visit to India from 11 January 2010 onward has raised tremendous positive expectations among the peoples of the two countries, media and policy makers for practical reasons. During her first term as Prime Minister of Bangladesh together with Indian Congress leaders like Mr. I. Gujral and regional leaders like Mr.Deve Gowda she was able to resolve some of the intractable issues like that of long term sharing of Ganges Water and the resolution of Chittagong Hill Tracts insurgency. Similar concrete achievements, if not more, are now being expected by the peoples of the two countries as both the Prime Ministers of India and Bangladesh came to power in recent past with comfortable majority and do have positive track records of taking the bulls by the horn. The title of the today's roundtable discussion, namely "Bangladesh India Relations: Exploring New Horizons" does symbolize that upbeat expectation amongst all of us. Given the inter state post 1947 political culture in South Asia of keeping resolution of territorial issues pending, such expectations seem to be reflection of too much of the sunny side on the part of Bangladeshi psyche. Meanwhile, the solemn declaration and its repeated affirmation of Sk. Hasina that Bangladesh's soil would not be allowed to be used by terrorists for attacking India followed by concrete action which lead to ULFA leaders surrender to Indian security apparatus have taken care of a serious security concern of Indian rulers and people on its eastern front. This has generated a huge surge of goodwill in the vocal Indian media whose Bangladesh critical columnists have not failed to note these unprecedented acts of friendship and tremendous risk to the person of Sk. Hasina and Bangladesh from the revenge seeking insurgent organizations of North east India. But again to many Bangladeshis who got frustrated from little or no implementation of many settled agreements by India despite expression of concrete and repeated measures of goodwill shown by Bangladesh like handing over of Berubari enclave, lowering of tariff to Indian products entering Bangladesh under SAPTA passed without any reciprocal gestures, this unilateral daring act of strategic risk taking appears to be one more act of friendship gesture going to waste. Consequently, any mismatch in give and take from the two sides during her ensuing visit to India is going to have tremendous impact on the Bangladesh Prime Minister's political capital and goodwill among her people.

INDIA-BANGLADESH RELATIONS: TOWARDS INCREASED PARTNERSHIP

The last decade has seen a new development in India's foreign policy. Both the Congress-led United Progressive Alliance (UPA) and the BJP-led National Democratic Alliance (NDA) governments have sought to improve political relations and deepen economic partnerships with neighbouring countries.

India's quest for self reliance, initiated soon after Independence, steadily reduced the salience of economic engagement with its neighbours. This approach cost India economically and diplomatically; trade barriers within South Asia have limited growth potential. Certain key unresolved issues between the two countries resulted in the under-exploitation of the potential for mutual growth. While India played a critical role in 1971 in the birth of Bangladesh, this did not however result in close bilateral ties. India was even present in Bangladesh's threat perception, with public opinion in Bangladesh accusing India of embracing a heavy-handed approach.

But the opening up of India's economy and the renewed political emphasis on building a peaceful periphery represented a unique opportunity for India to realise its ambition of resecuring strategic ties in its immediate neighbourhood. Additionally, geo-strategic equations with China, whose rise has cast a lengthening shadow over the subcontinent, presented an added urgency in New Delhi to transform its regional policy.

Bangladesh formed an important component in this strategy. India and Bangladesh, two sub-continental neighbours, have always shared strong cultural, linguistic and geographical ties. Historically the destiny of the Bangladeshi people has never been far removed from that of the other communities that make up the Indian sub-continent. Bangladesh has fought alongside India twice in the cause of the right of peoples to self determination, and the two countries have shared a porous border for over 40 years. Today, as the recent improvement in relations suggests, there is a growing realisation that increased cooperation will bring substantial socio-economic benefits that can no longer be overlooked.

Bangladesh Prime Minister Sheikh Hasina's landmark visit to India in 2010 was followed by Prime Minister Manmohan Singh calling on Dhaka in September 2011. These visits unveiled a sweeping agenda for the transformation of bilateral relations by committing the two leaders to resolve all major outstanding issues left behind since the partition.

The ambition in 2010 was to reaffirm their shared history and build a new basis for a cooperative relationship, with both sides making a substantive effort to overcome issues. A comprehensive framework of cooperation for development aimed at promoting trans-border cooperation in the management of shared water resources, hydro-power potential and eco-systems and in the areas of connectivity and trade and economic cooperation was signed between the two countries.

However, some of the progress that was made in the run-up to the second visit was undermined when the Teesta Waters Agreement did not fructify at the last minute. Given the emotion attached to the water issue in Bangladesh, there was some disappointment during Indian Prime Minister Dr. Manmohan Singh's visit to Dhaka. Neverthless, it is to be noted that the Joint Communiqué of 2010 and the Joint Statement of 2011 were major steps in charting the future course of relations between India and Bangladesh. It is now up to both the countries to restore confidence and rebuild upon what has already been achieved and advance the bilateral relationship.

DOMESTIC SITUATION IN BANGLADESH

The evolving political situation in Dhaka has always played a key role in determining Bangladesh's foreign policy and its relations with India. The 2008 general elections saw the Awami League come to power in Bangladesh, with the Sheikh Hasina-led government decimating Khaleda Zia's Bangladesh Nationalist Party (BNP) in the polls.

Over the years, India has enjoyed strong relations with Bangladesh under an Awami League government. This was further demonstrated by Bangladesh cracking down on insurgent groups operating within its borders and tempering anti-Indian Islamist sentiments within the country. The success or failure of Sheikh Hasina's policies will not only affect the future prosperity of Bangladesh, but will also impact the prospects of Indo-Bangladesh relations.

The spectacular manner in which the Awami League came to power in 2008 has allowed the government to undertake certain bold decisions that it was not capable of making during its previous term. In a bid to remove the caretaker system of government during elections, the government passed the 15th amendment to the constitution in 2011. The BNP, which is extremely critical of the amendment, is afraid that the Awami League will take advantage of the highly politicized nature of Bangladesh's institutions like the judiciary, police force and election commission and has threatened to boycott the elections.

The last time elections were boycotted by the opposition party, the army was forced to step in amidst allegations that the caretaker government was partisan. Crucially, going forward, India must be aware of developments occurring in real time in Bangladesh, lest it be caught off guard by unfavourable political changes.

One concern experts cite is that India may be relying too heavily on Sheikh Hasina and the Awami League to maintain stable relations with Bangladesh. While the Awami League shall remain in power till 2013, and might even return to power in an unprecedented fashion, it is imperative that India cultivate relations with the opposition party. It is no secret that India shares a certain affinity with Sheikh Hasina's liberal and pro-democratic government, but a propensity to vote incumbents out of power necessitates that India engages all shades of Bangladeshi public opinion.

Conscious of the present mindset of the people of Bangladesh, the BNP has also significantly toned down its anti-India stand of late. Certain BNP leaders have voiced the need to improve and strengthen India-Bangladesh relations, indicating that they can no longer exploit anti-India sentiments for narrow and immediate political gains. With the political situation precariously balanced in Bangladesh, taking this window of opportunity, the Indian government must look to the future and engage all sides of Bangladesh's political spectrum.

BORDER MANAGEMENT AND LAND BOUNDARY AGREEMENT

The India-Bangladesh border that stretches for over 4094 km and is extremely porous facilitates the illicit flow of goods across the border and illegal migration from Bangladesh into India. In fact, illegal trade and smuggling has led to violent incidents in the past with Bangladesh accusing India's Border Security Force (BSF) of shooting innocents. India, which has always maintained that the supposed innocents were in fact gangs of cattle smugglers, has now issued strict guidelines for the use of non-lethal weapons against illegal trespassers. With the majority of the trespassers evading security forces, it is evident that not enough resources are being allocated to the border. India's greater focus on the Indo-China and Indo-Pak borders has relegated the India's border with Bangladesh to relative obscurity over the last few decades, with the neglected border only receiving the central government's attention in the last decade only, due to rapidly escalating security concerns.

While both countries now recognise the significance of checking cross border crime they also acknowledge that the border guarding forces must exercise restraint. In July 2011 both nations signed the Coordinated Border Management Plan to effectively control cross border illegal activities. Both governments directed the concerned agencies to meet regularly to discuss coordination efforts, share information and identify vulnerable areas.

Related to the border issue is the problem of illegal migration from Bangladesh into India. Historically, migration has been a recurring cause of concern in India-Bangladesh relations; and Bangladesh's role in facilitating the movement of its population beyond its borders has always been a question mark. Today, with population pressures beginning to tell in several Indian states and influx from Bangladesh rising at an alarming rate, the issue has taken on great significance. Over and above the economic and demographic risk that migration poses to India through drain of resources and employment strains, migration has also led to a rise in crime and other subversive activities that pose a considerable challenge for India's security apparatus.

With the termination of the Illegal Migrants Determination by Tribunal Act (IMDT), the government took an important step in detecting and deporting illegal immigrants. However, in order for the Indian government to make considerable headway with the migration issue it needs the support of the sending country, in this case Bangladesh. Many European countries that are faced with the same migration problem are increasingly resorting to re-admission agreements in order to tackle the problem. Whether India should enter into a similar readmission agreement with Bangladesh remains unclear; yet it is evident that it needs to engage with Bangladesh on this issue. The Land Boundary Agreement signed on the 6th of September 2011 was meant to mark a watershed in India-Bangladesh relations and resolve a decade old boundary dispute between the two countries. This long overdue exchange of territory concentrated over 200 enclaves would give India a clear and demarcated border with Bangladesh and would bring these enclaves, which are like islands of Indian and Bangladeshi territory surrounded by each other's land, out of isolation and abject poverty.

The Indira-Mujib Land Boundary Agreement of 1974 (upon which the current agreement was built) was meant to do just that, but was not ratified by the Indian parliament. However, the agreement which has yet to be ratified by the parliament, was stalled when UPA ally Trinamool Congress and sections of the opposing NDA voiced reservations against the historic deal, arguing that the deal gives away too much territory to Bangladesh. The non-resolution of the enclaves remains a major problem for the current Bangladeshi government which has repeatedly been criticised by opposition parties for extending too much support to India.

INDIA'S FOREIGN POLICY IN COMPARISON WITH BANGLADESH'S FOREIGN POLICY

India's policies towards Bangladesh can be studied within the broad parameters of its policy towards its friendly neighbours. The basic objective of such policies can be acknowledged as:

(a) India's aspiration to see a forthcoming, secular and democratic regime in Bangladesh.

(b) To ensure that, Bangladesh does not pose any security challenge to India.

(c) To seek trade and transit for its North East (NE) region and have an integrated move towards socio - economic developments.

(d) To implement a bilateral approach to resolve all issues between the two countries.

These above mentioned four steps have substantially influenced India's policy towards Bangladesh. Unlike Pakistan, India always had the aspirations to become a regional super power through its own military and economic capacity. In this chase for supremacy, India has always considered Pakistan and China to be the major hindrances or impediment. India's clear fixation with these two countries has apparently reduced the significance of Bangladesh to her.

The foreign policy of Bangladesh, like that of any other democratic and secular state is a projection of the country's socio-economic and political commitments and restrictions in the international amphitheatre. Due to obvious reasons, India has always occupied the centre stage of Bangladesh's foreign policy. However many feel that India has displayed a lackadaisical attitude towards her. Unfortunately, Bangladesh has been perceived more as a safe haven for insurgents and illegal immigration.

Political and Sociological Faultlines

The polity of Bangladesh is marked by confrontation. There are two major and dominant political parties and their problem is that, these parties have not demonstrated any common move on how to deal with India on issues like water, transit, trade and NE insurgents. Each move is considered through a populist gauge and the perceived political mileage. One of them is over friendly to India, while the other one bears the extreme 'Anti-India' posture. Perhaps, India-Bangladesh relations have suffered cyclic phases of ups and downs, largely reflecting the shifting governments both in Dhaka and New Delhi. The public perception in Bangladesh is that, India, as a bigger country, should be giving more concessions to Bangladesh; since, it argues that it supported the war on humanitarian and political grounds.

Water Issues

One of the major irritant in the relationship has been the perennial debate over the 54 common rivers, running between Bangladesh and India. If one single issue that has degraded India in Bangladesh to the optimum, is Farakka. Because of Farakka,

Bangladesh has suffered and even India has not benefited out of it. Since the time Farakka issue had started becoming evident, anti-Indianism in Bangladeshi people became far more popular and to some extent, turned into an aspect of main stream politics and the relationship has turned into an extreme astringent one.

India undertook more projects on the common rivers; namely, river linking project, Tipaimukh Dam and Gazaldoba Barrage, etc. Bangladesh feels that both Gazaldoba and Tipaimukh, have been constructed or planned to deprive Bangladesh of an equitable share of water, which has been proved otherwise by India, scientifically. Bangladesh contests that anything, which amounts to denial of this right (of water) would be perceived by the Bangladeshis, as stabbing on their sovereignty and as an example of India's "hegemony," "high-handedness," "big brotherly attitude" and "a desire to dominate ". The sharing of the river waters, therefore, is a highly emotive issue for the policy makers, people and media in both the nations.

Security Related Issues

India's concern for security is axiomatic and recognizable. India's sympathies with democratic forces and its aversion to extra-regional presence are all geared to optimise its security interest, which is ensconced in its principal belief of a stable neighbourhood while engaging in a mutually beneficial relationship.

However, India on its own, can do very little to augment its security environment, and it requires the active cooperation and assistance of its neighbours. An increasing number of Bangladeshis have of late been getting involved in terror activities inside Indian territories. The issue of terrorist camps of Indian Insurgent Groups, inside Bangladesh had been one of the controversial issues between the two nations. To curb insurgency and ensure political stability, India has repeatedly sought Dhaka's assistance without which, it would be almost impossible for India to irradiate these radical groups.

The transformation of security scenario began, as the incumbent government led by Sheikh Hasina assumed power in Dhaka.

Bangladesh had taken decisive steps to limit the activities of militant organisations. Terrorist activities are being actively carried out by outfits based in both countries, like Banga Sena and Harkat-ul-Jihad-al-Islami. Bangladesh has apprehended and handed over some terrorists to Indian authorities. India is satisfied with Bangladesh's efforts as the United Liberation Front of Assam (ULFA) insurgency in Assam, has already begun to dissolve.

Bilateral Trade and Imbalances

Post independence India has grown many folds from a status of a struggling underdeveloped country to an economically recognised super power that has posted an impressive 8% average annual growth for over a decade. The economy of Bangladesh is also rising, however at a much slower rate of 6% to 8%. Although it will be correct to assume that Bangladesh is totally dependent on India due to its geostrategic location and other known reasons, it can also be assumed that India too has been benefiting economically due to its exports to Bangladesh. Therefore it is a complete matter of mutual dependence in the field of trade and economy. Issues like the Non-Tariff Barriers and Para-Tariff Barriers are seen by Bangladesh, as India's reluctance to open up its market and has lead to trade imbalances in favour of India.

Transit Facility to Indian States of NE

The geographical position of Bangladesh allows it to be a passage country, connecting the larger part of South Asia with the South-East Asia. Bangladesh has consistently denied India transit facility to the landlocked NE Regions of India. Although India has a narrow land link to this North Eastern region, which is famously known as "India's Chicken Neck" for better connectivity, India has always wanted transit facility from Bangladesh.

India's aspiration to develop insurgency-infested NE region, is inextricably linked to the issue of transit through Bangladesh. Bangladesh had agreed to accord transit facility to India through waterways, railways and roadways by signing Indo- Bangladesh Trade Agreement on 28 March 1972. However the Bangladeshi politicians have always been against providing transit to India on the pretext that they did not want Bangladesh to be unnecessarily dragged into a future Indo-China conflict. Therefore, despite economic benefits, providing connectivity to India, it remains a dubious issue; as it could have troublesome effect on Bangladesh's bilateral relationship with India or China in isolation.

Border Issues

India and Bangladesh share a land boundary of 4096.7 km, the fifth longest border in the world. This border is marked by porosity, complexities, spread over a varied terrain to include riverine, hilly and mountainous terrain; which has made guarding of this vast stretch of land, very tricky. The temperament of political relation between the two countries definitely has an influence on the borderland and vice versa.

The terrain and demographic composition of the bordering areas and lax governance make it convenient for populace of either side to slip into the other side. The wide-spread illegal migration from Bangladesh has reached such an astounding level, that it had begun to alter the demographic profile and threaten the socio-political fabric of the bordering. Recently a number of mass congregations and riots were witnessed in Assam to protest the deep seepage of the Bangladeshi migrants into the state. Thus, Indian prime concerns ie. illegal migration, cross border movement of Insurgent Groups and security of the state are entwined with the border. Killing of illegal migrants and trespassers (Bangladeshis or Indians) by BSF, rampant smuggling of arms and drugs, recurrent problem of cattle trade etc, are other border related problems which have negatively undermined the bilateral relation.

2001 BANGLADESHI-INDIAN BORDER SKIRMISH

The 2001 Bangladeshi-India border skirmish took place in the third week of April 2001 between companies of theBangladesh Rifles and the Indian Border Security Force on the poorly marked international border between the two countries.

Cause

The Partition of Bengal in 1947 left a poorly demarcated international border between India and Bangladesh (then-East

Pakistan). Ownership of several villages on both sides of the de facto border were disputed and claimed by both countries. The dispute over the demarcation of the Indo-Bangladeshi border worsened due to the existence of over 190 enclaves.

One of the disputed areas was a small sliver of land near the village of Pyrdiwah which the Indian Border Security Force (BSF) had occupied since the 1971 liberation of Bangladesh. The village was one of the Indian exclaves near the border of Bangladesh with the Indian state of Meghalaya. Bangladesh claimed that the village was within its territory.

Conflict

The April 16–19 fighting was the worst since the creation of Bangladesh in 1971. It took place around the village of Padua (known as Pyrdiwah in India), which adjoins the Indian state of Meghalaya and the Timbil area of the Bangladesh border in the Sylhet district. In that area, 6.5 kilometres of the border have remained in dispute for the past 30 years.

The trigger for the clash appears to have been an attempt by Indian forces to construct a footpath from an army outpost in Padua across a disputed territory some 300 metres wide to Indian Meghalaya. When the Indian Border Security Force refused to withdraw, the Bangladeshi border force attacked and retook Pyrdiwah village. As per the Bangladesh Rifles chief, the village had been illegally occupied by India since Bangladesh's war of independence in 1971.

A few days later, Indian border guards retaliated and tried to enter Boroibari, more than 100 km to the west of Padua/Pyrdiwah. Boroibari is another disputed area between India and Bangladesh. In a violent confrontation 16 Indian border guards died and 2 were injured. The attack also left 3 Bangladeshi border guards dead and 5 injured. About 10.000 civilians fled the area after some 24 were wounded in the shooting.

Result

Top Indian border security sources claimed that the BDR personnel had withdrawn from the occupied territories in the

Meghalaya sector, while in the Assam sector, the Indian BSF had vacated positions seized from Bangladesh. Fresh clashes erupted along the India–Bangladesh border just hours after both sides voiced regret for the recent killings, but by midnight of 20 April firing had again stopped.

An article reported that 6,000 Indian civilians had fled the region, and Indian government officials were attempting to convince villagers to return to their homes. Bangladesh later agreed to return 16 dead Indian soldiers the next day. Upon examining the bodies of the dead personnel, India alleged that the BSF men were tortured before being shot dead. On the other hand three Bangladeshi soldiers were also killed: two during combat and another who died of woundssustained during operations.

Aftermath

The Prime Ministers of Bangladesh and India, Sheikh Hasina and Atal Bihari Vajpayee, spoke over telephone and agreed to order a high-level investigation into the incident. Indian Foreign Ministry spokesman Raminder Jassal reported that both India and Bangladesh would improve diplomatic channels and promised to exercise restraint in the future. India and Bangladesh started talks in March 2002 to resolve their border disputes. By July 2001, the two sides established joint working groups to establish the un-demarcated sections of the border.

Officially, Bangladesh denied it had initiated hostilities. This was the first armed conflict between India and Bangladesh, two nations that had maintained friendly relations since Bangladeshi independence in 1971. The end of the brief conflict saw an upsurge of nationalism in Bangladesh. In parliamentary elections, the four-party right-wing alliance led by the Bangladesh Nationalist Party and Jamaat-e-Islami Bangladesh won a majority of 196 seats out of 300.

Both sides desisted from any further hostilities and began border talks to discuss disputes along their 4,000-kilometre (2,500 mi) border. Relations were cooled down shortly afterwards. India later began constructing a fence along the entire length of the international border with Bangladesh. India is still in the process of constructing the Indo-Bangladeshi barrier. Bangladesh protested that construction of the fence within 150 yards of the border was a gross violation of the Indo-Bangladeshi Treaty of Friendship, Cooperation and Peace. The Bangladesh government also protested frequent BSF incursions into Bangladesh, and shootings which resulted in the deaths of Bangladeshi citizens inside Bangladeshi territory. In a news conference in August 2008, it was stated that 97 people had been killed (69 Bangladeshis, 28 Indians, rest unidentified) trying to cross the border illegally during the prior six months.

POLITICS AND ORIGIN OF THE INDIA-BANGLADESH BORDER

The idea of protecting the Indo-Bangladesh border with a fence is not new. Regional politicians in Assam first proposed fencing the border in the 1960s in order to isolate the population of East Pakistan. During that period, the Government of Assam under Congress Chief Minister Bimala Prasad Chaliha launched a campaign to deport immigrants who had settled in Assam since January 1951.

He ignored Prime Minister Jawharlal Nehru's request to go slow on the issue. He along with his party also advocated clearing up an area in sufficient depth along the border to control Pakistani infiltration which was taken up by the government in Delhi at that time but not implemented. Assamese politicians were not able to convince the Central government on illegal migration from East Pakistan but they managed to sanction 180 additional police watch posts and erect a barbed wire fence in selected places on the Assam-East Pakistan border.

In the late 1970s and early 1980s there was a violent protest and anti-Bengali program in Assam, which led to the establishment of the Assam Accord. The mainstream Indian political leaders discuss the issue and place it on the national agenda in 1985. In 1986, the Indian government approved the Indo-Bangladesh Border Road and Fence project to prevent illegal (also called irregular) migration from Bangladesh. However, the progress of that project was very slow (Schendel, 2005).

The project was budgeted at Rs 3.7 billion in 1986· Progress on the fence construction on Bangladesh-Assam border was slow and irregular till 1998.

Apart from fencing the border, the All Assam Student Union (AASU) and the Asom Gana Parishad (AGP) demanded the enactment of the Illegal Migrants (Determination by Tribunal) Act (IMDT Act), which came into force in 1983. A number of criticisms were made of the Act with a demand for its amendment and abolition throughout late 80s and 90s by AASU, AGP and section of Assamese print media. In response to that the Supreme Court of India set aside the Act in a judgement in July 2005 and ordered the State Government of Assam to constitute a sufficient number of tribunals under the Foreigners Act to deal with illegal Bangladeshi migrants in Assam·

In December 2002, an estimation made by the Indian Ministry of Home Affairs (MHA) in 2004 claimed that Assam had a total of 26,490 foreigners staying illegally.

Earlier, the Bharatiya Janata Party (BJP)-led National Democratic Alliance (NDA) Government had claimed that there were 1.20 million illegal migrants living in Assam and around 20 million Bangladeshis living in other parts of India including big cities like Kolkata, Delhi and Mumbai. The number of Bangladeshis varies with each media or official report. The issue of Bangladesh migrants residing in India (apart from North-east) became a concern of the Indian media when it became a political agenda of the Hindu nationalist mainstream political party Bharatiya Janata Party (BJP) in the 1980s and 1990s. The next section will discuss the response of the Indian right wing political parties on the issue of Bangladeshi migrants in India.

MIGRANTS AS A SECURITY THREAT TO INDIA

Many Shiv Sena-BJP politicians claim that Bangladeshi migrants are a threat to Indian security. In 2001, the Supreme Court also expressed the concern that undocumented migrants from Bangladesh might pose a threat both to the economy and the security of the country· During the hearing of a Public Interest Petition filed by a lawyer O.P. Saxena representing the All India

Lawyers Forum for Civil Liberties (AILFCL), the bench of the Chief Justice and two other Justices of the Supreme Court said that the 'Bangladeshi migrants were eating into the economy of the country and had to a large extent become a security threat'. The bench also criticized the Union Government for being indifferent to resolve the issue and recommended that the government take exemplary steps to tackle the illegal migration, including deportation. In his petition, Saxena alleged that over one crore (10 million) Bangladeshi migrants had illegally crossed over to India and were causing a severe strain on the resources of West Bengal as well as poor North-eastern states. The case sought a direction from the Court to the union government to identify these Bangladeshis and deport them with the help of agencies such as National Human Rights Commission (NHRC)· Karlekar (2005) in *Bangladesh the Next Afghanistan* claimed that there had already been a security threat from Bangladesh in 1998 when it sheltered Anup Chetia, leader of outlawed United Liberation Front of Assam (ULFA). Media reports claimed that the outlawed ULFA had started several lucrative income-generating projects in Bangladesh to sustain its anti-India activities. These include three hotels, a private clinic and two motor driving schools in Dhaka, a number of groceries and drug stores in Sylhet, poultry farms in Mymensingh, and two schools in Narsingdi but this claim has not been substantiated by any other sources.

Karlekar (2005) also mentioned that Bangladesh poses a potential threat to India for its expanding Islamic militancy. He argued that the borders were particularly risky as most militant groups were based in the Indo-Bangladesh borderlands. The Indian NDA Government also viewed the past BNP-Jamaat coalition government as pro-Pakistan and anti-Indian (Wright, 2002). Karlekar among others has claimed that the geo-strategic location of Bangladesh makes the country an ideal base for Al Qaeda, Taliban and the ISI, allowing them to coordinate activities as far as Spain and Indonesia from there. In relation to that, so runs the claim, cross border migration has created many small pockets of illegal Bangladeshis in big cities like Delhi, Mumbai, Kolkata and adjacent border areas that can be used as bases to harbour terrorists to run militant activities in India and elsewhere.

Group of Ministers Report and Border Management Task Force

In 1999, India fought a military battle with Pakistan over the disputed Kashmir state from May to July known as the Kargil War. India was victorious in getting its Line of Control back from Pakistani invasion. After winning the war, a review committee known as The Kargil Review Committee (KRC) was formed to assess the country's overall security situation and capacity as well as enhance security measures at the national level.

The KRC Report found many deficiencies in India's security management system, particularly in the areas of intelligence, border management, and defence management. Prime Minister Vajpayee set up a Group of Ministers (GoM) cabinet to review the national security system in its entirety and consider the recommendations of the KRC report.

The members of the cabinet were LK Advani, Minister of Home Affairs, George Fernandes, Minister of Defence, Jaswant Singh, Minister of External Affairs and Yashwant Sinha, Minister of Finance. The GoM set up four task forces to assess the security situation and make further recommendations. The task forces were: 1)Task Force on Intelligence Apparatus 2) Task Force on Internal Security 3) Task Force on Border Management and 4)Task Force on Management of Defence

Dr Madhav Godbole, former Home Secretary during the demolition of Babri Mosque and the Mumbai riots in 1992-93, was appointed as the Chairperson of the Task Force on Border Management by the GoM· The report prepared by the Group of Ministers recommended the creation of a separate department for border management within the Ministry of Home Affairs under the overall charge of the Home Secretary.

The Group of Ministers Report in 2000 said that illegal cross-border migration had been occurring over five decades and estimated that there were 15 million Bangladeshis, 2.2 million Nepalese, 70,000 Sri Lankan Tamils and 100,000 Tibetan migrants currently in India (Ministry of Defence, 2000). It claimed that illegal migration was a grave threat to Indian security. However nothing regarding fencing the Indo-Bangladesh border was said. Some parts of the text were deleted intentionally from public view for security reasons; it is possible that fencing was part of it.

In January 2003, former Deputy Indian Prime Minister Lal Krishna Advani issued a national directive to all provinces to take 'immediate step to identify irregular Bangladeshis, locate them, and throw them out' (Ramachandran, 2005). A few weeks later, security forces on the Indo-Bangladesh border came dangerously close to a violent confrontation when the Indian Border Security Force (BSF) and its counterpart Bangladesh Rifles (BDR) attempted to 'push back' some 240 migrants across their respective territories (Ramachandran, 2005). During the year 2003, 18,801 Bangladeshis were deported by the Government of India and in the previous year, the number was 6,394 (Government of India, 2005).

The Indo-Bangladesh Border Fencing Project

The Government of India sanctioned the erection of fencing in two phases. The Indo-Bangladesh Border Works under Phase-I had been initiated in 1989. Fencing in 854.35 kilometres was erected and 2606.35 kilometres of road was completed as. Under Phase II, the government had approved additional fencing of 2429.5 kilometres and 797 kilometres road at an estimated cost of Rs 287.617 million (Government of India, 2006). This project was budgeted at Rs. 10.5 billion in 1998. It involved the construction of 900 km of border fence, 2800 km of border roads and 24 km of bridges along the India-Bangladesh border in the states of West Bengal, Assam, Meghalaya, Tripura and Mizoram (Schendel, 2005). The Assamese government and media were not satisfied with the fence on the Assamese side. As a local newspaper had put it, 'crossing the fence border remained as easy as slicing butter with a knife'.

In 2001, the Director General of the Border Road Organization calculated that 1 km of border fence cost Rs. 2.2 million and 1 km of border road Rs 4.5 million. A high BSF official admitted that 80 percent of the 4000 km border was unfenced, while the Indian External Affairs Minister claimed in a statement to Parliament that the border would completely be fenced in 2006-07. In 2001, BSF and BDR exchanged gunfire leading to the killing of BSF personnel which obviously had a negative impact on India-Bangladesh relations· Former Prime Minister of Bangladesh Sheikh Hasina resolved the dispute jointly with Indian Prime Minister Vajpayee· Work on erecting barbed wire fences along the Indo-Bangladesh border was again resumed by the NDA government headed by Vajpayee in 2002 (Karlekar, 2005).

The Indian government tripled its budget for border security in 2003. The work had been in actual progress from early 2004, when tenders were called and closed. Various public sector institutions of India undertook activities to fence different parts of the border, such as Indian Railways Construction Corporation (NBCC), Borders Road Organization (BRO), the Central Public Works Department (CPWD), and the state Public Works Departments in Assam, Tripura, Meghalaya and West Bengal.

In May 2004, the Central government of India changed and BJP-led National Democratic Alliance handed over power to the United Progressive Alliance (UPA) led by the Indian National Congress. After the newly formed government assumed power and formed their coalition government in 2004, the construction of fence was put on hold for review in June (Karlekar, 2005). According to Karlekar (2005), one of the main reasons was the strong opposition of the Bangladesh government that argued that the fence violated the India-Bangladesh Agreement in 1974 which prohibited the construction of any defence structure within 150 yard of the border and the fence was a defensive structure.

National level talks were held between the Home Secretaries of Bangladesh and India in Dhaka in September 2004 to cover security issues, implementation of the 1974 Land Boundary Agreement, cooperation in combating the problems of drugs and narcotics, border patrolling be security forces, cross border movements, visa regime and extradition treaty and agreements on mutual legal assistance in criminal matters (Government of India, 2005). Construction resumed after a meeting on 14 October 2004 in Delhi where the Cabinet Committee on Security decided to continue fencing the border. The UPA government allocated funds for border fencing, road and maintenance as well as for boats and aircraft for the BSF. India's seriousness about the fence was demonstrated by the fact that they spent Rs 2404.7 million for fencing the Bangladesh border during 2004-5. This was stated in the Indian Lok Sabha by the State Minister for Home Affairs Mr S. Raghupathy.

According to the Annual Report 2005-2006 of Indian Ministry of Home Affairs, fencing was necessary in order to prevent illegal infiltration and other anti-national activities from across the border. By the year 2004-2005, 1502 kilometers had been fenced. Similarly, work was completed on 2670 kilometers out of 3663 kilometers of roads to be constructed (Government of India, 2006). To date, a total of 2535.80 kilometres fencing has been completed in Phase I and II out of 4096.7 km long Indo-Bangladesh border. For border roads 3250.60 kilometres has been completed in Phase I and II (Government of India, 2007-08).

In 2007, India decided to replace the entire 861 km. of fence constructed under Phase-I in West Bengal, Assam and Meghalaya, as most of this fence have been damaged by adverse climatic conditions and repeated submergence. The replacement work has already commenced in the States of Assam and West Bengal. 193.70 km. of fencing has been replaced so far.

Illegal Migration and the Census of India 2001

According to the Census 2001 report released in 2005, the number of Bangladeshi migrants during the decade 1991-2001 was about 280,000, which was a decrease of 53% from almost 600,000 migrants between 1981 and 1991. In the 2001 Census, about 5.1 million persons were reported as migrant by last residence from across the international border from India's neighbour countries mainly Pakistan, Afghanistan, Sri Lanka, Nepal, Bhutan and Bangladesh.

About 97% of these migrants by last residence were from eight neighbouring countries including Afghanistan. Of these migrants, 3 million were from Bangladesh, 0.9 million from Pakistan, 0.5 million from Nepal and 0.1 million from Sri Lanka. About 65.2% of these migrants from neighbouring countries had migrated to India at least 20 years ago perhaps many of them during the time of partition and later during the Bangladesh liberation war in 1971.

The total number of migrants by last residence from neighbouring countries by duration of residence is 3.08 million from Bangladesh -all residents living in India for more than 20 years. The '20 years or above' category indicates migration at the time of the 1949 partition or the formation of Bangladesh in 1971. Yet the report also revealed the number of migrants who came from Bangladesh during the decade 1991-2001. In case of Bangladesh as the last place of residence, the total number of migrants with duration from 0 to 9 years is 279,878 in 2001and 591,572 in 1991. Another notable figure in the report was the flow of migrants from another neighbouring country Nepal-175,195 in 1991 and 261,451 in the 2001 census which is close to the total number of Bangladeshi migrants.

The decadal variation during 1991 –2001 has been negative - a reduction of 52.7% for Bangladesh and an increase for Nepal by 49.2%. It can be assumed that most of the migrants coming from Nepal were Hindu. According to the census 2001 in Nepal, 80.6% of the population is Hindu, 10.7% is Buddhist, 4.2% of the population is Muslim and 3.6% of the population follows the indigenous Kirant Mundum religion. Christianity is practiced by less than 0.5% of the population. It is very significant that the Shiv Sena-BJP government never complained about the migrants from Nepal, though statistics indicate the number of migrants was larger. They kept quiet on illegal Nepalese migrants as far as the literature and media are concerned. It can be interpreted that they did not take Hindu illegal migrants from Nepal as an economic or security threat to India. Another interesting feature of their campaign on detection and deportation of illegal Bangladeshi migrants is that, BJP appeared to be sympathetic towards Hindu migrants from Bangladesh. So this was not about jobs or security ;it is really an anti-Muslim campaign.

8

Bhutan-China Border Partition

Bhutan's 1,075-kilometer border are adhered to China and the rest 605 to India. Bhutan was once the bridge between Tibet and the east part of South Asia, and shares intimate religious, political, economic, and cultural bonds with Tibet. The Tibetan people cross the Himalayas along the Manas Chhu in east Bhutan and Paro Valley in west Bhutan to Assam, Bangladesh, and Bihar for religious, cultural, and trade activities. The twice-per-year bazaar fair in Bumthang, east Bhutan is a huge attraction for many Tibetan people. The Tibetan caravans offer wool, brick tea, edible salt, and musk in exchange for Bhutan's rice, paper, and dried pepper. Local governments of Tibet deploy officials in areas near Bhutan to purchase rice. It has been a ritual for Tibetans to travel a long distance along the Manas Chhu to embark on pilgrimage at monasteries near Guwahati, Assam. The influx of Tibetan refuges forced Bhutan to close its border with China in 1959, shutting down all cross-border trade activities. No formal trade or commercial relations has been established between Bhutan and China since then.

As a large part of Bhutan-China border is unclear, the focus on China-Bhutan relationship is to resolve border dispute. Border issues between Bhutan and China used to be incorporated into China-India border discussions. In 1959, then PRC Premier Zhou Enlai issued a letter to India Prime Minister Jawaharlal Nehru expressing China's wish to stage direct bilateral talk with Bhutan. The letter suggests Zhou's intention to separate China-Bhutan border issue from China-India border negotiations. Yet direct border negotiations between China and Bhutan did not begin until 1984. Since then, the capital cities of Beijing and Thimphu have been taking turns hosting the annual border negotiations. By 2004, 17 rounds of talk had been conducted, with the 17th round being held in Bhutan.

Core issues in China-Bhutan border disputes are as follows:

In the 10th round of border talk held in 1996, China proposed to exchange 495 sq km area of Pasamlung and Jakarlung valleys in the northern borders of Bhutan for Sinchulumpa, Dramana and Shakhtoe with an area of 269 sq km in the northwest Bhutan, which share borders with Sikkim, India, but no final decision was taken.

The 12th round held in Beijing in December 1998 centered on establishment of diplomatic and trade relations and ended with the signing of the Agreement between PRC and Kingdom of Bhutan on Peace and Stability in China-Bhutan Border Areas. The five-article agreement demands mutual respect and equal status regardless of the territory and power of a nation. In the agreement, China states its complete respect for Bhutan's independent status, sovereignty, and territorial integrity. The first article provides basis for friendly and good neighbourly cooperation between the two under the five principles of peaceful coexistence. It is understood between the two that differences in border issues had been alleviated and guiding principles for border issue settlement had been established through friendly negotiations in the previous 11 rounds based on the spirit of mutual understanding, mutual trust, and cooperation. The talks have deepened mutual understanding and strengthened traditional friendship between the two, and China and Bhutan are willing to strive together toward the shared objective of settling border disputes in fair and reasonable ways as soon as possible under the principles above. China and Bhutan hereby agree to maintain the status quo of the border as prior to March 1959 and ensure peace and stability of border region before a final solution is reached, and oppose unilateral efforts by either side to change the status quo. As for the progress in the last 11 rounds of border talk, as both sides have made clear their stance, both hereby agree to resolve the issue through friendly negotiations.

While both sides agreed on the need to maintain peace and stability in border region, no final decision was taken on territory exchange. The King of Bhutan once nodded his head on territory exchange in 1997. China again offered the above-mentioned 495 sq km area in the northern border of Bhutan in exchange for the 269 sq km in the northwest Bhutan. The talks came to a halt when the subject of territory exchange was raised. However, following the signing of agreement, Beijing immediately responded to the issues of mule routes and lumber exploration in Pasamlung, and assisted the Tibetan after they were harshly punished by Bhutanese border security troops in Pasamlung for entering Bhutan to collect Tibetan medical herbs. At that time, China was a little bit displeased with Bhutan's mentioning of new issues following years of border negotiations, and therefore agreed to let Bhutan's specialists determine the territory boundary and draw the map of both countries' territories, and also agreed to the use of standard names for areas under dispute to avoid confusion. The King of Bhutan once told the National Assembly that there are 4 areas under dispute, starting from Doklam in the west, along Gamochen at the border, to the river divide at Batangla and Sinchela, and down to the Amo Chhu River.

(1) Up to 89 sq km in Doklam are under dispute.

(2) Approximately 180 sq km in Sinchulumpa and Gieu are under dispute. The border line stretches from Langmarpo Zam along the river up to Docherimchang, through the river divide to Gomla, along the river divide to Pangkala, and finally down to the Dramana River.

(3) Starting from Dramana, along the border line up to Zingula, and along the line of river divide down to Gieu Chhu River, and finally to Lungkala

(4) Starting from the middle of Pasamlum, along the border line and the river divide to Dompala and Neula, going from Neula along the border line and the river divide to Kurichhu Tshozam, along the river divide to Genla then to Mela, and go all the way to the east.

By 1999 China and Bhutan had yet to resolve their border disputes. China sent delegation to Bhutan to carry on with border talks and managed to settle most of the major border disputes. The talks ended satisfactorily for both sides and China, for the first time, expressed their wish to provide financial assistance to Bhutan.

The 14th round of negotiation held in December 2000 saw Bhutan extending their border line further on the one provided by the China government. Bhutan also suggested that technical discussions between experts from both sides be held using maps. In July of the following year (2001), the King of Bhutan said to the National Assembly that border between Bhutan and China should stretch further along Doklam, Sinchulumpa and Dramana. The King also expressed faith that the border dispute between a small nation of Bhutan and a powerful, friendly nation of China would come to a successful settlement in the near future.

Several official interactions between China and Bhutan took place in 2001. The Bhutanese cultural delegation visited China in April, in July the Bhutanese delegation visited Beijing to conduct border talks, and in November the 15th round of border talk was held in Thimphu, capital of Bhutan. However, no final decision was reached with regard to the 3 places (Doklam, Sinchulumpa and Dramana) in question.

In July 2002, the Bhutanese Minister of Foreign Affairs revealed to the National Assembly that China had claimed to be in possession of the license of ownership of the 3 places. Bhutan asked China to extend the generosity of a superpower to a small country like Bhutan, but China replied that it cannot afford to be generous to every single neighbor considering that it has 25 other neighbours. Both sides agreed in the 16th round held in Beijing in October of the same year to create a mechanism in which the border would be examined by map experts from both sides.

No border talk was held in 2003. The 17th round, held in Thimphu in April 2004, saw both sides agreeing to assemble a team of specialists as soon as possible to examine the border. Both sides expressed wish to determine the border as soon as possible and decided to assemble a team of experts to examine the border as proposed by each.

Mutual visits continued, though not on a regular basis. During his visit to Bhutan in April 2003, Hua Junduo, PRC Ambassador to India, reiterated China's friendly, good neighbourly stance toward Bhutan. While there is no formal diplomatic ties between Bhutan and China, said Hua, the relationship is developing in a positive way, and actual relationship is more important than formal diplomatic ties.

Of all countries in Asia and China's neighbouring countries, Bhutan is the only one that has yet to establish formal diplomatic ties with China, preferring to keep a cautious distance from this powerful neighbor. The lack of formal ties has never affected Bhutan's support for China on the international scene. Examples of support include casting a vote in 1971 to keep China's place in the United Nations, inviting the PRC Ambassador to India to the coronation ceremony of King Wangchuck in 1974, speaking repeatedly in favour of China in the United Nations Human Rights Council meetings since 1995, and speaking against Taiwan's bid to host the 2002 Asian Games and the bid to join United Nations. Since 1979, leaders of both sides have been exchanging congratulatory messages on each side's National Day. In the 17th round of border talk held in 2004, King Wangchuck, during his meeting with head of Chinese delegation Wang Yi, reiterated Bhutan's friendly stance toward China, complimented China on its successful reform and opening up, and thanked China for its friendly and good neighbourly stance toward Bhutan. The King also pledged Bhutan's support for China in issues related to China's sovereignty such as Taiwan, human rights, and Tibet.

BHUTAN-CHINA RELATION : THE CHINESE FACTOR

While the Chinese State news agency Xinhua and others said that "a historic moment" at the sidelines of the United Nations Rio+20 Conference on Sustainable Development in Brazil was the first ever meeting between prime ministers of Bhutan and China, where expressions to establish diplomatic ties were discussed, the Bhutanese PM's media cell has said the Chinese local media has misreported that Bhutan and China will forge formal diplomatic ties.

Instead, PM Jigmi Y Thinley and officials from the Ministry of Foreign Affairs have been taking this opportunity on the sidelines of the meeting to meet people to campaign for the UN Security Council's seat.

Back at home, some quarters of the Bhutanese intelligentsia Bhutan TODAY spoke to have their own say. "That the news was splashed by China's State news agency is an embodiment of the fact that China wants to have diplomatic relations with Bhutan," an observer seeking anonymity said. According to him, if China engages with Bhutan it is in regards to its borders. "Given that Bhutan shares a long border with China, its interest in Bhutan might be 'strategic,'" he said.

Meanwhile, the Gangzur – Minjay member of the National Assembly (NA) Karma Rangdol and head of the Druk Phuensum Tshogpa's Foreign Relations Committee is for a relation with China in the "near future" but "not immediately". "We have to think about the relationship at a later stage but I am for it in the near future", he said, adding that relations should be built cautiously. However, Karma Rangdol said the decision depends on the next government as the present one's term is about to end. Underlining that Bhutan has diplomatic relations with over forty countries, he said relations with China could benefit Bhutan economically. "Because of geopolitical situation we can gain a lot," he said.

The Dewathang-Gomdar National Assembly member Ugyen Dorji says that establishment of diplomatic tie would facilitate settlement of the long standing border dispute between the two neighbours. "That's what Chinese are pressing for (diplomatic tie). They badly want us to establish diplomatic relations with them," he said, adding that he felt "positive" when the news first came. The two countries held the 19th round of border talks here in January 2010. Contrary to the "Indian angle," which people bring in whenever Bhutan-China relations are discussed, Ugyen Dorji said he does not think that a diplomatic tie with China will hurt the Indian government. He said the people and government of India are "broadminded as we are" and Bhutan would never hurt Indian sentiments. "The meeting of the two Premiers is nothing."

A political analyst said the dynamics of global politics has changed. "The relationship that India and China has evolved very positively in the last few years and the mutual respect and trust between India and Bhutan is unparalleled," he said. He added that along with time the "old order" should change. "As far as I know, New Delhi should be assured and Bhutan should move ahead." An observer said China would look for a formal tie with Bhutan if the former support the latter's bid for a seat in the Security Council. "If Bhutan wants to gain important seats in the United Nations, China's support would be important as China is empowered by veto right and its influence over other countries is strong," he said.

Trashiyangtsi MP Dupthob said the question is not about whether to build ties but about time. "It (to establish diplomatic tie) is inevitable as the three countries Bhutan, India and China have share common objectives," he said. As both the neighbours are strong, Bhutan will definitely benefit.

"After all, we have a long standing border issue with China, which even India would like to see resolved," he said. In an earlier interview with Bhutan TODAY, Indian Ambassador to Bhutan, Pavan K Varma said Bhutan's decision with regard to China is a matter of its sovereign will. "Bhutan, as sovereign country can take its own decision with regard to diplomatic relationship with any country including China," he had said. Meanwhile, the officiating foreign minister, Khandu Wangchuk also did not comment if Bhutan has plans to establish diplomatic ties with the second largest economy in the world. Lyonpo Khandu Wangchuk, who has also served as foreign minister in the past said: "We want good relations with all the countries".

Bhutan's foreign policy states that the government strives to promote goodwill and cooperation with nations, foster respect for international law and treaty obligations, and encourage settlement of international disputes by peaceful means in order to promote international peace and security. A 1949 treaty which gave India a say in Thimphu's foreign policy was revised in 2007.

CHINA AND BHUTAN: HISTORICAL & CONTEMPORARY CONTEXTS

China's embrace of its external periphery states was historically influenced by what is now construed as the Chinese notion of international system, that is, the tributary system (Zhang and Buzan 2012: 3). The Tibetan plateau probably with the exception of its Tang dynasty (618-907 AD) when Tibetan King Songtsen Gampo unified Tibet and forced the Chinese Emperor Taizong to enter into a marriage alliance gave birth only to what could be termed limited states. Whatever influence China ever had over Tibet or Tibet had over Bhutan and Nepal had an important logistical determinant. The communication and connectivity concerns required that even if Tibet was some form of a tributary state, the Chinese required Tibetans to be in charge of most of their affairs including even foreign affairs, occasionally letting them get away with near independence level of autonomy.

Only during the Qing Empire, China tried exerting relatively direct authority over Tibet. With Bhutan, the direct contact though was established in the 1720s, but it remained only informal (Library of Congress 1991) probably for two reasons: to secure their interests from the British and satisfy their urge of what B. R. Deepak calls "Manchu expansionism." A Centre for Bhutan Studies report (2004) captures this entire episode till its culmination in following words:

China was involved in Tibetan affairs since the time that Chinese Ambans (residents) were stationed in Lhasa in the 1720s under the Ching dynasty...The Bhutanese delegation to the Dalai Lama came into contact with the Chinese representatives in Lhasa although there was no evidence of any tributary relation with Beijing whatsoever. Relations with Tibet itself, was never better but it was severely strained after Bhutan supported the British during the 1904 Younghusband Expedition. The only contact with China was the occasional, informal meeting of a Bhutanese representative in Lhasa with the Chinese officials. Unlike Nepal, Bhutan never sent tributary missions to China... China made several efforts to exercise what it called 'historic' rights over Bhutan between 1865 when the Treaty of Sinchula was signed, and the signing of the Treaty of Punakha in 1910-a direct outcome of the claim the Manchu Government of China made on Nepal, Sikkim and Bhutan after its invasion of Tibet in 1910-12. China continued to make feudatory claim on Bhutan even after the 1910 Treaty of Punakha. It made a vague suzerainty claim over Bhutan during years just before the Chinese Revolution of 1911 to secure its southeastern border against increasing foreign aggression. The new Republic of China slowly let the claim die down, only for it to resurface later time and again.

Bhutan recognised China as a significant threat for the first time after the joint Chinese/Tibetan invasion of Nepal in 1792-1793 (Dutt 1981: 58-62). Since the Opium Wars until 1951 when Tibet finally went under the physical control of China after armed intervention by the People's Liberation Army (PLA), Bhutan and even Tibet had little to worry about China, as the British were the most powerful constant in the entire zone and China was being ravaged by wars both civil and foreign. China's tone changed from claim over Bhutan as the Manchu government did in 1910 to accepting Bhutan as a sovereign state after the 1960s. Nonetheless, the geostrategic balance that had prevailed in this region for decades stood altered forever after the British left.

Whatever the Chinese political claims to Bhutan are, it owes them to the largely cultural-religious Tibetan influence there for centuries. Indeed, the Tibetan claims had political and even military overtones as reflected in 8th century invasion of Tibet over Bhutan and subsequent strives that followed. However, the conflict was always of a regional texture preceded and followed by the arrival of another set of Tibetan lamas who preached Buddhism even as they started settling themselves and encouraging fellow Tibetans to follow them mainly in the Southern Valleys of Bhutan. In any case, even when there were clashes, it presented no existential threat to Bhutanese culture and way of life and the ground polity. Certainly, these wars served no grand geopolitical big game that spread far beyond the Bhutanese soils.

The Indian engagement in Bhutan was limited to religion and culture till the British developed interest in Tibet and then in Bhutan around mid-eighteenth century. Historically, Bhutan's political and economic interaction was with Tibet and Sikkim alone. The shift towards India began with the British engagement in Bhutan.

Bhutan completely alienated from its new northern neighbour China when the Dalai Lama escaped to India and the Tibetan revolt was ruthlessly suppressed in 1959. The fact that the most "dominant political and cultural element" in Bhutanese population comprises of the numerically prominent Ngalop – the people of Tibetan origin who migrated around the ninth century and introduced Tibetan culture and Buddhism to Bhutan – made them only more likely to realise the Tibetan crisis (Library of Congress 1991). Repeated claims regarding Bhutan by the communist government in China and Chinese leaders further pushed the Bhutanese government into a long period of self-imposed isolation from China even as the People's Republic officially denied any intention to subdue Bhutanese sovereignty.

After her independence, Chinese state laid its claim over Bhutan in 1954 itself by publishing a map in "A Brief History of China" thus beginning a long period of border conflict. The map depicted "a considerable portion of Bhutan...as a pre-historical realm of China." Four years later, in 1958, China not only published another map claiming large tracts of Bhutanese land but also occupied about 300 square miles of Bhutanese territory. An anxious Bhutan took resort to the less than a decade old British legacy India-Bhutan Treaty of 1949 Article 2 of which stipulated that : "On its part the Government of Bhutan agrees to be guided by the advice of the Government of India in regard to its external relations."

1960 marked another provocative declaration from a Chinese leader which gave Bhutan every reason to be cautious about Chinese intentions (Centre for Bhutan Studies 2004: 75): "Bhutanese, Sikkimese and Ladakhis form a united family in Tibet. They have always been subject to Tibet and to the great motherland of China. They must once again be united and taught the communist doctrine." The only silver lining in those initial years for Bhutan was that the Chinese did not attack

CHINA'S STRATEGIES TOWARDS BHUTAN AND THE COMPLEXITIES INVOLVED

The Chinese aims and objectives in Bhutan over last five decades point out towards a host of conflicting yet complementing interests that envelop issues pertaining to Tibet, India, and South Asia. More specifically, Bhutan could hold the key to China's legitimacy claims regarding Tibet and act as the last milestone in discrediting and demoralising India in its own backyard. Indeed China's continued motivation in engaging Bhutan relates to the strategic benefits its geography can deliver. However, China's Bhutan policy is certainly of a more comprehensive and subtle nature as Beijing is least inclined to align or link either its Tibetan concerns or its urgency to improve ties with India to factors which can be relied less upon or simply ignored. Thus the Chinese engagement with Bhutan seeks engaging Bhutan, getting its objectives fulfilled but without giving much due to Bhutan as it achieves them by enhancing cooperation where its own strength lies. Therefore, China looks for more of economic and tourism cooperation, hydroelectricity and infrastructure related cooperation and resource exploitation – areas where it has a decisive edge. Beijing probably believes that with the rise in economic and related interaction involving financial stakes, other benefits will simply accrue. China might not be wrong in having these expectations as obvious from the case of Nepal in particular. When stakes are high, Beijing has shown no hesitation in mounting military pressure along the border. That puts severe restrictions on buffer states like Bhutan whose greatest foreign policy success lies in not being taken as either granted or completely unreliable by India or China.

China's strategy towards Bhutan can be divided into the following three major aspects: border, economy and geopolitics.

Border: Military Intimidation, Diplomatic Seduction, Border Talks and Incursions, and Siliguri Corridor

Military intimidation followed by diplomatic seduction has formed an important part of China's policy towards Bhutan. After the closing of the border, trade and all diplomatic contacts in 1960, China resorted to significant military posturing against Bhutan at least twice – in 1966 and in 1979 along the border which remains the prime reason of dispute. In 1966, on the tri-junction of Bhutan, Chumbi Valley and Sikkim, the Tibetan grazers accompanied by Chinese troops entered Doklam pastures. China later "formally extended claim to about 300 sq. miles of northeastern Bhutan and also substantial areas north of Punakha, the former capital of Bhutan." When Bhutan requested New Delhi to raise this matter with Beijing, China rejected talking to India saying that the issues concerned China and Bhutan alone and "the Indian government has no right whatsoever to intervene in it." China followed up this incident by voting in favour of Bhutan's membership at the United Nations (UN) in 1971 which implied its recognition of Bhutan. However, Bhutan's strong support to India in the UN over Bangladesh issue the same year irked China dissuading them from building further momentum.

The coronation of the new King of Bhutan in 1974 where China sent a high-level delegation and Bhutan's vote in the UN in 1977 favouring the Chinese position against India's on who should represent Cambodia marked opening up of other vistas of cooperation.

For Bhutan, the Janata government in New Delhi made the task easier as its policy of "beneficial bilateralism" signaled normalisation of India-China relations. China wanted the border talks to begin but with Bhutan still unprepared, it ensured large-scale intrusions in 1979.

The negotiations finally began in 1984. In 1998, they agreed on Four Guiding Principles for further talks which included maintaining peace along the border, something China often violated to create pressure. After nineteen rounds of talks by January 2010, the two sides are said to have nearly finalised boundary demarcation (Bhutan Research 2012) and almost prepared to establish diplomatic ties with China. China also offered a sweet package deal to Bhutan that Bhutan has been reluctant to conclude. Medha Bisht (2010) wrote about the complexities involved in such a deal:

The protracted nature of Sino-Bhutan boundary talks and the continuous Chinese intrusions into Bhutanese territory reveals the strategic element embedded in the package deal. In November 2007, Chinese forces dismantled several unmanned posts near the Chumbi valley. This, analysts put it, has 'distorted the Sino-Bhutanese border near Sikkim,' with Chinese forces only a few kilometers away from the Siliguri corridor. Chumbi Valley, a vital tri-junction between Bhutan, India and China border, is significant as it is 500 km from Siliguri corridor—the chicken neck which connects India to North East India and Nepal to Bhutan. Meanwhile Chumbi Valley is of geostrategic importance to China because of its shared borders with Tibet and Sikkim. The North-Western areas of Bhutan which China wants in exchange for the Central areas lie next to the Chumbi Valley tri-junction.

Economy: Inclusion of Tibet, Historic-Contemporary Trade, Rail Connectivity and Long Term Economic Considerations

China and Bhutan trade totaled a pathetic USD 1 million in 2002. The situation has not changed much since. This could entail that for China, Bhutan is economically irrelevant. However, even with a small economy, Bhutan would be crucial to Tibet and Tibetans.

Bhutan would also be beneficial for China's "'Western development strategy', that could allow Tibet to regain a central position in the Himalayan region." It will also serve the 2000 Communist Party of China resolution which called for "Prosperous Borders; Wealthy Minorities program." Certainly, it would provide China with more leverage in Bhutan.

Today more than three fourth of Bhutan's trade is with India unlike till the 1960s when Bhutan had a flourishing trade with Tibet. The closing of Bhutan's Tibet trade and diversification of modern trade into new areas of commerce like tourism, industry and technology – areas where Bhutan lagged behind – has made Bhutan today an economically backward country. This is in complete contrast to the period even during the British domination when Bhutan served as a major trade point.

Sarkar and Ray (2005: 56) wrote: "According to an eighteenth century document, her (Bhutan's) annual trade was worth of Rs 200 thousand with Bengal and Rs 150 thousand with Tibet, including China." Françoise Pommaret (1999: 385-386) also writes that: "Bhutan carried out a substantial trade with her southern neighbours – Bengal (Cooch Bihar) and Assam (Kamrup) – at least from the 17th century, if not earlier."

Sarkar and Ray point out in the same article that Bhutan and Lhasa – the prime centres of trade and commerce in the Himalayan belt for centuries – were linked by four alternative routes facilitating round the year trade even in case of a political turmoil. They originated from Paro, Punakha, Bumthang and Trashigang in Bhutan to Lhasa in Tibet. Bhutan offered one of the shortest routes to Tibetan trade with Bengal (Trashigang) and Assam (Paro). This provides more reason for China to believe that Bhutan could again emerge as an economic hotspot in this region.

China's oft declared intentions to deepen economic cooperation with India's Northeast, Bangladesh and Bhutan point towards reviving above prospects and create many more. The mega rail projects that China is building up with significant investment along its entire Himalayan borders with India includes Yadong near the mouth of the Chumbi valley and Nyingchi near Arunachal Pradesh (Krishnan, 18 January 2012).

These rail routes have been planned to enhance connectivity of Tibet and link its markets with the Himalayan fringe-lands like Bhutan. Of course, it has military dimensions as well which has compelled India to improve connectivity of these neglected lands and listen to its smaller neighbours. Even bigger opportunities could be created via Bhutan when the proposed Silk Rail Route's southern corridor from Europe to Southeast Asia, via Turkey, Iran, Pakistan, India, Burma and Thailand reaches this region (Binyon 2013).

However, concerns remain. Mathou writes that Gangtok is a better location than Thimphu or Paro to become a trans-Himalayan trade hub. Binyon also underlines the implausibility of the re-emergence of the old Bhutan-Tibet trade pattern as a whole new Bhutanese trade pattern has emerged with India as a supplier and a market since 1960.

However, even with economic issues having the potential to remain the priority in the long run, Bhutan is too strategically positioned to be considered an economic priority alone. Economic ties are actually a real and probably genuine nevertheless shrewd pretext to keep Bhutan hooked up to the Chinese Caravan. A hub or not, China stands to benefit both economically and politically from engaging Thimpu.

Geopolitics: Chinese Foreign Policy, Dalai Lama .and Bhutan and India in South Asia

Concerning the Tibetan issue, the focus on Bhutan appears to be even more fundamental. Though Chinese policies inside Tibet have displayed little concern for Tibetan aspirations, it is entirely possible that by having Bhutan in good faith – a country that shares ethnic, religious, cultural and historic ties with Tibet – Beijing plans to assuage Tibetans' ill will against China. That Bhutan never invited the current Dalai Lama nor was his Gelugpa sect ever allowed to build any monastic institutions due to hierarchical feelings which subordinated Bhutan's Drukpa sect in Tibet only suits communist ideology to an extent.

Nevertheless, the most important geopolitical consideration for China in keeping Bhutan tagged remains India. The approach of Beijing over last five decades has been to minimise the role and importance of India in Bhutan. By consistently refusing to accept any Indian advocacy for Bhutan coupled with the "pressure tactics of border incursions," the Chinese have brought Bhutan to the negotiation table even though they been unsuccessful in making deep inroads in Bhutan.

China realises its limited leverage in Bhutan given critical Indian centrality in Bhutanese affairs and South Asia as well due to sheer geographic advantage that India enjoys. All that China wants from Bhutan is for it to follow an 'independent' policy which essentially means that Bhutan do away with its traditional policy tilt towards India. China blames India of dominating Bhutan unfairly in the name of 'hegemony' – calling it the Indian version of Monroe Doctrine. Thus, Beijing wants Bhutan to confer on Beijing a diplomatic status equal to that of New Delhi and accept a Chinese Ambassador (Ibid).

China's pragmatic foreign policy in contemporary times with the smaller South Asian countries – for example the studied non-interfering role it played when the Sri Lankan Tamil crisis required an Indian Peace Keeping Force – indicates that China fully takes into account the existing geographical and economic limitations of Bhutan. China realises the extent to which Bhutan can go against

India, and definitely does not expect a lean to China's side. However, it aims at neutralising Bhutan in the wake of any political or military conflict with India and use it as a base to further trade and commerce in Tibet and rest of South Asia. On a hopeful note, it might expect Bhutan to look up to China as an effective and reliable counterbalance to contain the inevitable Indian domination, something like Nepal. Bhutan has asserted its acceptance of China's core foreign policy concern i.e. One China Policy (Firstpost.com, 14 August 2012). Bhutan's transition from monarchy to parliamentary democracy saw the revision of the 1949 treaty with India in 2007 to one on a "more equal footing with both sides agreeing to 'cooperate closely with each other on issues relating to their national interests (Jacob 2012)'." The next in line could be Indian military presence there. As recent developments suggest, it could be a matter of time that Bhutan moves to balance its tilt towards India. In a world under growing Chinese domination and reducing geographical barriers, one can always expect an upward revision of Chinese strategies and objectives.

THE BORDER BETWEEN CHINA AND TIBET

China took advantage of this period of instability in Tibet to seize the regions of Amdo and Kham, making them into the Chinese province of Qinghai in 1724. Three years later, the Chinese and Tibetans signed a treaty that laid out the boundary line between the two nations. It would remain in force until 1910. Qing China had its hands full trying to control Tibet. The Emperor sent a commissioner to Lhasa, but he was killed in 1750. The Imperial Army then defeated the rebels, but the Emperor recognized that he would have to rule through the Dalai Lama rather than directly. Day-to-day decisions would be made on the local level.

Era of Turmoil Begins

In 1788, the Regent of Nepal sent Gurkha forces to invade Tibet. The Qing Emperor responded in strength, and the Nepalese retreated. The Gurkhas returned three years later, plundering and destroying some famous Tibetan monasteries. The Chinese sent a force of 17,000 which, along with Tibetan troops, drove the Gurkhas out of Tibet and south to within 20 miles of Kathmandu.

Despite this sort of assistance from the Chinese Empire, the people of Tibet chafed under increasingly meddlesome Qing rule. Between 1804, when the Eighth Dalai Lama died, and 1895, when the Thirteenth Dalai Lama assumed the throne, none of the incumbent incarnations of the Dalai Lama lived to see their nineteenth birthdays.

If the Chinese found a certain incarnation too hard to control, they would poison him. If the Tibetans thought an incarnation was controlled by the Chinese, then they would poison him themselves.

Tibet and the Great Game

Throughout this period, Russia and Britain were engaged in the "Great Game," a struggle for influence and control in Central Asia. Russia pushed south of its borders, seeking access to warm-water sea ports and a buffer zone between Russia proper and the advancing British.

The British pushed northward from India, trying to expand their empire and protect the Raj, the "Crown Jewel of the British Empire," from the expansionist Russians.

Tibet was an important playing piece in this game. Qing Chinese power waned throughout the eighteenth century, as evidenced by its defeat in the Opium Wars with Britain (1839-1842 and 1856-1860), as well as the Taiping Rebellion (1850-1864) and the Boxer Rebellion (1899-1901).

The actual relationship between China and Tibet had been unclear since the early days of the Qing Dynasty, and China's losses at home made the status of Tibet even more uncertain. The ambiguity of control over Tibet lead to problems. In 1893, the British in India concluded a trade and border treaty with Beijing concerning the boundary between Sikkim and Tibet.

However, the Tibetans flatly rejected the treaty terms. The British invaded Tibet in 1903 with 10,000 men, and took Lhasa the following year. Thereupon, they concluded another treaty with the Tibetans, as well as Chinese, Nepalese and Bhutanese representatives, which gave the British themselves some control over Tibet's affairs.

Thubten Gyatso's Balancing Act

The 13th Dalai Lama, Thubten Gyatso, fled the country in 1904 at the urging of his Russian disciple, Agvan Dorzhiev. He went first to Mongolia, then made his way to Beijing.

The Chinese declared that the Dalai Lama had been deposed as soon as he left Tibet, and claimed full sovereignty over not only Tibet but also Nepal and Bhutan. The Dalai Lama went to Beijing to discuss the situation with the Emperor Guangxu, but he flatly refused to kowtow to the Emperor.

Thubten Gyatso stayed in the Chinese capital from 1906 to 1908. He returned to Lhasa in 1909, disappointed by Chinese policies towards Tibet. China sent a force of 6,000 troops into Tibet, and the Dalai Lama fled to Darjeeling, India later that same year.

The Chinese Revolution swept away the Qing Dynasty in 1911, and the Tibetans promptly expelled all Chinese troops from Lhasa. The Dalai Lama returned home to Tibet in 1912.

Tibetan Independence

China's new revolutionary government issued a formal apology to the Dalai Lama for the Qing Dynasty's insults, and offered to reinstate him. Thubten Gyatso refused, stating that he had no interest in the Chinese offer. He then issued a proclamation that was distributed across Tibet, rejecting Chinese control and stating that "We are a small, religious, and independent nation." The Dalai Lama took control of Tibet's internal and external governance in 1913, negotiating directly with foreign powers, and reforming Tibet's judicial, penal, and educational systems.

The Simla Convention (1914)

Representatives of Great Britain, China, and Tibet met in 1914 to negotiate a treaty marking out the boundary lines between India and its northern neighbors. The Simla Convention granted China secular control over "Inner Tibet," (also known as Qinghai Province) while recognizing the autonomy of "Outer Tibet" under the Dalai Lama's rule. Both China and Britain promised to "respect the territorial integrity of [Tibet], and abstain from interference in the administration of Outer Tibet." China walked out of the conference without signing the treaty after Britain laid claim to the Tawang area of southern Tibet, which is now part of the Indian state of Arunachal Pradesh. Tibet and Britain both signed the treaty. As a result, China has never agreed to India's rights in northern Arunachal Pradesh (Tawang), and the two nations went to war over the area in 1962. The boundary dispute still has not been resolved.

China also claims sovereignty over all of Tibet, while the Tibetan government-in-exile points to the Chinese failure to sign the Simla Convention as proof that both Inner and Outer Tibet legally remain under the Dalai Lama's jurisdiction.

The Issue Rests

Soon, China would be too distracted to concern itself with the issue of Tibet. Japan had invaded Manchuria in 1910, and would advance south and east across large swaths of Chinese territory through 1945. The new government of the Republic of China would hold nominal power over the majority of Chinese territory for only four years before war broke out between numerous armed factions. Indeed, the span of Chinese history from 1916 to 1938 came to be called the "Warlord Era," as the different military factions sought to fill the power vacuum left by the collapse of the Qing Dynasty.

China would see near-continuous civil war up to the Communist victory in 1949, and this era of conflict was exacerbated by the Japanese Occupation and World War II. Under such circumstances, the Chinese showed little interest in Tibet. The 13th Dalai Lama ruled independent Tibet in peace until his death in 1933.

The 14th Dalai Lama

Following Thubten Gyatso's death, the new reincarnation of the Dalai Lama was born in Amdo in 1935. Tenzin Gyatso, the current Dalai Lama, was taken to Lhasa in 1937 to begin training for his duties as the leader of Tibet. He would remain there until 1959, when the Chinese forced him into exile in India.

BHUTAN'S ROAD TO DEMOCRACY LEADS TO CHINA?

There's a new anxiety in the top echelons of New Delhi about what's arguably India's only friendly neighbour, Bhutan. As the hill kingdom takes another baby step in its transition from monarchy to democracy with its second parliamentary election on July 13, there's realisation here that complacence has possibly allowed some disturbing developments there to go unnoticed. Friendship with Bhutan is often taken for granted by our foreign policy mandarins.

So, it was a rude shock when they learned last year from a Chinese press release that the new Bhutan PM, Jigme Thinley, has had a meeting with the then Chinese premier Wen Jiabao and the two countries were set to establish diplomatic ties. Given that Bhutan's foreign policy is, by and large, handled by New Delhi, such an important step without its knowledge created disquiet.

Although the PM's office in Thimphu sought to play it down, senior officers recalled that Thinley had said months after taking over as PM that he only saw growing opportunities in China and no threat. As part of Bhutan's outreach to China was the decision last year to procure 20 Chinese buses, typically the kind of purchase that would normally be booked with, say, Tata Motors. It raised eyebrows. It did not help that the person who got the contract for supplying the buses was reported to be a relative of Thinley. What's ironic is that in his poll campaign, Thinley is said to be impressing upon the electorate that he was the best upholder of Bhutan's ties with India, whereas he has possibly complicated them. Thinley's Bhutan Peace and Prosperity Party is again the main contender for power in this tiny, landlocked nation of 700,000 which saw transition to democracy from an over 100-year-old hereditary monarchy in 2008. Democracy in Bhutan was ushered in by Bhutan's benevolent fourth king Jigme Singye Wangchuck.

The last month saw the Bhutanese repose faith in the system with 55% of 380,000-strong electorate braving thunderstorms and landslides to exercise their franchise. As the world's largest democracy, India welcomed Bhutan's transition in 2008, but not everyone in South Block realised that the proposed model wasn't like India's Westminister model of parliamentary democracy. It's a diarchy in Bhutan with the monarch retaining certain overriding powers. Article 20.7 of Bhutan's Constitution says the cabinet shall be collectively responsible to the Druk Gyalpo (the king) and to Parliament".

The government must also enjoy the confidence of the king as well as parliament. Further Article 20.4 says "the PM shall keep the Druk Gyalpo informed from time to time about the affairs of the state, including international affairs, and shall submit such information and files as called for by the Druk Gyalpo". It now appears that the king wasn't quite in the loop as Bhutan expanded its diplomatic ties with 53 countries, as against 22 in 2008, as well as its overture to Beijing to enhance ties with China which has maximum significance for India. If he hasn't stepped in, it is to avoid any unintended signalling for the growth of democracy in Bhutan.

According to geostrategist Brahma Chellaney, the populist power of electoral politics has introduced a major new element in Bhutan with trans-boundary implications. "As a small, vulnerable country, Bhutan would like to have a good relationship with China. But since the time China gobbled up Tibet, Bhutan's spiritual homeland, Beijing has turned its attention to real estate in Bhutan, assertively laying claim to Bhutanese territory," says Chellaney. In foreign policy, any conflict between principles and national interest, the latter usually gets precedence. While celebrating the fledgling democracy in Bhutan, policy watchers wonder if New Delhi got blind-sighted to certain ominous signs.

BHUTAN AND CHINA, AND INDIA

India's strategic concerns about China arise from its emergence as the most influential player in Asia with the ability to shape the future balance of power that could be detrimental to Indian interests. Despite a dominant Indian desire at cooperation rather than competition with China, the vexed and unresolved boundary issue together with China's continued military modernization and incremental upgrade of its military posture in Tibet that enable rapid force deployment, backed by logistical capability and communication infrastructure complicates the relationship.

China's attempts at strategic balancing in South Asia by forging military and economic ties with all of India's neighbours, some of whom have fractious ties with New Delhi, and by expanding its naval power in the IOR further exacerbate bilateral tensions.

Bhutan, China, India and Nepal

Latest manifestation of this is the Chinese attempts to build in roads into Bhutan. The Chinese Premier Wen Zia Bao and Bhutanese Prime Minister Jigme Thinley's meeting on the side lines of Rio + 20 Summit was a result of Bhutan's ambition for a non permanent seat in the UNSC in 2013, which china appears to have exploited.

Implications of Chinese Moves

Chinese success in Bhutan together with moves in Nepal, where it is enhancing its economic, military and infrastructural footprints will have grave serious strategic implications for India. The landlocked Himalayan Kingdom of Bhutan has borders of some 470 km with Tibet and 650 km with India. India has a special relationship with the Bhutanese Kingdom having signed a Treaty of Friendship way back in 1949, which was updated in 2007, that provides among others unilateral guarantee for the defence of Bhutan.

Whereas China officially does not recognise Bhutan and has no diplomatic relations, however it does conduct periodic talks to reduce border tensions. China claims some 300 sq miles of Bhutanese territory mainly in the Chumbi valley, the Torsa Nala, and some areas opposite Haa (Western Bhutan). The Chinese also claim some grazing areas in the north.

Strategic scenario on India's Northern borders will get greatly compounded if Bhutan and neighbouring Nepal were to fall into the Chinese sphere of influence. Bhutan sit's at the centre of Sino Indian Eastern sector, as long as it remains neutral any Chinese military adventurism in the Chumbi valley and Tawang would largely be through attritional mountain offensives invoking Indian reaction in self defence. However, if Bhutan and Nepal were to come within the Chinese sphere of influence, the precarious land route along the the Siliguri corridor a virtual Chicken Neck of seven north eastern states would become vulnerable prone to being cut off by any determined Chinese push – isolating the entire eastern sector. It is for this reason Bhutan's neutrality is extremely important and absolutely imperative as it forms a barrier and buffer to Chinese desires of expansion to the South towards the Siliguri plains. Chinese designs in Bhutan plainly pose a threat in being to Indian security.

Two other issues are of importance. China is rapidly developing road infrastructure opposite the Chumbi Valley including plans to extend railway network from Lhasa to Zangmu, as well as Shigatse and possibly to Yadong at the opening of the Chumbi Valley. These developments point to Chinese attempts at upgradation of operational posture. What should be of concern to India is the fact that in the event of hostilities it is unlikely that China will respect Bhutanese neutrality. The defence of Bhutan therefore is irrevocably linked to the defence of India.

Strategic Perspective

It can thus be surmised that the Chumbi valley forms an essential ingredient of the China's forward policy. Chumbi Valley, a vital tri-junction between Bhutan, India and China, is significant as it is located mere five kilometres from the Siliguri corridor—the chicken neck which connects India to North East India and Nepal to Bhutan. At the same time, Chumbi Valley is of geostrategic importance to China because of its shared borders with Tibet and Sikkim.

It is this geo strategic context that has made New Delhi sit-up and take notice of recent Chinese overtures to Bhutan. China and Bhutan have held a range of boundary talks and both sides are moving towards a joint field survey, in order to harmonize the reference points and names of the disputed areas. The focus of the joint-field survey was supposed to be on the disputed areas in the western sector which constitute the pastoral lands of Doklam, Charithang, Sinchulumpa and Dramana.

This exclusive focus on the North-Western sector is important due to its close proximity to the Chumbi Valley. China realizes that to get requisite leverage against India, which it considers moving rapidly towards strengthening its military posture through structured modernization and communication infrastructure build up. For China, Bhutan and Nepal are critical cards against perceived Indian military maneuvering. It needs however to be underscored that the China- Bhutan reconciliation can only come with the settlement of the boundary issue where China seeks the Dhoklan plateau overlooking Chumbi Valley while making tradeoffs in the grazing grounds in North Bhutan. This complicates the China threat theory.

The moves in Bhutan together with rapid Chinese inroads into Nepal would greatly contribute towards China's desire to establish a continental bridge through Tibet. Bhutan on the other hand would provide PLA with the requisite launch pad to cut off the Siliguri Corridor either as pre emptive action or in concert with larger territorial designs. Trading off some territory in the North to Bhutan in lieu of the pastoral land of the Doklam plateau therefore appears to be a pragmatic step towards achieving larger strategic objective.

Nepal, Bangladesh, Myanmar and Sri Lanka are countries where India has ceded strategic space to China through acts of omission and commission land locking it from North and East. Restoration of diplomatic relations between China and Bhutan therefore would inevitably constitute a strategic shock for India.

India's Strategic Calculations

Strategically, Bhutan sits between Sikkim in the West and Arunachal Pradesh in the East. It's neutrality is an important construct in providing depth to the Chumbi Valley leading to Siliguri Corridor and Tawang – the centre of Tibetan spiritual abode in India. Should Bhutan diplomatically ally with China – these two vulnerabilities would be greatly exposed with all the attendant military ramifications. Access to Chumbi Valley through Bhutan, in addition to the traditional routes would severe and isolate North East in the event of a war with China. Simultaneously, Bhutan would open the Western flank of Tawang – Tenga sector exposing the threat to plains of Assam.

Indian economic investments in Bhutan are exemplified by Bhutan becoming a hydropower exporter to India. By 2020, India expects Bhutan to export 10,000 MW of power to India. In addition, there are a large number of other economic programmes afoot. As per Medha Bisht of IDSA, India is considered a trusted friend and an ally in Bhutan. At present, there is no anti-India lobby in the country and, given the geographical imperatives of Bhutan, India is likely to remain the most important partner in its foreign policy calculus in the coming years. Bhutan also leverages India's role as its strategic partner.

While geopolitics shapes the bilateral relationship in a major way, one need to take note of the fact that Bhutanese society is changing fast. With the youth constituting almost 50 per cent of the total population, a new generation is emerging in Bhutan. As evident in the India – Bhutan power cooperation, Bhutan is getting increasingly assertive in negotiating various issues with India. India needs to address these growing nuances, which could soon emerge as visible sores in India – Bhutan bilateral relations.

In initiating diplomatic ties with China thus, Bhutan will have to make some stark strategic choices. Replacing India with China would mean economic and ecological tradeoffs in a balancing strategy aimed at maintain harmonious relations with its two big neighbours. Bigger issue is how far Bhutan is ready in becoming a pawn in Chinese designs in Tibet and against India. The ultimate formula to settle the boundary dispute would dictate the extent of this engagement between the two.

Bhutan's strategic choices are thus of great geostrategic and military concerns to India. How it makes them would depend on the range and depth of Indo-Bhutan relations. Above discourse need not only be seen from the perspective of geo politics alone.

Is China pushing reconciliation with Bhutan to convert it into a continental bridge linking with the Bay of Bengal of course through connectivity with India to create another "Silk Route", in this regard recent resolution of boundary dispute between China and Tajikistan to create an access to Afghanistan in pursuit of its economic investments provides a possible window into Chinese designs. In case China is able to develop close political and economic ties with Bhutan and incrementally bring it into its circle of influence it will become a win – win situation for China and matter of grave concern for India.

The issue for India is that as sovereign independent nation state it has the rights to pursue an independent foreign policy commensurate with its larger interests. While being closely aligned with India it has sought to pursue a policy of neutrality. Will the Chinese overtures change this? How should India respond what are the policy choices, is the dilemma that India will need to deal with.

9

Inter-Communal Relationships amongst South Asian Partition

Since Independence in 1947 and the creation of two separate nation-states, the Indian Subcontinent has regularly witnessed ethnic violence (several wars of varying intensity opposing India to Pakistan in 1948, 1965, 1971, 1999), partitions (1947 and 1971), bloody riots, in which different communities have been confronting each other along various lines: religious (Hindus *vs* Sikhs, Hindus *vs* Muslims), ethnic (Punjabis *vs* Bengalis, Sindhis*vs* Muhajirs, and so on), and national (Indians *vs* Pakistanis, Pakistanis *vs*Bangladeshis).

These episodes of violence have at times reached astonishing levels, as during the 1947 Partition when hundreds of thousands lost their lives while millions had to flee what had been the homeland of their forefathers for centuries. This was nothing less than an ethnic cleansing beforehand. In India, ethnic violence has taken on such an importance that a specific word has even been coined to define the tensions between the major ethnic groups, Hindus and Muslims in particular: communalism.1 In Pakistan, the creation of a separate country along religious lines has not subsumed other identities, as the 1971 Partition between East and West Pakistan (and the subsequent creation of Bangladesh) has shown: ethnic and linguistic identities were successfully mobilized against an authoritarian centre.

These periods of violence have however been (fortunately) followed by longer periods of relative peace and stability, and even 'outright' reconciliation, when tensions and animosities even appeared as a (quasi)-aberration. This was the prevalent mood when India and Pakistan embarked upon their peace process in 2004.

Our interest now lies in the relationships between South Asian2 sub-groups in a diasporic3 context, while keeping in mind the dominant situations in home-societies as well. Through the exploration of the similarities and differences between the diaspora and the countries of origin on the one hand, between different host-societies where South Asians have settled down on the other, we would like to assess whether there is any specificity of the diaspora. Does the situation observed in the diaspora reinforce the theories that are put forward to explain ethnic conflicts and ethnic violence? Or does it on the contrary invalidate them? Are there any internal dynamics, and if so, to what extent are they independent from the events and turmoil of the Subcontinent? These are some of the questions that we will try to address here.

We are using here the plural as South Asians form very heterogeneous communities.

Three countries have been selected for this study, the United States, the United Kingdom and France. The United Kingdom has long been the paradigmatic country of the migration from the Subcontinent. The United States has become the home of fairly successful and increasingly visible South Asian diasporas4 but it also witnessed an event that reshaped its ethnic landscape and its relation with the Other: September 11. As for France, apart from the fact that all the contributors to the special issue are based in France, this country offers a contrasting example with the Anglo-Saxon model in terms of integration and the place of religion in society.

MIGRATION AND IDENTITY: DIASPORIC CONSTRUCTIONS OF THE SELF AND THE OTHER

Migration is often a very disruptive experience that generates a sense of insecurity, resulting from uprooting and marginality. In their adaptation strategies, immigrants redefine their self-perceptions and their collective identities.

Recent scholarship has insisted that collective identities, far from being immutable, are constructed, multiple and flexible. All the contributions to this volume highlight in particular the role of Otherness in fashioning identity. This transactional aspect of identity is reinforced in a context of migration: diasporic constructions of the Other(s) are remarkable for their multiplicity and their instability. In the host country, South Asians interact with other South Asian groups, with different ethnic minorities and with the majority population, who all potentially represent powerful figures of Otherness. And the representations and relationships thus generated are highly instable, as they depend on complex interactions between the global context, the regional (relations between South Asian states), the national (public policies towards ethnic minorities) and even local ones (community relations might not follow the same patterns on the East and the West Coast of the United States or in Bradford and Southall).

Migration tends to reinforce antagonist perceptions of 'us and them', and to strengthen national/ethnic/religious identifications. Peter van der Veer has offered the most comprehensive analysis of the dialectical link between migration and nationalism (Van der Veer 1995). Although nationalist discourse is opposed to expatriation, and to the mixing of population and the transgression of national boundaries it implies, migration fosters nationalism both among the indigenous population (through defensive, xenophobic forms of nationalism) and among migrants, through exacerbated expressions of national identity, defined along ethno-religious lines. In this process mutually exclusive religious nationalisms are fashioned. They are based on a reinvention of the past, on naturalizing the link between people, culture and territory and on antagonist constructions of the others.

In the process of the redefinition of diasporic identities, religion tends to become a major component of ethnic identity. This is due to the disruptive nature of migration that propels some migrants to turn to what they perceive as unchanging values and traditions of their past. This also owes to the political framework of the host society where the ethnicity5 of minority groups is mainly defined in religious terms and used as a basis for mobilization and politics of recognition. Finally the experience of migration often leads to a self-conscious reflection on religious traditions, beliefs and practices. This redefinition of things religious tends towards rationalization, homogenization, drawing of clear-cut boundaries with other religious groups and exclusion of heteropraxy (popular practices for instance). Interactions with others (indigenous populations, South Asians and other minority groups) prove an important component in this process of redefinition: what was taken for granted at home has to be explained, sometimes advocated in a hostile environment and finally transmitted. The issue of religious and cultural transmission to the next generation is indeed perceived as crucial.

The existing literature

Most studies have so far focused on the relationships between immigrants, their homelands and host-societies, but very few studies deal with the issue of inter-ethnic relationships amongst South Asian diasporas. Among the major exceptions, is the book edited by Crispin Bates (Bates 2001) where several case-studies of inter-ethnic relationships are examined both in the Subcontinent and in the diaspora: ethnicity and community politics in Fiji (Kelly), Mauritius (Nave), East Africa (Twaddle), Trinidad (Chatterjee), Pakistan (Leonard and Waseem) and India (Hansen), to mention a few.

Interestingly, no European country has been chosen as a case-study in this otherwise highly interesting book, not even the UK (owing probably to the lack of researchers who have shown any interest in the topic, though the issue of South Asians in the UK as such has been very thoroughly studied by the best specialists). At any rate, as Crispin Bates has underlined in the introduction of the book, many researchers have tended to neglect this issue as they see it as unproblematic:

> It is assumed that the identities of migrant communities say Indian Hindus and Pakistani Muslims, male and female, are largely brought with them, and that they are based upon primordial and age-old forms of identity to be found in the Indian Subcontinent. The conflict between these 'communities', and the expression of

gender and caste differences, are then often accepted as inevitable or natural, and only their articulation and the choice of methods for their management and amelioration remain a cause for concern.

The international activities of militant political and religious organizations such as the VHP6 and the JI7 are likewise predicated upon the assumption that the interests and identities of Hindus and Muslims everywhere are essentially the same (Bates 2001: 2-3).

Apart from Bates, Laurent Gayer, a contributor to this volume, has also addressed the issue of inter-ethnic relationships: in his Masters dissertation (Gayer 1998), he draws a comparison between the patterns of relationships between South Asian populations in London and Paris. He shows how diasporic populations can invent a common identity in opposition to the racism of the host-society as is observed in London for instance, while at the same time they can reinvent (and not simply import) the conflicts affecting their homelands (Hindu/Muslim communalism, Sikh separatism, and so on).

Inter-ethnic relationships and long-distance nationalism

Apart from a couple of studies, not much has been written on this topic. And yet these diasporas are not only increasingly important at the demographic level (20 million Indians, 4 million Pakistanis, 4 million Bangladeshis)8 and more and more diversified, but they are also getting increasingly involved in the politics of both their host-society and their homeland. Besides, as a result of the migration process, many of these immigrants experience a redefinition of their identities, some identities may become subsumed (like language or caste-based) while others may be given a new salience, and even take precedence over other identities (like religion), which is likely to have implications on inter-ethnic relationships. But such a process can vary from one country of immigration to another, depending on the models of integration prevalent in each country and on other variables. The fact that the various sub-groups often overlap makes this issue all the more interesting and complex. The cases of Indian/Pakistani/Bangladeshi Muslims on the one hand, and of Sikh/Muslim/Hindu Punjabis on the other illustrate it. Historically, those who have left India have been among the most politicized and defensive of their identities, and have even occasionally indulged in violence. The examples of the Ghadarites in Canada and in the United States at the beginning of the twentieth century, and of the Indians in South Africa, who were the first ones to mobilize against British rule under the leadership of Gandhi, are a case in point (Bates 2001: 8). As for the contemporary period, Benedict Anderson and others have also highlighted that the diasporic experience may generate long-distance nationalism. This is how Anderson defines it (Anderson 1998: 74):

Nonetheless, in general, today's long-distance nationalism strikes one as a probably menacing portent for the future. First of all, it is the product of capitalism's remorseless, accelerating transformation of all human societies. Second, it creates a serious politics that is at the same time radically unaccountable. The participant rarely pays taxes in the country in which he does his politics: he is not answerable to its judicial system; he probably does not cast even an absentee ballot in its elections because he is a citizen in a well and safely positioned in the First World, he can send and guns, circulate propaganda, and build intercontinental computer information circuits, all of which can have incalculable consequences in the zones of their ultimate destinations. Third, his politics, unlike those of activists for global human rights or environmental causes, are neither intermittent nor serendipitous. They are deeply rooted in a consciousness that his exile is self-chosen and that the nationalism he claims on e-mail is also the ground on which an embattled ethnic identity is to be fashioned in the ethnicized nation-state that he remains determined to inhabit. The same metropole that marginalizes and stigmatizes him simultaneously enables him to play in a flash, on the other side of the planet, national hero.

Interestingly, the sub-group, quoted by Anderson, which is usually given as a quasi-paradigmatic example, is from South Asia: indeed, expatriates from the Sikh community have played a significant role in the Khalistani movement (which campaigned for a separate Sikh State carved out of the Indian Union). Moreover, some recent reports have shown the important role of migrants, settled in particular in North America and the United Kingdom, in financing religio-political movements in India9 while other studies have brought to light that the remittances of Pakistani migrants in the Gulf were partly used to finance religio-political movements in the homeland (Zaman 1998). This implies not only that long-distance nationalism can be observed among all major communities beyond national, ethnic or religious affiliations, but given the heightened sense of nationalism (generated by both endogenous (dislocation leading to insecurity) and exogenous (racism of host-societies) factors) that many migrants experience, it may have implications on inter-ethnic relationships amongst diasporas as well. This also means that in diaspora, along with identities, the inter-ethnic relationships are being redefined, and cannot be simply considered as the replications of the legacy of conflict.

The links that are maintained with home-societies also suggest that many expatriates tend to closely follow the developments in the Subcontinent. Hence some events, like wars, partitions, riots, nuclear tests, destruction of sacred sites, and so on, are likely to have an impact on inter-ethnic relationships in the diaspora. But other events that take place outside the Subcontinent, such as September 11, can also affect these relationships.

But beyond transnationalism, it is important as well to examine—through the historical evolution, the mutual perceptions, the organization patterns, and so on—the points of cleavages and of rapprochement between communities. Spaces and vectors of conflict are also worth studying, all the more so as violence as such in the diaspora is first and foremost symbolic. The media, Internet, the lobbies have all a crucial role to play in the process.

The explanations for ethnic violence

Several theories have been put forth to explain ethnic violence. Ashutosh Varshney's study of the relationships between Hindus and Muslims in India (Varshney 2003) shows that these theories can be classified into five major categories: essentialism, instrumentalism, post-modernism, constructivism, institutionalism. To these, Varshney adds a sixth category, linking ethnic conflict and civil society. He believes that all the former ones are inadequate because they neglect local issues and overlook the importance of civil society.

Essentialists explain conflicts by referring to historically deep-rooted animosities based on inherent and irreconcilable differences of race, culture or religion. Hence, ignoring the many instances of cooperation and coexistence between different communities, including Hindus and Muslims who share common conceptions about social life, essentialists argue that their animosities have always existed, and hence that conflicts are inevitable. Essentialism poses a problem not only because of its racialist undertones, but as Varshney underlines, because it also 'makes it hard to explain why, if animosities are historically deep and so rooted in cultural differences, tensions and violence between groups tend to ebb and flow at different times, or why the same groups live peacefully in some places but violently in others'.

The instrumentalist argument focuses on how the respective leaderships strategically manipulate ethnicity for the sake of economic and political power (Brass 1991), even though the leaders themselves may not believe in ethnic identity. It does not however offer, as Varshney pinpoints, a convincing explanation of why ethnicity is mobilized by the leaders at all. By simply claiming that building bridges may be at times in the interest of the leadership, and creating cleavages in their interest in other instances, it does not make clear why interests can be perceived in totally different ways or why people should blindly follow the leadership (Varshney 2003).

As for post-modernists, they lay the stress on the narratives promoted by the elite, deeply implicated in the formation of knowledge. In the South Asian case, the census is one of the most striking and well-known examples of categorization that has had an incidence on the self-definition of communities (Metcalf 1995). However, its importance in creating separate identities between different communities, mainly Hindus and Muslims, and between castes, should not be over-emphasized as post-modernists have tended to do: categorizations, like census, did not create separate identities as such but certainly helped to crystallize them (Gaborieau 2001).

The constructivist view argues that many of the identities that are taken for granted have in fact been elaborated in recent time (Hobsbawm 1983, Anderson 1983). In a society like India, constructivists, such as Gyanendra Pandey, claim that the main contemporary ethnic cleavages were created by the colonial power and, the impact has been such that their divisions have had a long time effect (Pandey 1990). But once again, if the role of the British in widening the gap between communities cannot be denied, it should not be over-emphasized since, to take once again the examples of Hindus and Muslims, the delimitation of identities, as fluctuating as it could be, was a reality even before the British came to India (it could be observed as early as the thirteenth century); the two communities have even been confronting each other from the seventeenth century onwards. Hence the pre-colonial period was not the Golden Age where communal harmony was the dominant norm, as post-colonial literature would have it (Pandey 1990). But the fixation of identities and confrontations, that remained fragmentary and localized, did not mean for all that that these communities nurtured a centuries-old hostility that would have prevented any kind of cohabitation, as the essentialists argue.

Last but not least, institutionalism connects ethnic conflict or peace, on the one hand, and political institutions, on the other (Varshney 2003: 35). The nature of multiethnic societies, whether they are consensual (or consociational) or majoritarian democracies, and have federal or centralized governments, proportional representation or first-past-the post electoral system, will have an incidence on ethnic peace or conflict. For instance, in a multiethnic society in which ethnic groups are geographically concentrated, federalism may be more suitable for ethnic peace than a centralized political system (Varshney 2003: 38). Although institutionalism is one of the most relevant theories, it does not explain variance in ethnic violence or peace at the local or regional level. Reflecting on this, Varshney suggests a sixth theory, which links ethnic conflict and civil society. For him, only such a framework of analysis can account for local or regional variations. Relying on a thorough study of several cities in India where ethnic conflict has been either recurrent or hardly present, he shows that in cities where there are strong associational forms of civic engagement such as integrated business organizations, professional associations, reading clubs or TRADE unions, polarization along ethnic lines and outbreaks of ethnic violence are less likely to take place. However, his study, based on statistical data, hardly takes into account power struggles between ethnic groups and between social groups and the State.

Now it remains to be seen how relevant these theories about ethnic conflict (which may not necessarily be violent) or peace are when applied to the relationships between South Asian communities in diaspora. We have already pointed out their shortcomings in explaining ethnic conflict in home-societies. Interestingly, in a diasporic context, though none of these theories can, in a fully comprehensive way, account for ethnic conflict, almost all of them can be, to some extent, usefully mobilized. Essentialism is not helpful as such for the researcher, but its use by the respective leaderships in creating cleavages (and less frequently in building bridges) between the communities arouses his interest.

Given the renewed importance of leadership in a diasporic context, instrumentalism becomes a useful analytical tool. Post-modernism and constructivism can also be useful to understand the existing categorizations put in place in some of the host-societies as they may generate feelings of common belonging, and hence promote ethnic peace (like the 'South Asian' category in the United States or the 'Asian' category in the UK, which 'forcibly' lumps together all South Asians, regardless of their national, ethnic or religious affiliations); these are issues above all of self-perception and self-ascription. In other cases, some people try to differentiate themselves as much as possible from the rest of South Asians (for instance, a fraction of Hindus manifested their difference from other 'Asians', Pakistanis in particular, especially after the Rushdie affair) or from other ethnic groups in the host-society (like Indians trying to look as different as possible from disadvantaged groups such as Hispanics and African-Americans). Last but not least, institutionalism can be summoned to explain that though political institutions as such may not matter in promoting ethnic conflict or peace between the members of a given ethnic group, the 'institutionalized' policy of the host-society towards their minorities (in other words, the models of integration of each country) does have an impact on the inter-ethnic relationships within the group. As for the connection between civil society and ethnic peace, the institutionalist vision is also relevant in that it helps to explain why in countries with strong civil societies, like the United States and the UK, the promoters of ethnic peace can exert an influence on ethnic affairs. But once again, not a single theory can achieve a global and comprehensive explanation. Therefore, we have to rely on a combination of the different models to assess the situation.

THE PREVALENCE OF LOCAL CONTEXTS: MIGRATION HISTORIES, NATIONAL IDEOLOGIES AND STATE POLICIES

The contributions in this volume insist on the prevalence of the different local contexts in extent patterns of relationship among South Asian diasporic communities. In each of the three countries that are studied, France, the UK and the US, a unique combination of historical processes, political ideologies and state policies regarding immigration has fashioned a specific national context and particular ways of dealing with immigration, immigrants and ethno-religious pluralism. The classic opposition between Anglo-Saxon multiculturalism and the French model of republican integration clearly needs to be qualified by taking into account two elements. Firstly, the very different histories of migration in these three countries have been as instrumental as national ideologies in fashioning these two 'models'. Secondly, a convergence of issues and policies related to immigrants is to be observed: multiculturalism is increasingly questioned in the United Kingdom and quotas and affirmative action are being debated in France.

Although South Asian migration to the US is the oldest as it started in the late 1880s, with the arrival of Punjabis on the West

Coast, it has become numerically significant much more recently, with a second migration wave that started in the mid-1960s, after the US liberalization of immigration policy. This legislation also privileged educated and qualified people and this explains the very high socio-economic profile of South Asians in the US today —which contrasts with that of their counterparts in France or the United Kingdom. With approximately 3 million people, South Asians amount to 1% of the total American population.

In the United Kingdom, South Asian migration history owes much to the colonial past: the earliest migrants came as subjects of the British Empire and so did those who settled *en masse* in the 1950s, as their status of British subjects was perpetuated within the Commonwealth. A new legislation strictly limiting immigration from 1962 along with a Race Relations policy, which strived at fostering good relations between the different ethnic groups, initiated a second wave of mass migration, mostly made of the wives and children of the 1950s settlers. The majority of them were from unqualified, rural background and they came to the UK as part of a chain migration process. In the 1970s, they were joined by urban, qualified migrants, who mostly arrived from East Africa. Today, with 2.3 million people, South Asians represent the first ethnic group of the country (over 50% of the ethnic minorities population) and 4% of the total population, according to the 2001 census.

South Asian migrants settled in France came more recently and in much smaller numbers: they came mostly in the late 1970s and now they amount to no more than 130,000. The Pondicherrians represent a special case: thanks to their French nationality, they came much earlier, in the 1950s, after Pondicherry became part of the newly independent India. Amongst migrants directly coming from South Asia,11 they constitute the only group having a colonial connection with France. Since the French people have no colonial representation or categorization of South Asians—apart from Pondicherrians—South Asians in France have been subjected to lesser levels of racism and discrimination than North Africans in France or Asians in the UK. Because of the French model of individual integration and because of all these aspects pertaining to a specific migration process, the emergence of well structured South Asian communities in France has so far been delayed.

The historical phases of migration constitute another important variable. Early migrants tended to have more interactions across ethno-religious boundaries for instance: it was the case with the pioneers of the 1930s and 1950s in the UK, with Punjabi Muslims and Sikhs in California in the early 20th century and interestingly with South Asians migrants in Paris today as Chatterji argues in this volume. The nature of migration, whether it is individual or chain migration, is also an important factor in the extent of interactions with the Other. Chain migration, like in the UK, tends to limit the need and the opportunities to interact outside self-sufficient community networks. In France, South Asian migration is composite: while the majority of migrants arrive as part of a chain migration process, a significant proportion do so on an individual basis. As for the United States, most of the migrants in the 1960s and 1970s migrated on the (individual) basis of their qualifications; in the following decades, however, an increasing number arrived thanks to the family reunification provisions, and hence became part of a chain migration process as well. However, South Asians in the United States do not form major ethnic enclaves (except in some areas like Coney Island, in New York, which is largely dominated by Pakistanis, or Devon Avenue in Chicago, which has a more mixed South Asian population) and daily interactions with other South Asians tend to be much more limited than in the UK.

The second phase of migration started with the arrival of families, the coming of age of a second generation and the institutionalization of ethnic communities. South Asians in the UK experienced this phase as early as the 1970s. The emergence of a second and now third generation has given rise to a composite and hybrid type of identification as British Asian: as we shall see later, this identity label which transcends the ethno-religious and national boundaries associated with home societies and the parents' generation has become a category ascribed by the dominant society. It is given shape by racism and discrimination and is reappropriated by the youth through the creation and consumption of a common diasporic culture. This phenomenon is much more recent in the US than in the UK and has been reinforced in the aftermath of September 11. As for France, as we have noted, South Asian migration history is still going through the pioneer phase, despite the emergence of a second generation, especially among Pondicherrians, Sri Lankan Tamils and Pakistanis. Interestingly, in the absence of any valid category (*Sud-Asiatique,* South Asian, is not used in France and *Asiatique,* Asian, refers to Chinese and formerly Indochinese people), South Asians tend to be lumped together as Indians or Hindu. Whether this could constitute the nucleus of a common identity remains to be seen.

Finally the place of immigration in national ideologies and the related policies has to be assessed. As is well known, immigration has been central in the definition of the American national identity as the 'nation of all nations'; the country defines itself as a society of immigrants. But very early on, liberal views on immigration coexisted with exclusionist policies.

After the Chinese, South Asians were classified as 'aliens ineligible for citizenship' in the early 20th century and the introduction of national quotas in 1924 strictly limited their entry to the country. This period of exclusion, discrimination and xenophobia is an important aspect of the history of the South Asian presence in the US and the post-September 11 period also sheds light on this uneasy past.

Paralleling immigration legislation, the question of integration of these immigrants has emerged as an early preoccupation. In reaction to the predominance of WASP values and principles in the definition of an American identity (even in the melting-pot model), multiculturalism emerged as a new paradigm in the 1960s in leftist circles, under the influence of the civil rights movement. In the multicultural framework that has been operating since then, ethno-cultural identities are to be defended as distinct and equally valued components of national identity.

Ethnicity has hence become the only available basis of collective self-definition and mobilization (Lacorne 1997). As the ethnic group constitutes the basic socio-political unit, individuals are encouraged to identify with communities defined on ethno-religious terms.

Although official census categories refer to the national origin of immigrants, religious affiliation is prevalent in the definition of ethnic identity.

But this is also to be explained by reference to the specific role of religion in the fashioning of American national identity, its relation to the State and its relevance in socio-political debates till today (Lemarchand 1997). Religion has indeed played a crucial role when the country was founded by dissidents of European Protestant churches who had sought refuge from religious persecution. As a result, the American Constitution has established the separation between the State and the Church in such a way that it also guarantees freedom of religion and religious pluralism.

The American conception of this principle of separation contrasts with the British system of Church and State (since it is opposed to any established religion) and with the French model of *laïcité* (as it has not emerged out of confrontation with the Church). It is also rather flexible and permeable. Although officially confined to the private sphere, religion is in fact omnipresent in the public space, in social life and political debates.

Finally, the American religious landscape, continuously modified and enriched by immigration, is particularly lively since the US has the highest level of religious practice amongst developed countries. The relationship between the State and religion is very different in the UK: the Church of England is the official Church of the State, according to the Establishment Act of 1701.

For a long time, it meant that Catholics and Dissenters were denied freedom of religion and were prevented from holding any public office. British modern history is thus characterized by the interdependence of politics and an established religion (and the subordination of the latter to the former) and by religious conflicts between Catholics and Protestants on one side and Anglicans and Dissenters on the other (Baubérot & Mathieu 2002). As stated by Baubérot and Mathieu, religion has remained an integral part of the country's cultural identity well into the 20th century. Despite an overall low level of religious practice, especially among followers of the Church of England, religion remains important in the public space and in social debates, as exemplified by the compulsory teaching of religious education in State schools. Whereas identities are mainly defined along racial terms for Whites and Afro-Caribbeans, South Asian identities tend to be drawn along religious lines.

As compared to the US, immigration occupies a very different position in British history and British collective representations. The debates and policies regarding immigration have been shaped bearing in mind the importance of Commonwealth immigrants. They combine an increasingly restrictive immigration legislation and policies promoting the integration of migrants and the coexistence of the different communities. These policies have been used to legitimize the legislative stance: in other words, to ensure the successful integration of already settled immigrants, further immigration had to be stopped. Immigration became a political issue much earlier than in France, immigrants being confronted to racism and discrimination from the local population and the institutions (Lapeyronnie 1993).

If a large consensus was achieved as early as the 1960s on immigration policy, policies of management of the diversity introduced by immigration were—and still are—the subjects of heated debates. The initial policy of assimilation was quickly replaced by an ideal of integration that had to be achieved through the promotion of racial equality. Discrimination based on racism (both institutional and social) was identified as the major threat to the integration of immigrants and to social peace (Crowley 1994). Anti-racism is therefore an important component of the Race Relations legislation: racial discrimination was made illegal, equal opportunity in the access of ethnic minorities to public services and employment was promoted and new resources and powers were allocated to local authorities to enforce this policy. This had several consequences: racial (meaning ethnic) categories were created and one had to belong to pre-defined communities in order to benefit from the legislation. To understand on which basis ethnic categories have been constructed, let us examine the Mandla case. In 1979, the headmaster of a local private school refused to admit a Sikh boy unless he removed his turban to comply with rules about the school uniform. The Sikhs viewed it as indirect racial discrimination as defined by the 1976 Race Relations Act, and referred the case to the newly created Commission for Racial Equality, which then appealed to the House of Lords. Interestingly, the crux of the matter lied in establishing whether Sikhs were an ethnic/racial group or not, as only groups defined along ethnic lines and not merely on a religious basis could benefit from the 1976 Act. Ultimately, the Lords stated that Sikhs were indeed an ethnic group and made ethnicity the basis of collective identification and mobilization (Crowley 1994).

According to another provision of the Race Relations legislation, local authorities were entrusted with the implementation of this policy. Accordingly, the competition for resources and for recognition amongst ethnic groups occurs mainly at the local level. The local authorities which are in charge of education and social services leave it to voluntary and community organizations to provide adequate service. These organizations entirely depend on annual grants from local authorities and enter thus in a fierce competition. Indeed 'rights and resources are claimed in the name of communities that must compete with each other' (Baumann 1996).

Since it lies on an opposition to racism, multiculturalism recognizes the right of ethnic communities to maintain separate cultures. Ethnic communities are hence defined by reference to reified cultures, which are in turn characterized by their internal homogeneity and binding. Unlike Whites and West Indians, South Asians have been encouraged to identify and mobilize along religious lines. British multiculturalism has therefore resulted in the politicization and ethnicization of these affiliations, in a way clearly reminiscent of colonial policies (Beckerlegge 1991).

As for France, in sharp contrast with the US, immigration holds a marginal role in the national ideology: traditionally, France does not perceive itself as a country of immigration (Schnapper 1991). And in contrast with its early politicization in the UK, from 1945 to the mid-1970s, immigration remained solely linked to economic requirements: it was central to French economic development, but remained very marginal in political debates. But once labor migration was curbed, again for economic reasons, and the first wave of migrants gave way to the arrival of their family, France was confronted 15 years later with the same issues as in the UK, namely the integration of its migrant population. The French model of integration is usually described as universalistic and egalitarian, based on the ideal of republican individualism that rejects any public expression and recognition of cultural diversity (Lapeyronnie 1993). Cultural assimilation is supposed to be achieved on an individual basis, as the republican model does not acknowledge ethnic communities or any other intermediary social body between the State and individuals. Particular identities, considered as an obstacle to social progress, are to be abandoned. The contemporary rendition of the concept of *laïcité*, epitomized for instance by the 2004 Act which banned the wearing of religious signs in State-run schools,12 is regarded as the prime instrument of republican integration: religion is to be confined to the private sphere and public expressions of faith (as the wearing of Islamic headscarves or Sikh turbans) are considered as a threat to the entire republican framework.

ETHNIC ENTREPRENEURS: KEY PLAYERS IN THE RELATIONSHIP BUILDING PROCESS

If exogenous factors, like local contexts, are important in order to understand the complex intricacies at play in inter-ethnic relationships, so are more endogenous factors. Among them, leadership plays an important role: ethnic entrepreneurs are often crucial actors in either building bridges or widening gaps between sub-groups in the larger South Asian communities.

Host societies tend to transform the resources of migrants: some identities are devaluated and relegated to the private sphere, new economic opportunities appear, communities regroup along ethnic or religious lines to conform to the expectations of the State. As a result, potential entrepreneurs are offered a new set of resources that vary from one country of migration to the other. And identity becomes one of the resources that can be mobilized by the entrepreneurs.

The migration process as such creates the ground for the emergence of ethnic leaders or entrepreneurs. Their emergence can first be seen as an answer to the need of newly arrived migrants. For instance, when Pakistani men first landed in the UK, most were poorly-educated and could hardly speak English. They were therefore at loss in dealing with British institutions and so they turned to community members for help. In this context, anyone who was educated, had a good knowledge of English and was seen as being able to deal with British authorities, could easily achieve a position of influence, and hence be promoted to the status of a 'leader'. After the phase of settlement was completed, the need for patrons did not subside, as new needs arose in response to the sense of disruption and marginalization due to the migration process. Maintaining ethnic and religious traditions and recreating a 'Pakistani community' became very important (Shaw 1988: 141-4). People who were able to 'organize' the community and set up institutions that would help perpetuating these traditions were fairly easily INVESTED with authority within the community. As a result, new types of leaders, like imams and Sufi pirs, came to play a decisive entrepreneurial role, as the mobilization against Salman Rushdie revealed (Blom 1999).

Beyond ethnicity, religion and place of immigration, a similar phenomenon exists amongst other South Asian communities in the UK and elsewhere, including amongst educated, prosperous and fairly well integrated migrants. Such is the case in the United States or in Canada, where feelings of stigmatization and uprooting are experienced, no matter how successful the migrants are in their host societies. They also express similar needs for *desi* representatives that will help them maintain their ethnic heritage.

However, it is interesting to note that this tendency is particularly acute in countries which promote multiculturalism. It is much less visible in countries where integration at the individual level, like France, is called for. Indeed, multiculturalism encourages the construction of a public ethnic identity instead of a purely private one (Taylor 1992). This publicization can take various forms, like ethnic parades, ethnic awareness weeks, endowed chairs in universities and political lobbies. But, migrants are also submitted to pressures in host-societies to organize into groups that are culturally 'homogenous' and to have ethnic leaders as spokespersons for the community. As Kurien rightfully notes, 'the need to have a distinctive, coherent heritage puts pressure on members of ethnic groups to be ethnic in certain formulaic ways, including *constructing a monocultural homeland in order to be part of a multicultural society*' (Kurien 2004: 365). This in return can have serious implications on inter-ethnic relationships amongst South Asians, since leaders re-appropriate the prevalent notions of the host society and tend to promote essentialist and exclusivist conceptions of ethnicity, that do not leave much room for the Other, including the Other South Asian. Beyond the construction of exclusionist identities, another point to be noted is that unity is not only seen as a primordial prerequisite for any kind of influence within the community as well as in the host-society but also as a form of 'moral obligation' upon the community (as both a reaction to Partition and to the *fitna* tradition, a major feature of power-relationships in the Subcontinent, marked by constant shift of allegiance and alliances. However, South Asians have been characterized by a high propensity for internal divisions which decrease the effective impact of any single group whatever be its agenda.

The migration process leads some migrants to yearn for positions of leadership, seen as a compensation for the downward mobility that many of them experience. This longing for influence is stronger in multicultural societies where leaders of ethnic groups can become political actors, albeit usually only at a local level. Hence, this logic often encourages potential leaders to adopt positions that will ensure them both a status within the community and acceptance as legitimate representatives from the host society, even if these positions are defined along narrow ethnic or religious lines.

For example, Pakistani leaders in the UK tend to seek influence by using the emotional issue of Islamic values (Shaw 1988: 143), whereas Indian Hindu representatives in the United States use redefined versions of Hinduism, (mostly) along *Hindutva*13 lines, to gain power within the community (Kurien 2004). For many self-styled Pakistani spokespersons, the use of Islamic references is seen as the right way of gaining the support of migrants who mostly look for means of curbing acculturation. For some Indian Hindu activists in the United States or Canada, and particularly for the supporters of *Hindutva*, a somewhat homogenized version of Hinduism can have a unifying effect in an alien land. Besides, as Jayant Lele notes in reference to the Canadian context, the label 'Hindu' has the 'advantage' of avoiding to have to deal with the compromising problems of the Sikhs14 and the Muslims (Lele 2003: 94). This may adversely affect the inter-ethnic relationships amongst South Asians, as leaders from all sides, neglecting the huge diversity of their home countries, tend to promote essentialized and exclusionist conceptions of their own cultures, in order to have access to resources in the double system of relations in which they operate: status amongst fellow migrants, political power and recognition from the host-society.

As opposed to the United States and the United Kingdom, where the settlement process has already taken place in the past decades and where there is a sizeable elite, most South Asian migrants in France still belong to the first generation and primarily hail from underprivileged social categories, with a fairly low educational background.15 This situation has considerably hampered the leadership formation process as most migrants are still busy settling down and have a low visibility.

While this pioneer stage and the profile of South Asian expatriates explain the strength of economic ties over other forms of bonding, it does not account alone for this relative lack of leadership. The local context does indeed play a crucial role. The French model of integration does not encourage any type of mobilization at the community level, and hence do not officially recognize community leaders as such.

However, in some conflictual cases (like the 'veil affair' for young Muslim girls and the turban issue for Sikh schoolboys), the French government has been confronted with the need for 'ethnic representatives'. Interestingly, in the case of the Sikhs, despite the official policy of *laïcité*, the representatives they have reached for are hailing from the local *gurudwara*. As for the Muslims (who are mostly from North and Sub Saharan Africa), the French authorities have lately engaged in a process of looking for 'legitimate' leaders in response to various 'challenges' (the *hijab*, and the perceived threat of fundamentalism, for instance). But this process is fraught with hurdles not only because of the internal diversity of Muslims but also because there are competing leaderships that are either recognized (or even nominated, as a legacy of the colonial period) by the French government, or by the 'community', but hardly ever by both.

In other words, depending on their countries of settlement, ethnic entrepreneurs mobilize the resources that are locally available: they form lobbies in the case of the United States (Mohammad-Arif 2000, Therwath in this volume), or opt for racial categorizations in the case of the UK. Accordingly, community leaders define the groups that they can mobilize.

The situations described above seem to suggest that a diasporic situation combined with migration to a multicultural society is bound to reinforce the cleavages between South Asians rather than bridge them. However, the picture does not look as grim: ethnic politics can also be promoted in progressive ways as the increasing dynamism of peace-making South Asian organizations in North America and the UK reveals.

Beyond confrontation, the emergence of a diasporic South Asian identity?

South Asian diasporic subjectivities are fashioned as much by confrontation, violence or competition as by cooperation, solidarity and peace-making. This second strand of diasporic activism tends to be neglected by social scientists who have usually focused on the first aspect (except for Gayer 1998, Shain 1999), although both are interconnected.

The experience of migration has also fostered a common South Asian identity that transcends national, ethnic or religious cleavages. This pan-ethnic, inclusive type of identification emerges at first as an exo-definition by the host society, whose representations, categorizations and policies tended to lump together people from the sub-continent. The experience of racism, discrimination and marginalization has been particularly important, especially in the UK where the colonial legacy has greatly impinged on patterns of integration and inter-ethnic relations of the former colonized communities. This is also true of the post-9/11 situation in the US, as explained by Mohammad-Arif in this volume. Through censuses for instance, multicultural approaches have also led to the formation of new categories like South Asians in the US or Asians in the UK.

These perceptions from the host society are reappropriated by the diasporic communities, mostly by the second or third generation and an ascribed type of identification becomes an asserted one. Here the generation divide is clearly important: the youth, born and/or brought up in the host country, tends not to support the ethno-religious or national divisions that they associate with their parents' generation, these 'uncles and aunties' mentioned by Therwath in this volume (although communal and fundamentalist organizations do recruit among sections of the youth). The trauma of Partition is still very present for the first generation of migrants and influences their representations of and relations to the South Asian Other. As in South Asia itself, the memory (both individual and collective) of these tragic events is transmitted to the second generation, particularly amongst Punjabis, but not to the third generation. If it still means something at all to the youth, Partition operates as a negative point of reference and encourages them to transcend the divisions and promote cooperation both in South Asia and in the diaspora.

This common diasporic identity promoted by the youth is grounded on perceived cultural commonalities: food, movie, music and dress. This South Asian hybrid culture exemplified and produced in the diaspora is also increasingly consumed in the home societies.

In fact an important dimension of this diasporic identity is its relation to the homeland, whether with reference to political involvement (and the many instances of long-distance nationalism), economic investments (through remittances) or emotional links. Interestingly, the initiatives and organizations promoting cooperation among South Asians partake not only of those classic patterns of involvement in the homeland but also of new and increasingly diverse ones, like diaspora philanthropy. Development projects, hospitals, schools and colleges, libraries, public infrastructures are thus funded by expatriates. Diasporic philanthropists and actors of reconciliation are motivated by a sense of responsibility towards their home society and have been influenced by the values and modes of action of the host society.

With a common sense of belonging forged by the experience of migration and an ethic of responsibility towards the homeland, several progressive organizations have emerged in the diaspora, especially in the US and the UK, in the last twenty years. As detailed by Mohammad-Arif in this volume, these organizations were primarily concerned with the plight of South Asian migrants in their host society and have only recently extended their action to the home societies.

She explains the rise of this new kind of activism by the changes in the socio-demographic profile of immigrants (with the youth and women contesting the hegemony of first generation (male) leaders) and the traumatic events such as the nuclear tests in India and Pakistan. It also illustrates the maturation of civil societies both in the diaspora and in the sub-continent (mostly in India and less so elsewhere).

Some of these diasporic activists have focused on the fight against communalism (the rise of *Hindutva* in India and the diaspora being their main target), and the promotion of peace through people to people contact and mobilization against the nuclearization of the sub-continent. Through their cooperation with organizations based in South Asia, to which they give an international platform, they have been instrumental in the emergence of a transnational network of South Asian peacemakers (like the Indo-Pak Forum for Peace), which was very active during the World Social Forum held in Bombay in 2004.

But what is the real influence of these diasporic actors? They have achieved important victories, with the banning of Sewa International in the UK16 or with the anti-Modi campaign, preventing him to enter the US. However, their real impact within their own communities tends to be rather limited: their following is mostly restricted to intellectual, academic and militant circles and their mobilization potential can in no way compete with their opponents. Their legitimacy to speak for the 'silent majority' remains to be established.

The contributors

In his contribution, Laurent Gayer reflects on the complexity to investigate on diasporic constructions of otherness (hence the paucity so far of empirical studies), as they are remarkable for their plurality and their volatility, in interaction with multiple contexts, local and transnational ones. Breaking away from reified conceptions of diaspora and their homeland, he stresses the dynamic dimension of diasporic identifications, while exploring local patterns of conflict and cooperation amongst South Asians in Southall. He demonstrates in particular how internal and external group boundaries are constantly questioned and challenged, be it towards a diasporic reinvention of communalism or the promotion of commonalities and of a pan-ethnic identity.

Miniya Chatterji, in the only article of this volume on France, examines how in Paris' so-called *'quartier indien'*, an area of intense migrant economic activity, community boundaries are being drawn among South Asian Muslims. She attempts to identify how 'sub-groups' are being redefined in migration, by tracing out the nature and depth of bonds and bridges shared by South Asian Muslims. She argues that, at such an early stage of settlement, economic activity seems more prevalent in defining these internal group boundaries than religion, national origin or language.

Christine Moliner focuses on Sikh representations of the Muslims and the relationships between those two groups sharing a common regional identity, both in the Sub-continent and in the diaspora. She does so diachronically, arguing that historical constructions of the Muslim as the Other (often, but not always, as the enemy) have been instrumental in Sikh identity formation process, since the 18th century onwards. And synchronically, she traces the reshaping of these representations in the post-colonial UK that is home to important Sikh and Muslim populations and the ways they impact on inter-community relationships.

In her article, Aminah Mohammad-Arif examines the inter-ethnic relationships among South Asian diasporas in the United

States, focusing more particularly on Hindus and Muslims, both Indians and Pakistanis. She argues that the importance of religion in the redefinition of individual and community identities combined with the settlement in a multicultural society, like the United States, has implications on the relationships between South Asians, as it has tended to (re)create cleavages. However, the proponents of exclusionist identities have been increasingly facing competition from secular forces, whose constructions of identities obey to different logics and repertoires that go beyond religion, and are inclusive of all communities to the extent of calling into question the borders drawn by History.

Ingrid Therwath addresses here the issue of Indian-American lobbies in the United States: their growing influence has been widely reported in the (ethnic) media, but even more striking are their internal divisions, giving way to the constant formation of new groups (a phenomenon known among South Asians as the 'everybody wants to be president syndrome'). In the face of these divisions, Islamophobia has provided a unifying force, whose roots can be found in the articulation between local and transnational factors: on the one hand the support to the Hindu nationalist ideology in the context of the (American) war against terrorism, on the other hand the furthering of the India-Israel-US strategic partnership.

Conclusion

While most contributors to this volume agree that the redefinitions of identities in a diasporic setting have had fairly adverse implications on inter-ethnic relationships, a common line of argument between the different contributions is the importance of local contexts in (over)determining the bonding and bridging process amongst South Asians. Conceptions of foreigners, classification patterns, institutional frameworks, as well as migration policies and agendas of each country are all crucial elements that need to be taken into account (Massicard 2005: 279). Some countries indeed encourage mobilization (whether along sectarian or progressive lines) on a community basis (namely multicultural societies), while others do not officially recognize communities as such, like France, and hence the issue of inter-ethnic relationships is not endowed with the same importance. But in France too, contradictions may surface as this society has been increasingly facing a tension between principles of assimilation of minorities at the individual level and policies towards more recent migrants that partly call into question these very principles, like affirmative action. At any rate, local dynamics are essential in the understanding of some of the identity investments and positions that are at stake (Massicard 2005: 274), as they influence the bonding or 'breaking' process within communities.

But not negligible either is the role played by the length of the migration process as well as by the social background of expatriates, as the degree of settlement in the host-society and the presence and visibility of an elite have an impact on the leadership formation, and related to it, on the community formation.

At any rate, all these groups, beyond their ideology, also operate in a double framework, articulating transnational interests with local concerns. As a result, though South Asians are far from impervious to events taking place in their home-societies, the inter-ethnic relationship issue in the diaspora obeys to a specific dynamic, related to a whole range of factors that goes well beyond a mere replication of the conflicts taking place in the Sub continent.

GILMARTIN ON ZAMINDAR LONG PARTITION

Over the last couple decades, histories of the partition of India and its consequences have proliferated. But Vazira Zamindar's study stands out for the originality of its conception and its importance in making sense of this seminal event. Zamindar is well aware of the complex history of political negotiation and conflict that led to the British decision to divide the subcontinent in 1947, but this is not the focus of her book. Nor is the violence that marked the drawing of the partition boundaries between India and Pakistan, though this plays an important part in her story. Rather, Zamindar's book is a study of the ways that the logic of partition--and of the migrations that it set off--fundamentally shaped the very process of state-building and bureaucratic consolidation that produced the Indian and Pakistani states. It is in this sense a book, as the title suggests, about The Long Partition, the long-term process of official engagement (by both Pakistan and India) with migration, return, and belonging, that helped to constitute, amidst much contingency and bureaucratic violence, the meaning of separate nations and states. Partition eluded easy "closure" in the years after 1947, she argues, as it was a development that put "the very process of making modern nation-states to trial and scrutiny".

The strength of Zamindar's book lies in her dramatizing clearly that the making of these states occurred against the backdrop of the thousands of complex personal and family decisions made in these years by migrants (and non-migrants) themselves. Few historians have, in fact, shown so clearly how the histories of everyday, personal decisions inescapably shaped the parameters in which high-level state-making and nation-building occurred. Zamindar focuses in particular on Delhi and Karachi, and on the multivalent issues that shaped decisions to migrate or stay in those two new capital cities.

Though violence and the fear it produced played a major role, such decisions were grounded also in the everyday worlds of family, work, marriage, and property. Zamindar documents these concerns through interviews conducted in both Delhi and Karachi, and through the traces that such varied motives and entanglements have left behind in bureaucratic and court records.

In juxtaposing such personal worlds with official efforts to formulate and define a rationality of state control over the process of migration, Zamindar in fact shows clearly both the power of bureaucratic control and violence in disrupting everyday lives, and the contingencies that made it impossible for either the Indian or Pakistani states to fully or easily deploy a logic of state rationality on partition's aftermath. In fact, it is one of the great strengths of Zamindar's account that one is left in the end with a sense both of the power and violence of the process of state-building that partition engendered, and, at the same time, of the state's inevitable limitations in the face of the complexity of everyday life that defined partition's migrations.

The contradictions in post-partition state-building are traced by Zamindar through a series of illustrations, none more compelling than her careful delineation of the critical problem of evacuee property, an issue she shows to be far more complex than has usually been portrayed. On the one hand, control and redistribution of evacuee property represented a key framework in which the state asserted its claims to rationalizing developmental authority by using "rehabilitation" to normalize state oversight over a property-owning society in the wake of partition's migrations. But, on the other hand, as Zamindar shows, this process in some cases only thinly masked state participation in coerced displacements from property, in which Muslims in India were, in effect, expropriated to make "room" for Hindu and Sikh migrants. A full "exchange" of minority populations was in fact negotiated only in the Punjab, but resettlement of evacuees, including pressure on "intending" migrants to give up property, became a mechanism, in both India and Pakistan, of state control over minorities. Indeed, issues of migration, in Delhi for example, became increasingly caught up not only with questions about migration to Pakistan (which did not necessarily want more Muslim migrants from India), but also with the designation of Muslim zones within the city, as a mechanism of protecting Muslims, or (depending on the arguments being put forward) clearing Muslims and thus freeing up evacuee property in other parts of the city.

In fact, Zamindar's book raises critical questions about the meaning of "voluntary" migration in the wake of partition. Much of the law surrounding migration and citizenship in the years after partition was predicated on the notion that migrants made free choices in terms of their decisions to settle in India or Pakistan, but in fact, as Zamindar shows, the issue of "choice" was extremely complex and can hardly be assessed independently of the personal and bureaucratic worlds (including those regarding property) in which many migrants and non-migrants were enmeshed. The very process of state-building in these years was caught up with the problems in reconciling the legal notion of "choice" (as it arose in migration cases) with attempts to establish fixed (and thus, in the end, unchosen) categories of citizenship. As Zamindar notes of one court case as India sought to fix the meanings of citizenship in the wake of partition, "allowing an individual... to choose his own nationality, was to open a Pandora's box in this social and political landscape" (p. 208). Such contradictions were doubly evident in cases involving women and children. And yet, to escape entirely the paradox of choice surrounding the interpretation of migration and citizenship was impossible, as her discussion of the complex history of government issuance of permits and passports makes clear.

Among the most compelling arguments running through Zamindar's account are those highlighting the complex relationships between citizenship based on territory and that based on religion. Implicit of course in the subcontinent's territorial partition was a vision of territorial nationality, a vision embraced, as Zamindar makes clear, by both India and Pakistan. And yet, the couching of the demand for Pakistan before 1947 in terms of a "two-nation theory" based on religion complicated efforts to come to terms with this transformation. In the case of Karachi, policies on migration were marked by considerable tension, as Zamindar shows, between a Muhajir community (whose views were often reflected in the Urdu newspaper, Jang) that saw Pakistan's embracing of migrants as a key to the state's religious/ideological identity. Yet, the government of Sind was far less welcoming of migrants, as, ironically, was the government of Pakistan, which worried about its state capacities being overwhelmed by a wholesale migration of Muslims from India. In India, post-partition policies came face to face with the "Muslim question," the problem of reconciling a territorial view of citizenship and nationality with the notion that Muslims, as a special category, had to specially prove their identification with India (their "choice") in ways others did not. Zamindar's book in fact provides a powerful historical backdrop for understanding the special disabilities faced by Muslims as Indian nationhood and identity solidified in the wake of partition. Yet, at the same time, her work also shows the complex legal and ideological negotiations that marked the efforts of the bureaucracy and the courts to come to terms with the complexity of the varied positions of Muslims in India and their relationship to Muslims (family, friends, spouses) across the newly drawn borders.

Zamindar's history of The Long Partition is an important contribution to the subcontinent's history literature for many reasons. First, it persuasively makes the case that we view India's partition not as a single event, but as a long-term process, with critical consequences for our historical understandings of the cultural framework within which state-building and nation-building took their distinct courses in Pakistan and India. Second, it suggests the critical importance of treating the histories of Pakistan and India together in these years. One of her most powerful arguments lies in her contention that the history of migration tied together the histories of the two states in ways that makes it highly problematic to write their histories after 1947 entirely separately. Third, it illustrates dramatically the importance of linking together the history of everyday life and that of the state, for it is clear from her presentation that neither can be fully understood without the other.

Last, and in some ways most intriguingly, her work suggests critical frames in which it is important for historians to reconsider the entire story of India's partition, after 1947 and before as well. Though Zamindar herself does not take on the story of the events leading up to partition, the various tensions surrounding migration and its meanings in the years after 1947 raise critical questions for framing the larger story. Partition can no longer be viewed as an aberration in the larger histories of nationalism and state-building that define the subcontinent's twentieth-century history; rather it crystallizes critical questions about the relationship between state-building, national identity, everyday life, and individual choice that marked the end of the colonial era.

VIOLENCE, GENDER, AND THE ONGOING PARTITIONS OF SOUTH ASIA

There has recently been a spate of revisionist writing on the 1971 war that led to the foundation of Bangladesh. Yasmin Saikia's new book stands out for its people-centered approach as it provides fresh insight into this moment of conflict and violence, which moves beyond the official narratives of events that have been endorsed and promoted by the Pakistani, Indian, and Bangladeshi establishments. Instead of focusing on high politics and taking sides, Saikia privileges the human stories of "individual losses and personal tragedies suffered by both men and women", which form the basis of what she terms a "people's history of 1971".

The book is primarily concerned with probing the causes and effects of violence, particularly against vulnerable groups such as women, before, during, and after the war. In this, Saikia draws her inspiration from the scholarship on the 1947 partition of British India into India and Pakistan, which has done a masterful job of weaving the story of violence into our understanding of the historical events of independence and partition.

In some ways, thus, the book suggests that the horrors surrounding 1971 were the culmination of the unfinished business of the 1947 partition and our inability in South Asia to come to terms with the brutality towards women and children in the name of community, nation, and religion displayed at this moment. It is clearly intended to serve as a lesson for people in South Asia and an attempt to heal the wounds of 1971.

The book is divided into three parts. The first part provides the conventional historical narrative of 1971 and discusses why it needs to be dismantled in favor of a more people-sensitive account of the war and its aftermath. It places 1971 within the theoretical parameters provided by the scholarship on the 1947 partition and its impact on ordinary people, particularly in terms of gender violence, as well as scholarship on moments of mass violence from other parts of the world, such as the Holocaust, apartheid South Africa, Rwanda, and Darfur.

Part 2 produces verbatim the testimonies of ten women, ranging from the victims of sexual violence to social workers to female soldiers, and their experiences during 1971. Saikia provides thoughtful and scholarly introductions to each testimony, which helps the reader navigate the range of emotions these raw memories evoke and place them in a more meaningful context.

Part 3 is a postscript that discusses the memories of male perpetrators of the violent crimes committed during this period in an attempt to go beyond the nationalist narratives of these men as heroes. The self-reflective nature of these memories as the men make halting attempts to come to terms with their crimes and thus redeem their humanity, and perhaps also seek forgiveness from their victims, makes for poignant reading.

Excavation of women's and some men's memories of violence and redemption forms the core of this highly readable monograph. The account of Saikia's interactions with her subjects as she traveled across Bangladesh to collect their stories is a fascinating study in the power of oral historical testimonies and the shaping of the book itself—from a set of disparate memories wrenched from the deep recesses of women's minds to a sophisticated historical retelling of the war of 1971.

As Saikia notes, the act of recovering the memories of women who are barely able to articulate the nature and extent of the wounds inflicted on them has to be an act of interaction between the teller and listener, the latter shaping the testimony into a deeply personal and gendered history of violence that lies outside the realm of recorded histories. "Listening," she argues, "exorcises memories and loss, granting them new meaning and educating those who remember and listen".

Saikia makes the powerful argument that history has to serve as more than a tool for identity formation in the subcontinent if we are to truly decolonize our past and present. Thus the collective memories that serve to dislodge official nationalist historical narratives cannot merely be an account of the heroic deeds of a community; rather, they have to take into account both its successes as well as moral failures in the past. This will ensure that the historical retelling is imbued with an "ethical dimension" that recognizes the ability of war to dehumanize individuals even as it provides an opportunity to recover humanity in the face of untold suffering.

As a result, even as it systematically unpacks nationalist narratives, the book is careful not to take sides and suggests that the focus should not be on apportioning blame to one group or another, but rather on "search[ing] for an answer to the fundamental question of what was lost and regained during the war". The book does not shy away from recognizing the brutality of the Pakistani army towards the Bangladeshi freedom fighters and Bengali women or the sheer scale of violence unleashed against the Urdu-speaking, pro-Pakistan Biharis by the Bangladeshi freedom fighters. Moreover, the book points out that the violence against many of the victims of these atrocities is ongoing, both metaphorically in their systematic silencing by the state and literally in the statelessness of Biharis as they continue their struggle for survival in refugee camps in Bangladesh, unwanted by either Pakistan or Bangladesh, as well as in the vilification and exploitation of the *birangonas*, Bengali women rape survivors who were labeled as such by the Bangladeshi state.

The book renders and discusses the testimonies of women in a deeply compassionate manner as it struggles to understand the cost of war in the name of nationalism in South Asia. Saikia underlines the fact that a people's history of 1971 is necessary because it allows us to uncover, at the moment of intersection between memory and history, and past and present, the violence that undergirded the formation of nation-states in South Asia.

It also forces us to remember the dehumanization of women in the history of nation-state formation in the region, by militarized nationalism, systematic state policies, random men as well as friends and neighbors. In this story, thus, women emerge as far more than nameless victims of violence, as they become the voices of our conscience, compelling us to rewrite the celebratory narratives of our nationalist pasts. One wishes, however, that Saikia had at greater length and more explicitly addressed issues of state formation in Bangladesh in light of the processes unleashed by the violence, particularly in terms of the production of political practices and institutions.

The book struggles to find meaning in the violence that it so starkly and disturbingly reveals to its readers. As a South Asian, I was profoundly moved and ashamed while reading the book (which attests to its power), but at the same time I was left curiously dissatisfied regarding why the violence occurred and how we are to account for in the present and prevent it in the future. While there is no doubt that the telling of the story itself is enough, one wonders whether the framework the book provides for understanding the level of violence and women's responses to it in terms of the concept of *insaniyat* (humanity) is adequate. Why does *insaniyat* disappear in times of war in South Asia, if it is indeed such a deeply ingrained idea in its multiple cultures, as the book seems to suggest?

Moreover, how are we to ensure that the victims and perpetrators of violence are given the justice they deserve? Saikia herself suggests that a war crimes tribunal would not be appropriate because of the lack of interest in such an endeavor from the Pakistani and Bangladeshi governments as well as the acrimonious nature of public discourse in the countries, which continues to be deeply divided and vengeful.

In this situation, she suggests that the "religio-cultural site of lived Islam" can provide an "emancipatory space" where women's experiences can be recognized and grievances addressed in a "vocabulary understood by the people". She asserts that the victims of rape can invoke their rights under the Islamic concept of *hūquq-al-ibad* (rights of persons) that would oblige the perpetrators to admit to their crimes, leaving the possibility open for forgiveness from the victim. While this sounds fine at a theoretical level, it paints a too-rosy picture of lived religion which assumes that the institutions of lived Islam are somehow above the deeply patriarchal discourses of nationalism and community and would be willing to listen to and learn from the experiences of women during war, and mete out justice to their male perpetrators.

Saikia does admit, however, that there are no easy answers to the questions raised by violence and the initial challenge is to provide a space for women and men to speak about the multiple sites of violence while also compelling the Pakistani and Bangladeshi governments to admit to their culpability in promoting violence against the vulnerable. This book is an admirable step in that very direction.

The book is written in a lucid style and the stories told by the women make for compelling reading. It will find a large readership in South Asia. I also think that it is time that we, historians and teachers of South Asia, begin to include Bangladesh more centrally in our narrative of postcolonial South Asian history. This book, by bringing together the themes of gender, violence, nation, and community, would serve as an ideal vehicle to teach these themes in undergraduate survey and more topical courses on South Asian history and politics. Further, because it is a product of an eclectic research methodology that includes rich ethnographic fieldwork alongside more traditional archival sources, the book would serve as a wonderful teaching tool in graduate courses on memory, oral histories, and the making of archives.

10

Surrender of Pakistani Forces in East Pakistan and Making Bangladesh

The *Instrument of Surrender* of Pakistani forces stationed in East Pakistan was signed at Ramna Race Course in Dhaka at 16.31 IST on 16 December 1971, by Lieutenant General Jagjit Singh Aurora, General Officer Commanding-in-chief of Eastern Command of the Indian Army and Lieutenant GeneralA. A. K. Niazi, Commander of Pakistani forces in East Pakistan. As Aurora accepted the surrender, the surrounding crowds on the race course began shouting anti-Niazi and anti-Pakistan slogans.

India took approximately 90,000 prisoners of war, including Pakistani soldiers and their East Pakistani civilian supporters. 79,676 prisoners were uniformed personnel, of which 55,692 were Army, 16,354 Paramilitary, 5,296 Police, 1000 Navy and 800 PAF. The remaining prisoners were civilians – either family members of the military personnel or collaborators (razakars). The Hamoodur Rahman Commission report instituted by Pakistan lists the Pakistani POWs as follows: Apart from soldiers, it was estimated that 15,000 Bengali civilians were also made prisoners of war.

Foreign Involvement

The Soviet Union sympathised with the Bangladeshis, and supported the Indian Army and Mukti Bahini during the war, recognising that the independence of Bangladesh would weaken the position of its rivals—the United States and China. The USSR gave assurances to India that if a confrontation with the United States or China developed, it would take counter-measures. This assurance was enshrined in the Indo-Soviet friendship treaty signed in August 1971.

The United States supported Pakistan both politically and materially. President Richard Nixon and his Secretary of State Henry Kissinger feared Soviet expansion into South and Southeast Asia. Pakistan was a close ally of the People's Republic of China, with whom Nixon had been negotiating a*rapprochement* and where he intended to visit in February 1972. Nixon feared that an Indian invasion of West Pakistan would mean total Soviet domination of the region, and that it would seriously undermine the global position of the United States and the regional position of America's new tacit ally, China. Nixon encouraged countries like Jordan and Iran to send military supplies to Pakistan while also encouraging China to increase its arms supplies to Pakistan. The Nixon administration also ignored reports it received of the "genocidal" activities of the Pakistani Army in East Pakistan, most notably the Blood telegram. This prompted widespread criticism and condemnation both by Congress and in the international press.

Then-US ambassador to the United Nations George H.W. Bush—later 41st President of the United States—introduced a resolution in the UN Security Council calling for a cease-fire and the withdrawal of armed forces by India and Pakistan. It was vetoed by the Soviet Union. The following days witnessed a great pressure on the Soviets from the Nixon-Kissinger duo to get India to withdraw, but to no avail.

It has been documented that President Nixon requested Iran and Jordan to send their F-86, F-104 and F-5 fighter jets in aid of Pakistan.

When Pakistan's defeat in the eastern sector seemed certain, Nixon deployed a carrier battle group led by the aircraft carrier USS *Enterprise* into theBay of Bengal. The *Enterprise* and its escort ships arrived on station on 11 December 1971. According to a Russian documentary, the United Kingdom deployed a carrier battle group led by the aircraft carrier HMS *Eagle* to the Bay, although this is unlikely as the *Eagle* was decommissioned at Portsmouth, England in January 1972.

On 6 and 13 December, the Soviet Navy dispatched two groups of cruisers and destroyers and a submarine armed with nuclear missiles from Vladivostok; they trailed U.S. Task Force 74 into the Indian Ocean from 18 December 1971 until 7 January 1972. The Soviets also had a nuclear submarine to help ward off the threat posed by USS *Enterprise* task force in the Indian Ocean.

China

As a long-standing ally of Pakistan, the People's Republic of China reacted with alarm to the evolving situation in East Pakistan and the prospect of India invading West Pakistan and Pakistani-controlled Kashmir. Believing that just such an Indian attack was imminent, Nixon encouraged China to mobilise its armed forces along its border with India to discourage it. The Chinese did not, however, respond to this encouragement, because unlike the 1962 Sino-Indian War when India was caught entirely unaware, this time the Indian Army was prepared and had deployed eight mountain divisions to the Sino-Indian border to guard against such an eventuality. China instead threw its weight behind demands for an immediate ceasefire.

When Bangladesh applied for membership to the United Nations in 1972, China vetoed their application because two United Nations resolutions regarding the repatriation of Pakistani prisoners of war and civilians had not yet been implemented. China was also among the last countries to recognise independent Bangladesh, refusing to do so until 31 August 1975.

AFTERMATH

India

The war stripped Pakistan of more than half of its population and with nearly one-third of its army in captivity, clearly established India's military dominance of the subcontinent. In spite of the magnitude of the victory, India was surprisingly restrained in its reaction. Mostly, Indian leaders seemed pleased by the relative ease with which they had accomplished their goals—the establishment of Bangladesh and the prospect of an early return to their homeland of the 10 million Bengali refugees who were the cause of the war. In announcing the Pakistani surrender, Prime Minister Indira Gandhi declared in the Indian Parliament:

"Dacca is now the free capital of a free country. We hail the people of Bangladesh in their hour of triumph. All nations who value the human spirit will recognize it as a significant milestone in man's quest for liberty."

Pakistan

For Pakistan it was a complete and humiliating defeat, a psychological setback that came from a defeat at the hands of intense rival India. Pakistan lost half its population and a significant portion of its economy and suffered setbacks to its geo-political role in South Asia. Pakistan feared that the two-nation theory was disproved and that the Islamic ideology had proved insufficient to keep Bengalis part of Pakistan. Also, the Pakistani military suffered further humiliation by having their 90,000 prisoners of war (POWs) released by India only after the negotiation and signing of the Simla Agreement on 2 July 1972. In addition to repatriation of prisoners of war also, the agreement established an ongoing structure for the negotiated resolution of future conflicts between India and Pakistan (referring to the remaining western provinces that now composed the totality of Pakistan). In signing the agreement, Pakistan also, by implication, recognised the former East Pakistan as the now independent and sovereign state of Bangladesh.

The Pakistani people were not mentally prepared to accept defeat, as the state-controlled media in West Pakistan had been projecting imaginary victories. When the surrender in East Pakistan was finally announced, people could not come terms with the magnitude of defeat, spontaneous demonstrations and mass protests erupted on the streets of major cities in West Pakistan. Also, referring to the remaining rump Western Pakistan as simply "Pakistan" added to the effect of the defeat as international acceptance of the secession of the eastern half of the country and its creation as the independent state of Bangladesh developed and was given more credence. The cost of the war for Pakistan in monetary and human resources was very high. Demoralized and finding himself unable to control the situation, General Yahya Khan surrendered power to Zulfiqar Ali Bhutto who was sworn-in on 20 December 1971 as President and as the (first civilian) Chief Martial Law Administrator. A new and smaller western-based Pakistan emerged on 16 December 1971.

The loss of East Pakistan shattered the prestige of the Pakistani military. Pakistan lost half its navy, a quarter of its air force and a third of its army. The war also exposed the shortcomings of Pakistan's declared strategic doctrine that the "defence of East Pakistan lay in West Pakistan". Hussain Haqqani, in his book *Pakistan: Between Mosque and Military* notes,

"Moreover, the army had failed to fulfill its promises of fighting to the last man. The eastern command had laid down arms after losing only 1,300 men in battle. In West Pakistan 1,200 military deaths had accompanied lackluster military performance."

In his book *The 1971 Indo-Pak War: A Soldier's Narrative* Pakistani Major General Hakeem Arshad Qureshi a veteran of this conflict noted,

"We must accept the fact that, as a people, we had also contributed to the bifurcation of our own country. It was not a Niazi, or a Yahya, even a Mujib, or a Bhutto, or their key assistants, who alone were the cause of our break-up, but a corrupted system and a flawed social order that our own apathy had allowed to remain in place for years. At the most critical moment in our history we failed to check the limitless ambitions of individuals with dubious antecedents and to thwart their selfish and irresponsible behaviour. It was our collective 'conduct' that had provided the enemy an opportunity to dismember us."

Bangladesh

Bangladesh became an independent nation, the world's fourth most populous Muslim state. Mujibur Rahman was released from a West Pakistani prison, returned to Dhaka on 10 January 1972 and to become first President of Bangladesh and later its Prime Minister.

On the brink of defeat around 14 December, the Pakistani Army, and its local collaborators, systematically killed a large number of Bengali doctors, teachers and intellectuals, part of apogrom against the Hindu minorities who constituted the majority of urban educated intellectuals. Young men, especially students, who were seen as possible rebels were also targeted. The extent of casualties in East Pakistan is not known. R.J. Rummel cites estimates ranging from one to three million people killed. Other estimates place the death toll lower, at 300,000. Bangladesh government figures state that Pakistani forces aided by collaborators killed three million people, raped 200,000 women and displaced millions of others. In 2010 Bangladesh government set up a tribunal to prosecute the people involved in alleged war crimes and those who collaborated with Pakistan. According to the Government, the defendants would be charged with Crimes against humanity, genocide, murder, rape and arson.

Hamoodur Rahman Commission

In aftermath of war Pakistan Government constituted the Hamoodur Rahman Commission headed by Justice Hamoodur Rahman in 1971 to investigate the political and military causes for defeat and the Bangladesh atrocities during the war. The commission's report was classified and its publication banned by Bhutto as it put the military in poor light, until some parts of the report surfaced in Indian media in 2000.

When it was declassified, it showed many failings from the strategic to the tactical levels. It confirmed the looting, rapes and the killings by the Pakistan Army and their local agents. It lay the blame squarely on Pakistani generals, accusing them of debauchery, smuggling, war crimes and neglect of duty. Though no actions were ever taken on commissions findings, the commission had recommended public trial of Pakistan Army generals on the charges that they had been responsible for the situation in the first place and that they had succumbed without a fight.

Simla Agreement

In 1972 the Simla Agreement was signed between India and Pakistan, the treaty ensured that Pakistan recognised the independence of Bangladesh in exchange for the return of the Pakistani POWs. India treated all the POWs in strict accordance with the Geneva Convention, rule 1925. It released more than 90,000 Pakistani PoWs in five months. Further, as a gesture of goodwill, nearly 200 soldiers who were sought for war crimes by Bengalis were also pardoned by India.

The accord also gave back more than 13,000 km^2 of land that Indian troops had seized in West Pakistan during the war, though India retained a few strategic areas. But some in India felt that the treaty had been too lenient to Bhutto, who had pleaded for leniency, arguing that the fragile democracy in Pakistan would crumble if the accord was perceived as being overly harsh by Pakistanis and that he would be accused of losing Kashmir in addition to the loss of East Pakistan.

Long term consequences

- Steve Coll, in his book *Ghost Wars*, argues that the Pakistan military's experience with India, including Pervez Musharraf's experience in 1971, influenced the Pakistani government to support jihadist groups in Afghanistan even after the Soviets left, because the jihadists were a tool to use against India, including bogging down the Indian Army in Kashmir.
- After the war, Zulfikar Ali Bhutto authorised the highly secretive and clandestine atomic bomb program, as part of its new deterrence policy, to defend itself and never to allow another armed invasion from India. Many Pakistani scientists, abroad working at the IAEA and European and American nuclear programs immediately return to what remain of Pakistan and took participation in making Pakistan a nuclear power.
- Writing about the war in Foreign Affairs magazine Zulfikar Ali Bhutto stated 'There is no parallel in contemporary history to the cataclysm which engulfed Pakistan in 1971. A tragic civil war, which rent asunder the people of the two parts of Pakistan, was seized by India as an opportunity for armed intervention. The country was dismembered, its economy shattered and the nation's self-confidence totally

undermined.' This statement of Bhutto has given rise to the myth of betrayal prevalent in modern Pakistan. This view was contradicted by the post-WarHamoodur Rahman Commission, ordered by Bhutto himself, which in its 1974 report indicted generals of the Pakistan Army for creating conditions which led to the eventual loss of East Pakistan and for inept handling of military operations in the East.

Important dates

- 7 March 1971: Sheikh Mujibur Rahman declares that, "The current struggle is a struggle for independence", in a public meeting attended by almost a million people in Dhaka.
- 25 March 1971: Pakistani forces start Operation Searchlight, a systematic plan to eliminate any resistance. Thousands of people are killed in student dormitories and police barracks in Dhaka.
- 26 March 1971: Sheikh Mujibur Rahman signed an official declaration of independence and sent it through a radio message on the night of 25 March (the morning of 26 March). Later MajorZiaur Rahman and other Awami League leaders announced the declaration of independence on behalf of Sheikh Mujib from Kalurghat Radio Station, Chittagong. The message is relayed to the world by Indian radio stations.
- 27 March 1971: Bangladesh Force namely Mukti Bahini {consisting Niyomito Bahini (Regular Force) and Gono Bahini (Guerilla Force)} was formed under the Commander-in-Chief (C-in-C) General Mohammad Ataul Ghani Osmany.
- 17 April 1971: Exiled leaders of Awami League form a provisional government.
- 3 December 1971: War between India and Pakistan officially begins when West Pakistan launches a series of preemptive air strikes on Indian airfields.
- 6 December 1971: East Pakistan is recognised as Bangladesh by India.

- 14 December 1971: Systematic elimination of Bengali intellectuals is started by Pakistani Army and local collaborators.
- 16 December 1971: Lieutenant-General A. A. K. Niazi, supreme commander of Pakistani Army in East Pakistan, surrenders to the Allied Forces (Mitro Bahini) represented by Lieutenant General Jagjit Singh Arora of Indian Army at the surrender. India and Bangladesh gain victory.
- 12 January 1972: Sheikh Mujibur Rahman comes to power.

INDIA AND BANGLADESH: CALCULUS OF TERRITORIAL DISPUTE SETTLEMENT

The prime ministers of India and Bangladesh signed a landmark protocol to their 1974 Land Boundary Agreement, providing for final settlement of their long-pending boundary issues. Given that instances of territorial dispute settlement in this sovereignty-conscious region have been few and far between, this exercise in statesmanship is both commendable and long overdue. A review of the principles and processes underlying the compromises reveals useful insights into territorial dispute settlement at New Delhi's end.

The India-Bangladesh boundary is no ordinary one. Hastily constructed in the dying days of British colonialism, it was the longest international boundary created during the age of decolonisation. The border was intended to separate a contiguous majority area of Muslims from that of non-Muslims — but for only about a quarter of its length does it separate a Muslim-majority in Bangladesh from a Hindu-majority in India. As many as 162 tiny enclaves (111 Indian and 52 Bangladeshi) dot a section of the frontier: in the extreme an Indian enclave sits within a Bangladeshi enclave, itself situated within a larger Indian enclave, all surrounded by Bangladeshi territory!

Shifting rivers, mapping errors and 'adversely possessed lands' — that is, lands unwittingly encroached upon and (illegally) occupied by both countries — added to the maze of identity, loyalty and insecurity along the Bengal borderland. Sixteen Indian and three Bangladeshi border guards were killed in 2001 following a show of force in a disputed area along the border. Demarcating a boundary has unsurprisingly been a protracted affair.

According to the recent agreement, the Indian enclaves in Bangladesh and the Bangladeshi enclaves in India are to be swapped, enabling unbroken territorial continuity – with minor exceptions – for both states. New Delhi's claim to compensation for the additional acreage ceded to Bangladesh is waived. The bewildered 51,000 residents in these enclaves will presumably be offered the choice of either relocating or, more likely, having their citizenship switched – although this is not accounted for in the Protocol. The 'adversely possessed lands' are to be mutually vacated, something that will be done in conjunction with the swapping of enclaves. Finally, the remaining disputed points are to be marked and delimited, enabling India thereafter to share its first fully demarcated land boundary with a neighbour.

The Protocol lays down weighty precedents for New Delhi's territorial dispute settlement practices. Especially notable is admitting an uncompensated swap of territory – during the course of exchanging the enclaves – in effect ceding land to which it holds undisputed title. Minor exchange of disputed territory by New Delhi is not groundbreaking. In 1951, India and Pakistan agreed to exchange two disputed territories on the India-East Pakistan (now Bangladesh) border. And in 1959 the two countries prepared modalities for future exchange of territories pending boundary demarcation. Letting-out undisputed territory on a 'perpetual lease' is not groundbreaking either. In 1974, New Delhi leased a narrow strip of territory (Tin Bigha corridor) to the then newly-inaugurated independent government of Bangladesh. The Indian Supreme Court interpreted the lease as a form of 'undisturbed possession' for Dacca's use which did not divest India of its sovereign rights.

But uncompensated cession of undisputed territory along its land border is altogether unprecedented. It also sets a useful precedent for that significant patch of disputed territory that will necessarily have to be ceded to China in the context of a Sino-Indian boundary arrangement in the foreseeable future. With New Delhi already having ceded a small, uninhabited island to Sri

Lanka along their maritime boundary line in the mid-1970s, and with the Indian judiciary vesting treaty-making authority wholly to the executive, the swap of enclaves on the India-Bangladesh border should pass constitutional muster.

Two fundamental principles and processes that underlie New Delhi's calculus of territorial dispute settlement are particularly noteworthy. First, an imperative of good neighborliness has been a fundamental pre-requisite for settlement — New Delhi was willing to meet the Bangladeshi Prime Minister mid-way, even beyond, but only after the latter had met India's security concerns and walked the extra mile to extend the hand of friendship. Significant credit for the settlement belongs at the Bangladeshi end.

Second, and more important, is a practice of Indian boundary diplomacy which has seen New Delhi admit to the exigencies of 'zamini haqeeqat' (ground realities) in disputed border areas — formally seeking to resolve territorial disputes according to the status quo, with least disturbance to local inhabitants. 'Ground realities' is formally acknowledged in the India-Bangladesh Joint Statement. Paired with the acceptance of a political parameters-based approach to dispute resolution, it has also unlocked potential for resolving the long-dormant Sino-Indian boundary dispute.

India and Bangladesh should use the goodwill generated through the settlement to resolve their long-pending maritime border dispute. That dispute consists of: (a) demarcation of the coastal boundary line around a tiny island at the point where a common boundary river meets the estuary on the Bay of Bengal, and (b) overlapping EEZ boundary and resource development claims emerging from the concave geography of the Bengal coastline.

For the former, international arbitration on the tried-and-tested lines of the 1968 settlement between India and Pakistan that divided a semi-submerged tract at the mouth of the Arabian Sea may provide a model for determining the coastal boundary. For the latter, New Delhi should desist from unilateral surveying of the overlapping maritime zones pending judgment of their respective claims at the Permanent Court of Arbitration (PCA) at The Hague.

Better still, submitting to settlement principles in the analogous Myanmar-Bangladesh maritime baseline claims case, currently under fast-track International Tribunal for the Law of the Sea (ITLOS) proceedings would be an act of graciousness on New Delhi's part. Best of all would be joint survey and development of the overlapping India-Bangladesh maritime zone without prejudice to the ITLOS or PCA verdicts. In doing so, New Delhi would also set a portentous precedent for claimants in the South China Sea.

BANGLADESH INDIA BORDER ISSUES

Bangladesh shares with India a land boundary of 4,096 Kilometers of which 6.5 kilometers including some riverine parts in Comilla Tripura area remain un-demarcated. Despite the Mujib Indira Agreement of 1974 resolving the boundary and enclave issues almost 36 years ago, 51 enclaves measuring 7,083.72 acres are in adverse possession of India forcing their Bangladeshi residents to live in abysmal conditions. Some acres of land in the district of Sylhet too is reportedly have been occupied by the Indian Border Forces since independence. Besides, continued killing of over a thousand unarmed Bangladeshis by Indian BSF since 1990 is a negation of the most elementary norms of inter state behavior unheard of in modern inter state relations between two supposedly friendly countries having normal political, commercial and cultural relations. It is as if life of individuals and repeated promises not to snuff that out on the slightest pretext is of no consequences in a region which has given birth to two major religions of the world.

On the maritime side the boundary too remains un demarcated together with the issue of the ownership of the South Talpatty/ New Moore Island now forcibly occupied by India despite Bangladesh's protest. On the other hand new measures like drawing of a new unusual maritime base line, etc.. keep on emerging side lining recourse to meaningful negotiation and stead putting more pressure on Bangladesh's legitimate interests and positions.

The list seems quite lengthy as old issues remain unresolved while new ones are being added with the passage of time and ever increasing state of politico economic activities and relations. So what can be done to redress the situation, bring a measure of respectful behavior and establish good neighborliness that seems to be the stated aim of both the countries? Will these problems and others which will come up in other presentations by concerned and knowledgeable persons in this session could be positively influenced or resolved through the exercise of unilateral goodwill measures at leadership level on bilateral plane? Or why some of these issues have not been suitably addressed in sub regional or regional forums which we did set up with high hopes and the kind of which other countries are so successfully using? Could we once again look into some Eurocentric practices to overcome our own generic problems?

What is Border Security and Management

In the light of the complexities of issues and stakes involved given the high level of expectation which may not pass as pragmatic in the light of South Asia's dominant neighborly culture we need to take a look into the border security and management issues between the two countries from the perspective of the best practices of the European countries which gave the present world the very concept of statehood and its social derivatives like democracy and conflict resolution mechanisms, confidence building lessons at the inter state level.

The Organization for Security and Cooperation in Europe (OSCE) which has 56 members including some from the Central Asian and Caucasus regions recognizes that border security and management is a matter of the national sovereignty and responsibility of States. While promoting open and secure borders in a free, democratic and more integrated manner they commit themselves to upheld the principles of international law, in particular, international human rights, refugee and humanitarian law as well standards and recommendations laid down by the relevant international organizations. They reaffirm the norms, principles, commitments and values enshrined in the Helsinki Final Act, all of which apply equally and unreservedly and other similar instruments developed to date to address the threats of terrorism, organized crime, illegal migration, and the illicit trafficking in weapons, drugs and human beings. At the regional and sub regional levels: In the same spirit, the participating States reaffirm their obligations and commitments in all regional and sub regional formats in which they are members and undertake to promote their co operation in all relevant organizations and agencies in order to ensure consistency in policies and standards and to avoid duplication of efforts;

Bilaterally: In a spirit of solidarity, and aiming at good neighborly relations, the participating States respect their bilateral agreements on border related issues and undertake efforts to promote sharing of experience and good practices.

Main Objectives of Cooperation

Co operation by the participating States is aimed at promoting the implementation of border related commitments; foster compliance with border related security and management standards recognized by the participating States, as well as their improvement,*inter alia,* based on sharing of good practices.

The participating States promote co operation between their border services, customs authorities, agencies issuing travel documents and visas, and law enforcement and migration agencies, as well as other competent national structures, with a view to achieving the following aims:

To promote free and secure movement of persons, goods, services and investments across borders, in conformity with relevant legal frameworks, international law and OSCE commitments, *inter alia,* through enhancing the security of travel documents and encouraging, as appropriate, circumstances that could allow liberalization of visa regimes, in the spirit of the commitments under the documents mentioned above;

To reduce the threat of terrorism, including by preventing cross border movement of persons, weapons and funds connected with terrorist and other criminal activities;

To prevent and repress transnational organized crime, illegal migration, corruption, smuggling and trafficking in weapons, drugs and human beings;

To promote high standards in border services and competent national structures;

To promote dignified treatment of all individuals wanting to cross borders, in conformity with relevant national legal frameworks, international law, inparticular human rights, refugee, and humanitarian law, and relevant OSCE commitments;

To create beneficial conditions for social and economic development in border territories, as well as for the prosperity and cultural development of persons belonging to all communities residing in border areas, with access to all opportunities;

To foster prospects for joint economic development and help in establishing common spaces of freedom, security and justice in the OSCE area;

To ensure the security of the international transport circuit for supply of commodities.

Guided by the OSCE co operative approach, they believe that:

1 That their common prosperity and security can be enhanced through an increase in beneficial cross border movements of people, goods, services and investments.
2 Issues of a regulatory nature raised by cross border movements can best be addressed through direct co operation between the border services and competent national structures of the participating States, based on relevant agreements. This co operation should take place at the bilateral, regional and multilateral levels.
3 Sovereign national authorities, and in particular the border services responsible on each side of the border, have the best knowledge of the issues at hand. Cross border dialogue, transparency and confidence building constitute the first logical steps towards generating solutions with added value to the benefit of all.
4 Since every border has a particular character and may call for specific policy choices, each participating State has the sovereign right to choose how to secure and manage its borders, taking into account relevant political, military, economic and social considerations.

In sum, the concept is to treat the matter of security as common, cooperative and indivisible basis and to base their work on security and border management on the basis of pragmatism and realism while a spirit of solidarity and partnership based on mutual interest and respect sustains that. Periodic review and monitoring of activities are undertaken to learn from the many diverse circumstances.

Conflict resolution is effected through peaceful dialogue while the OSCE Court of Conciliation and Arbitration is the tool available to States recognizing its jurisdiction, for consultation and to provide confidential legal opinion Besides there are methods and arrangements for training, capacity building and initiating confidence building measures of participating states.

INDIA'S TIES WITH BANGLADESH: AREAS OF COOPERATION & CHALLENGES

Cooperation in Counter-terrorism

Over the years the war against terrorism and its causes have come to be viewed as a collective effort of all members of the international community. International terrorism cannot be fought unless we cooperate. With terror groups acquiring transnational networks, they now possess the ability to cross national lines and establish sanctuaries in nations that they perceive to be the weakest link. Once there, they exploit the differences between nations and cultures.

Facing an evolving terror threat and with Indian investigative agencies encountering several difficulties with other countries while following up terror related cases, Indian counter-terrorism efforts were provided a major boost, when Sheikh Hasina responded to Indian security concerns and began clamping down on anti-India terror outfits operating out of Bangladesh territory. Both governments voiced the need to work together on security issues and "reaffirmed their unequivocal and uncompromising position against terrorism in all its forms and manifestations, including insurgency". As a commitment towards this course, Dhaka recognised that certain Pakistan-based terror groups had formed close connections with militant networks in Bangladesh on account of its proximity to India and the porous nature of their shared border.

Sheikh Hasina and the Awami League have been true to their word and have severely restricted the activities of Indian insurgent groups such as ULFA and terror groups such as LeT and Harkat-ul-Mujahideen. It is this context that Bangladesh handed over ULFA leader Anup Chetia and reopened Chittagong arms haul case of 2004. Soon after the Mumbai terror attacks the Indian government conveyed to Dhaka its concerns about Bangladeshi links to the terror outfits responsible for the assault. Quickly following up on Indian concerns, Bangladesh arrested Abdul Rouf Daud Merchant, an operative of the mafia gang headed by Dawood Ibrahim.

It is time for India to reciprocate what has largely been a gesture of goodwill on Bangladesh's part; the progress that India and Bangladesh have jointly made on counter terrorism must now transcend the narrow bounds of security cooperation and permeate other bilateral issues in their relationship.

All-round Progress

In many ways, that has already started happening. At a symbolic level, during her visit in 2010, Prime Minister Sheikh Hasina was conferred the prestigious Indira Gandhi Prize for Peace, Disarmament and Development for 2009 at a ceremony at Rashtrapati Bhavan in New Delhi. The government of Bangladesh also conferred the Bangladesh Swadhinata Sammanona (Bangladesh Freedom Honour), the highest Award of Bangladesh for foreign nationals, on the former Prime Minister of India, Smt. Indira Gandhi, for her extraordinary contribution to the historic Liberation War of Bangladesh.

Befitting the shared legacy of the great poet laureate Rabindranath Tagore, the two countries jointly celebrated the 150th Birth Anniversary of Rabindranath Tagore in 2011 in a manner befitting his vision and spirit. The joint celebration enthused the people on both sides to explore the common cultural heritage and linkages and had promoted exchanges not only among Tagore experts, but also a whole range of artists, singers, dancers, dramatists, poets, writers and actors which has led to greater understanding among the two sides. It was also agreed that the 90th Anniversary of the publication of Bidrohi by Poet Nazrul Islam would be jointly celebrated.

There has been progress on other fronts too. While it was decided to amicably demarcate the maritime boundary between India and Bangladesh, it was also agreed that Bangladesh will allow the use of Mongla and Chittagong sea ports for movement of goods to and from India through road and rail. Work on the proposed Akhaura – Agartala railway link to be financed by a grant from India would also start shortly, even as exchange of travel between the people of both countries was enhanced with the starting of "Maitree Express" between Kolkata and Dhaka.

India has offered 300 scholarships annually to Bangladesh for a period of five years for study and training of its students in universities and training institutions in India, covering a wide range of disciplinest. Further, recognising the urgent need of trained doctors and specialists in the field of healthcare in Bangladesh, the two Prime Ministers agreed to set up a programme for training of Bangladesh doctors in premier Indian medical institutes.

Both Prime Ministers also recognised that poverty eradication and ensuring food security were great challenges to both the countries. They also recognized the need to give added focus on rural development policies, transfer and diffusion of technology and development, in particular to enhance agricultural productivity.

Border haats have also been opened in Baliamari (Kurigram)-Kalaichar (West Garo Hills) and another one is proposed in Balat (East Khasi Hills)-Dalora (Sunamganj). This is a fulfilment of the long standing demand of the local people of the area and it is hoped that the resulting economic activity would contribute to the economic upliftment of the people of the area surrounding the border haats.

Recognising the urgency of protecting and conserving the fragile ecosystem of Sundarban, the world's largest mangrove forest, work on the conservation of the Sundarban and the Royal Bengal Tiger of the Sundarban have started. Clearly, over the last decade, both the countries have witnessed a qualitative transformation in virtually all areas of bilateral cooperation making the relationship a truly multi-faceted one. But as in many such relationships, there are continued challenges to overcome too.

Challenges and Potential Concerns

India and Bangladesh share a 4094 km border with India contiguous to Bangladesh on three sides. Such proximity has contributed to hostilities in the past, and both sides need to resolve certain issues in order for the relationship to move forward.

Trade

Trade has always been an irritant in India-Bangladesh relations. The unfavourable trade deficit for Bangladesh and a number of tariff and non-tariff barriers to trade on the Indian side has caused significant resentment amongst Bangladeshi's, who believe that India has devised numerous trade barriers that deny mutually beneficial trade. The unrecorded trade between the two nations adds to the trade deficit, and the potential loss of customs duties is a major problem for Bangladesh due to the volume of illegal goods flowing into the country. The greater part of this trade is characterised as quasi legal or informal, and involves the participation of locals living along the border area who usually bypass the customs posts or work in collusion with anti-smuggling agencies.

Non-tariff barriers (NTBs) remain the single greatest impediment to increasing trade. The non-tariff barriers introduced by India as pointed out by Bangladesh's Commerce Ministry include packaging requirements, laboratory testing for food and cosmetic products, inadequate infrastructure facilities such as warehousing and trans-shipment yards, customs clearances, visa restrictions and poor connectivity to customs stations.

Over the past few years both countries have agreed to work together on the issue of removal of tariff and non-tariff barriers with the aim of facilitating greater trade ties. India has allowed Bangladesh duty free access to its markets for 10 million pieces of readymade garments, removed 46 items from the negative list and even allowed Nepal and Bhutan transit access to Bangladesh. India has also begun dismantling some of its NTB practices; testing facilities for Bangladeshi exports are being set up at the Petrapole border and sanitary tests for food items such as the Hilsa fish are now taking place in Kolkata and not Petrapole.

Trade between Bangladesh and India rests at US$ 5.099 billion during the financial year 2010-11. However, the geographical proximity between the two countries represents a significant potential for expanding trade relations. Due to the relative size of their respective economies, the trade relationship between India and Bangladesh is of greater significance for Bangladesh; nevertheless increased economic integration between these South Asian neighbours would mean better connectivity for India's North Eastern States that remain in political and economic isolation even today. While a case for greater economic engagement between the two countries can be safely made, it is yet unclear whether India should pursue a Free Trade Agreement (FTA) with Bangladesh or presently maintain a general import liberalisation process as advocated under SAFTA. As India opens its markets unilaterally there might be a different political context for FTA negotiations.

Bibliography

Alam, Aftab : *US Policy Towards South Asia: Special Reference to Indo-Pak Relations,* Raj, Delhi, 1998.

Amitabh Sikdar: *India and China : Strategic Energy Management and Security,* Manas, Delhi, 2009.

Anderson, J.: *Transnational Democracy: Political Spaces and Border Crossings,* Routledge: London and New York, 2002.

Anderson, M. and Bort, E.: *Boundaries and Identities: The Eastern Frontier of the European Union,* Edinburgh: International Social Sciences Institute, University of Edinburgh, 1996.

Anil, K.C.: *Military and Democracy in South Asia : Challenges, Politics and Power,* Sumit Enterprises, Delhi, 2009.

Bartlett, C.A. and Ghoshal, S.: *Transnational Management: Text, Cases and Readings in Cross-Border Management,* Boston: Irwin/McGraw-Hill, 2000.

Benjamin, Joseph : *China-Pak Relations : Prospect and Retrospect,* Reference Press, Delhi, 2004.

Bhat, T.P. : *India and China : Trade Complementarities and Competitiveness,* Bookwell, Delhi, 2008.

Chitkara, M.G. : *China-Pak Relations Challenges Before New Millennium,* APH, Delhi, 2001.

Coakley, J.: *The Territorial Management of Ethnic Conflict,* 2nd edn London: Frank Cass, 2003.

Deepak, B R : *India and China : 1904-2004 : A Century of Peace and Conflict,* Manak, Delhi, 2005.

Diener, Alexander C., and Joshua Hagen. *Borders: A Very Short Introduction.* New York: Oxford University Press, 2012.

Dixit, J.N. : *India and Regional Developments : Through the Prism of Indo-Pak Relations,* Gyan, Delhi, 2004.

Donnan, H. and Wilson, T. M.: *Borders: Frontiers of Identity, Nation and State,* Oxford: Berg, 1999.

Gao, Mobo: *The Battle for China's Past: Mao and the Cultural Revolution,* London, Pluto Press, 2008.

Ghosh, Ajoy : *Indo-Pak Conflict : Threat to South Asian Security,* Reference Press, Delhi, 2003.

Gupta, Alka R. : *Indo-Pak Security Discourse : South Asian Context,* Radha Pub, Delhi, 2010.

Gupta, S.: *Disrupted Borders: An Intervention in Definitions of Boundaries,* London: River Oram Press, 1993.

Huntington, S.P.: *The China Defence Modernisation Military and the State,* N.Y., Vintage Books, 1964.

Imtiaz, A.: *State and Foreign Policy: India's Role in South Asia,* New Delhi, Vikas, 1993.

Jha, Prem Shankar : *India and China : The Battle Between Soft and Hard Power,* Penguin Books India, Delhi, 2010.

Kunju, N. : *Indo-Pak : Nuclear Cold War,* Reliance, Delhi, 2002.

Nayyar, K K : *National Security : Military Aspects,* Rupa, Delhi, 2003.

Ohmae, K.: *The Borderless World: Power and Strategy in the Interlinked Economy,* New York: Harper, 1990.

Phuskele, Preeti : *India and China : Emerging Superpowers,* ICFAI University, Delhi, 2009.

Prabir De: *India and China in an Era of Globalisation : Essays on Economic Cooperation,* Bookwell, Delhi, 2005.

Rosen, P.: *Societies and Military Power: India and its Armies,* Ithaca, Cornell University Press, 1996.

Schneider, S. and Barsoux, J.L. : *Transnational Management: Text, Cases and Readings in Cross-Border Management,* Boston: Irwin/McGraw-Hill, 2000.

Thampi, Madhavi : *India and China in the Colonial World,* Social Science Press, Delhi, 2010.

Theodore, William : *The Buddhist Tradition in India, China and Japan,* New York: Vintage Books, 1972.

Velez-Ibanez, Carlos: *Border Visions and Management.* University of Arizona Press, 1996.

Wilson, Thomas M., and Hastings Donnan: *A Companion to Border Studies.* Hoboken, NJ: Wiley-Blackwell, 2012.

Index

P

S

V

Z

□□□